Asiatic Russia

Asiatic Russia

Partnerships and Communities in Eurasia

Editors
Suchandana Chatterjee
Anita Sengupta
Susmita Bhattacharya

Maulana Abul Kalam Azad Institute of Asian Studies, Kolkata

SHIPRA

ISBN: 978-81-7541-487-7

First Published in India in 2009

Asiatic Russia: Partnerships and Communities in Eurasia

Published by :
SHIPRA PUBLICATIONS
115-A, Vikas Marg, Shakarpur, Delhi-110092 (India)
Tel. : 91-11-65277210, 22500954, Fax : 91-11-22458662
Email : info@shiprapublications.com
www.shiprapublications.com

Contents

Introduction

An examination of the background to the conference, organized jointly by the Maulana Abul Kalam Institute, Kolkata and the Institute of History, Novosibirsk, the list of proceedings and the contributions indicate that the conference (and the volume) have gone much further than a standard academic meeting on a subject of interest to two partner-research institutes on well fixed and delimited themes. There has been an ambitious attempt here to bring together Indian and Russian perspectives – covering almost the whole gamut of serious research in the two countries on major aspects of the history and politics of Asiatic Russia. At a time when it is clear that Indian statesmen are increasingly attempting to think of South Asian interests within the framework of global demands and requirements of the broadest order (whether in relation to the WTO or to the Nuclear non-proliferation regime), this interest in the northern regions of Asia must be deemed to be significant. The conference must be taken as an implied critique of research agenda that focus on a narrow preoccupation with neighbourhoods, or circumscribed foreign policy initiatives that move further afield but are equally narrow in their range. The conference indicates not only the complex matrix that preoccupies Indian scholars but also draws upon representatives of an important part of the Asian continent to engage with this matrix.

The conference was the outcome of discussions at a meeting of scholars in Novosibirsk in June 2007 (whose proceedings was published by the Maulana Azad Institute as *Siberia in Focus* (Towards Freedom, Kolkata 2007). The meeting in Kolkata, subsequently, in February 2008, went much further than the original symposium. It provided the opportunity for a more substantial exchange between researchers at the Institute and four major institutions in Siberia. It also acted as a forum for Russian scholars to acquaint themselves with a broad range of informed opinion from India, from a number of institutions, on subjects concerning Asiatic Russia.

The conference achieved the two crucial aims of its initiators. It ensured the stimulation of a broad-ranging and deep interest in Asiatic Russia in India, drawing out connections thereby between what has occurred there, and the course of events, past and present, in Central Asia, the PRC and South Asia. It also provided an occasion to demonstrate the willingness of Russian scholars to engage with opinions voiced in South Asia concerning the region and its development. At a time when, in India, study of the FSU is limited to Central Asia or European Russia, and, in Russia, perspectives were either parochial or tilted to European and US debates regarding concepts of Russia's evolution, this was an important departure. It is with major justification therefore that it has been thought necessary to ensure publication of the proceedings of the conference.

In this volume, statements and analyses are broad-ranging and general in nature, and introduce historiography or political comment. There are seldom large bodies of archival material that are the basis of conclusions – or, for that matter, dense statistical analysis or theoretical initiatives. On the other hand, the points at issue are not those that are part of standard publicist literature – nor are the papers the equivalent of brief encyclopaedic entries. The volume is intended to be the foundations of mutual awareness between Russian and Indian scholars of the Eurasian region, and to sustain the connections that the conference established.

* * *

In the present volume, a number of Russian papers have established the broad historical outlines of what constitutes the Russian settlement of Siberia and the Russian Far East. The also address the shape crucial problems have taken in the past and the nature of such problems today. Most are united in a critical assessment of the way a centre-periphery approach to these areas have thrown up problems for their effective development. This, it is clear, is a feature of the past and the present, though the dimensions of what have taken place vary. Significantly, running slightly against the grain, among the Russian papers, in an important (almost "metropolitan" view of the problem) Felix Iurlov argues against the tendency for the tensions to lead to demands for what is tantamount to a Siberian Republic.

Natal'ya Ablazhei and Evgenii Vodychev have provided an

important outline of colonization and located the character of settlement and urbanization in Siberia against this background. They trace the early impetus in trapping and mining and the more aggressive development of Soviet times, which culminated in the formation of large urban units and the stress on oil and natural gas production. Acceptance of the importance of this area for the development of the USSR, regrettably, failed to evolve a measured evaluation of what such importance implied, or what the needs and requirements of the region were. Rather, there developed a bald assertion (and pursuance) of the "region for country" principle (i.e. that the area had to be exploited for the welfare of the country as a whole). The historical dimensions of this story are more specifically examined in A.K. Kirillov's paper on the "metallurgical" and "Trans-Sib" strategies that developed over time in the pre-Soviet period, i.e. the centring of settlement and development on extractive industries, or the communications' infrastructure. The author indicates the mixture of state and private interest that forwarded both. He draws out the way settlement focused initially on the initiatives both of the state and the Demidov family – and the limitations of each (in the way the initiative to mould extractive units developed), moving on to the way the Trans-Siberian railway was able to galvanize both industry and agriculture, creating important centres such as Barnaul as it went on. The voice of protest that a rude exploitation of the region threw up in late imperial times, well before the revolutions of 1917, is well taken up in M.V. Shilovskii's discussion of G.N. Potanin and N.M. Yadrintsev's writings concerning the identity of Siberia and the difficulties that had been the region's lot.

A vigorous statement of the processes that have been at work here is stated in a number of papers. Denis Anan'ev deals with the contrast between the factors that shaped the American West and those that shaped Russian colonization of Siberia. He stresses the variety of institutions in the case of the English presence in North America and the uniform bureaucracy that ruled European Russia and Siberia in the Petrine era and after. This, he argues, as well as the "frontier experience" that Turner has associated with the American West, determined the democratic nature of that frontier and made its fate different from that of Siberia. Such insights are followed up for both pre-revolutionary and post 1917 periods by V.V. Alekseev in his piece on the system of integration of Asiatic Russia – which stresses the trapping, agrarian settlement, and industrialization dimensions of the integration of the region, expressing a critique of the devastation of Soviet rule and the amelioration of the situation after 1991. E. T. Artemov takes a similar stand (on the imperial Russian and Soviet pasts) arguing against the rhetoric of late Soviet rule that Russia east of the Urals was a drag on the country as a whole – a drag that had distorted its essence as well as its development. Artemov pointedly stresses the anomalies that shaped the organization and exploitation of this space.

Integration and the connectivity of resources, a group of presentations stress, is crucial not only to the understanding of the region but also to its future. This is part of V.Yu. Malov's presentation – which discusses projects for Siberia's future stimulated by the Baikal Economic Forum of 2000. These projects take up a comprehensive evaluation of possible transport development and its probable impact. The nature of communications' infrastructure and the limitations of the past (the inadequacy of the structures evolved under Imperial Russian and Soviet rule) as far as transport corridors are concerned is laid out in V.A. Lamin's comprehensive account of the significance of the Siberian corridors when seen against world corridors and transport networks. Marina Baldano again focuses on this subject – with more specific attention to the history of the Trans-Siberian railway and its potential for the future. B.V. Bazarov, meanwhile, examines a subregional component here of the trade relations between Russia, Mongolia, and China, dealing in depth with the potential of this relationship. He makes an important case for viewing the relationship as a promising support to possible future improvements in the commercial exchanges of the region as a whole.

An important caveat also comes from Russian research. The factors outlined above can only be examined and developed in their correct light if adequate attention is paid to healthy approaches to migration and the trans-border dimension – approaches that are not always forthcoming. Viktor Diatlov, whose path-breaking studies of migration in Siberia are well acknowledged in scholarly circles, points out the substantial misreading to which statistics as well as impressions of Chinese migration into Siberia are subject. Diatlov examines a number of these statements that are often made without data – and, when data is available, misinterpretation is rampant. Diatlov has delineated the nature of Chinese migration into Siberia – and does not deny its existence and the role it plays in reshaping Siberia and the Russian Far East. But he warns that it must be examined more closely than is the case.

Russian perspectives, significantly, avoid the broader matters of religion and (barring Diatlov's paper) ethnicity - matters that raise questions concerning the various identities that feature in the region as a whole. These are significant since they tend to transcend borders and hence require careful treatment that is not statist in character. Stephan Dudoignon, working from French traditions of scholarship on Islam, presents a useful outline of the work that has been done in research groups in the "School of Omsk" (in Russia) concerning the significance and nature of Islam in Siberia – work in which anthropology and history have jointly been the means to examine genealogies and narratives that frame the identity of various Muslim communities of the area. While Dudoignon's own interest in the literature comes from the light it throws on how Islam engaged with an unusual range of pressures in the region, the research he cites also indicates the broad range of Islam in Siberia – which forms the basis for a wider global interaction.

These issues are gradually making their way into Indian awareness of the region as a whole, which grows out of an amalgam of different perspectives. Madhavan Palat sets the tone of one of these points of engagement when he dwells on engagement with the problems that Siberian colleagues have made their pivot – the role of Siberia in Russia. In his keynote address, where he establishes a pointed evaluation and critique of the current orthodoxy in the West (not wholly ignored in metropolitan circles in Moscow, one may add) that Imperial Russian and Soviet appropriation of Siberia and the Russian Far East were done on terms that were not cost effective or efficacious. The corollary (not normally accepted in circles in Moscow) is that the area cannot be effectively exploited by the Russian Federation, and requires to take into consideration its identities and contiguities (in North America, China and Central Asia) to realize its fullest potential. Palat states a firm rejection of notions that assume only one path of development for any given area to the total abandonment of other perspectives. In an important contribution, P.L. Dash points to similar conclusions as he examines the foundations for suggestions of disaggregating the Russian Federation – finding that they are impractical.

How, as a consequence, the region should be studied in India poses a conundrum and Anita Sengupta and Suchandana Chatterjee attempt to deal with it. Sengupta assesses the way debates on geopolitics have created a framework in the past (during the 19th and 20th centuries) for viewing the "heartland" that includes large sections of Asiatic Russia and that Halford Mackinder considered crucial to global strength; the way such debates have become the reference point for the present, as sections of the region attempt to find the terms to project and define their interests. Clearly, such terms do not coincide with the way in which Indian policy makers and scholars define their own global position – if these terms are to be associated with the well-stated preoccupations with non alignment, globalization and regional security – but it is clear that if Indians are to deal with the area, this is the imagination with which they will have to contend.

Chatterjee, developing a research preoccupation with Central Asia, and pursuing a clear unease with the boundaries of the region of the five "-stans" in cultural and social terms, examines the increasing projection of regional histories and myths in Siberia. She also examines the work and popularity of Russian protagonists of Siberian particularism (the same Potanin and Yadrintsev who have been mentioned by Siberian contributions) and fresh readings of their work today. Her comprehensive evaluation of recent literature on Siberia flags a host of studies and collections of material that have located the region more firmly in a broad spectrum of territory, religion and ethnicity.

A formidable example of unstructured sensibility in Siberia – of the type Chatterjee finds interesting – is provided by Rashmi Doraiswamy's discussion Valentin Rasputin's "Fire" one of the hallmarks of perestroika. Highlighting Russian sensibility that went against the grain, Doraiswamy examines what the roots of such writing might have been – and the overall social significance of it, dwelling on the record of disavowal of Soviet beliefs and values with which the author is said to have been associated.

Ajay Patnaik's follows a similar concern to that exhibited by Chatterjee – i.e. he is preoccupied with Siberia's broad Asiatic connections. But he argues his case out within the framework of a wholly different set of relationships and factual material. He links Central Asia with Asiatic Russia as a whole at a political and economic level, indicating the compulsions that connect the area to the PRC, Korea, Central Asia etc and showing how only the interweaving of these connections can ensure the development of the area to the satisfaction of the economic aspirations of the

Federation as a whole.. Providing another side of this picture, Sreemati Ganguli - in an exercise that is methodologically comparable - examines the determination of Russian foreign policy to ensure its predominance in the region as a while.

Moving out of a firm awareness of Central Asia and its relevance to India, in contrast to Chatterjee, Patnaik and Ganguli who pose their problem more firmly as a problem of how to think about Siberian and Central Asian identities and links, P. Stobdan, one of India's leading Central Asianists, points out the revival of Buddhist sensibilities in the region as a whole, running from Ladakh to Buryatia. Both the papers of Sharad Soni on Tuva and K. Warikoo on Buryatia echo such a perspective. Again concerned with India's interests, Sudha Mahalingam represents the keen eye of the policy maker – taking stock of Asiatic Russia as a source of oil and natural gas – and demonstrates the vast resources of Asiatic Russia that cannot be ignored by India. She touches on Indian investments in Sakhalin as she proceeds.

* * *

Arriving at a balance sheet of the presentations, it is clear is that while Russian papers made a determined effort to indicate the state of debate in Russia itself, Indian papers tend to indicate the complex character within which the region exists in the world of scholarly exchange. Equally, they also firmly show the considerable interests that India has in the region – whether through cultural connections or the pull of economic interests. Significantly, on the Indian side, this does not lead to any comment on the way this has come to affect policy or even social engagement in the area (the paper of P. Stobdan being a rare exception). Given the stress in studies of Indian foreign policy and external relations more generally on official doctrine, perhaps this should come as no surprise. Undoubtedly, as awareness grows of the complex character of the region (Central Asia/Asiatic Russia), through exchanges such as those indicated in this conference, more pointed speculation will become regular.

Certainly, today, both business interests and cultural connections are fanning out from India over Central Asia as a whole and into Asiatic Russia. This is partly associated with official policy – but this is only the tip of the iceberg. "Global Indians" working out of various trading enterprises, as well as a host of Russian associations and societies are responsible for the phenomenon. The process, it is almost certain, will compel scholarly interest in comparative studies which hark back to an earlier engagement in the School of International Studies and other Indian bodies where the experience of Eurasia was intended to inform an Indian speculation on the South Asian experience generally. The proceedings of this conference, it is hoped, will contribute to this reorientation of the compass.

Prof. H.S. Vasudevan
Director
Maulana Abul Kalam Azad Institute
of Asian Studies

Kolkata

1

An Identity for Siberia

Madhavan K. Palat

Siberia has latterly attracted attention as the unlikely site of yet another contest between the Cold War rivals, Russia and the West, as the progressive disintegration of the Soviet state continues to play out. What was once conceived of and had acted as a single bloc, rechristened the Soviet Empire stretching from Germany to the Pacific, has fragmented into so many distinct or indistinct blocs and groupings, or nations and states, that new essences to each of these regions are being discovered or asserted with unfailing regularity. Where the political substance cannot be adequately described, entire "spaces" (*prostranstva*) called the Central Asian, Inner Asian, Middle Asian, Siberian, and most popularly Eurasian, have been reconstituted; and, if all else fails, the ancient, discredited and deservedly forgotten geopolitical, indeed geological, concepts of the continental heartland have been dusted off the shelves to provide political struggles against the Russian state with a theoretical foundation that would be as unshakeable and as inexorable as the geology of the continental drift. The Russian and Soviet state has been cleansed of East Europe, now reimagined as Central Europe; the Baltic, the Ukraine, Moldova, and various parts of the Caucasus and Central Asia have been wholly or partially amputated; and the vast and seemingly inert space of Siberia now remains to be lopped off as an ungainly and toxic appendix. The salience of Siberia in the post-Soviet world of the twenty-first century is due to the question of the essence of Russia; and the essence of Russia is one of the many entry points into the grand strategic debate on the unfinished agenda of the Cold War, the positioning of the Russian state in the world strategic balance. Is Siberia to be a part of Russia or merely ethnically and culturally

Russian for the most part in the manner that Austria is German without being Germany?

Siberia has been positioned in the context of the debate on Russia being European or Eurasian: if Russia is European, then somehow Siberia does not belong in Russia; but if Russia is Eurasian, Siberia seems naturally to be a part of Russia. This is not a polemic necessarily between Russia and the West, for it cuts through Russia as much and many Russians themselves assume positions which might be upheld or deplored as Western, that is, that Russia is strictly European and her salvation lies in her becoming properly European. The reform of Russia and of the Soviet Union through Gorbachev's perestroika of the eighties and Eltsin's liberalization of the nineties were carried out with the seductive appeal of Russia becoming European and shedding the dross of her "Asiatic" heritage and its gratuitous diversions. As Russia scraped off these poisonous encrustations she would enter the utopia called Europe; and just as communism was so long "on the horizon" during the long Soviet night, so the brilliant sparks of Europe flickered on the horizon during this new post-Soviet play of light and shade.

The polemic about Russian Europeanness possesses a peculiarly Russian flavour that must be emphasized. Only in Russia after the Cold War has Europeanization, modernization, development, prosperity, and the utopia that all this cheerfully promises, imperatively demanded the surrender of priceless assets. These assets were not merely the non-Russian stretches of the Soviet Union like Central Asia and the Caucasus, but now encompass even Russian expanses like Siberia. Japan was driven from its colonial empire in military defeat; France began with a military defeat and followed it up with a bitterly contested decolonization; Britain was driven from empire through astute Gandhian non-violence; but Russia alone cast off its white man's and other burdens apparently over-enthusiastically, without any military defeat to drive her out, nor any other compelling imperative. It seems perplexing; and by the same token, the campaign against Siberia remaining a part of Russia seems equally perplexing.

As with socialism and central planning, the Soviet system differed by organizing a polyglot state that sought to reduce differences between regions rather than exploit them in colonial fashion. The Soviet Union was not an empire like the European ones although it had evolved from a colonial and dynastic empire. But western polemicists could equate the Soviet Union with a colonial empire; forced Soviet modernization did appear to be russifying and colonial all too often; and Stalin even toasted the Russians as the elder brother to the non-Russians. A further divergence appeared, in polemical terms, with the European decolonization and contraction to within Europe, leaving the leadership of the western world to the USA. Now Russia seemed to be in possession of the last colonial empire of the western world; but, unlike the wise imperialists who abandoned the colonies and exploited asymmetries to good profit wherever possible, Russia foolishly remained committed to empire by investing in it to develop the underdeveloped, throwing vast resources into central planning at the expense of European Russia, and thus slowed down the growth, prosperity and utopianization of Russia. What were once regarded as assets were in fact liabilities, which now included the Caucasus, Central Asia, and even Siberia. As Europe had abandoned its various empires, limited itself to Europe, and prospered in the course of it, and as Japan had forsaken its Co-Prosperity Sphere and flourished so spectacularly in consequence, so Russia should shrink to Russia proper. It signalled the defeat of the Soviet Union in the final and third world war of the twentieth century, the Cold War. Now Russia like the rest of Europe would shrink in defeat into its national essence, become committed to Europe, and leave the leadership of the world to the USA. It has happened with Soviet world-wide ambitions, it has happened with the Near Abroad or the former Soviet Republics, and it would now happen with Siberia also. This was the final, post-Soviet meaning of Russia reforming and becoming Europe or building the "common European home" dreamt of or propagated by Gorbachev.

This belongs to the reforms process inaugurated by perestroika, that of Russia discarding the non-Russian parts of the Soviet Union in order to constitute a Russian national state to carry out the reform more vigorously. Powerful interests and currents of opinion coalesced in the eighties and early nineties to demand and legitimize the shrinking of Russia to Russia proper by abandoning the Soviet Union and the non-Russian territories of the Union. The radical democrats under Eltsin's leadership challenged the central power structures of the CPSU by creating their base in the then Russian Federation of the Soviet Union. Their primary purpose was not to dissolve the Union but to secure the support of all the radical forces that opposed the anti-reform establishment within the Party; and these radical forces included both the reforming democrats and the non-Russian nationalist leaders in the various Republics. All were invited to feast on the carcass of the Party that was going to slaughter, and they responded with an insatiable lust. Each Republic was to go its own independent way, and by that implacable logic, Russia was also to chart a course separate from the rest of the Union.[1] To this were added highly influential conservative and nationalist Russian voices best represented by Solzhenitsyn.[2] They argued that Russia drained her energies by commitments to the non-Russian parts of the Soviet Union. These commitments were of various kinds, and each author chose his favourite slant, but collectively they amounted to demanding that Russia divest herself of her non-Russian territories in order to prosper. The most appealing and seductively simple or simplistic argument was that Russia had invested vast amounts of capital on the less developed regions of the Soviet Union, capital that could have been invested in Russia proper.[3] With such investments came debilitating military commitments as in the Caucasus and Central Asia or Afghanistan. To those obsessed with culture, Russia was losing or had lost much of her distinctive culture by melding into a polyglot and mongrelized Soviet culture. To impatient reformers, the backward regions of Central Asia and the Caucasus slowed down the process of reform and democracy owing to their primitive authoritarian habits. Only the diehard partocrats remained devoted to this dinosaur. If the reason for the dissolution of the Union was the inner party struggle to gain control of the reform process and carry it to its extreme, these were the legitimizing arguments that seemed self-evident to those who advanced them in those heady days.

The reform of the Soviet system and the dissolution of the Union were carried out in ideological and political terms by the reforming democrats and in national terms by the Russians, to the applause of their strategic partners in the West who rubbed their eyes in disbelief at their dream script being acted out before them almost without prompting. All the charges that were brought up against the non-Russian territories could now be dredged up against Siberia also, with the exception, a large exception of course, of national composition and culture since Siberia is after all overwhelmingly, indeed almost entirely Russian, indeed more so than France is French or England is English.[4] With the unerring instinct of the true cold warrior, Brzezinski argued that the Russian Federation should pursue the logic of the reform to its conclusion and virtually fragment into three parts, a loose confederation of European Russia, a Siberian Republic, and a Far Eastern Republic.[5] All three would become more compact and creative, Russia without excess imperial burdens, and the Siberian and Far Eastern Republics without being stifled. While Russian nationalists understandably have not followed Brzezinski's well-meant advice, the economic argument of the reformers can still find purchase. It lies in the same charge brought against non-Russians during perestroika, that Russia has invested too much in Siberia with too little return. What has been spent in Siberia was and continues to be a sacrifice by Russia, not an investment. There is good economic and developmental reason therefore to do something else with the non-performing Siberian asset.

The problem with Siberia has been laid out, along with its solution, by two scholars from the Brookings Institution, the American think tank.[6] They have claimed that Siberia is both larger and colder than any single territory or country in the world, therefore the costs of inhabiting it and exploiting it have been excessive, and that the solution lies in a major resettlement or a transfer of the population of Siberia southward and eastward into warmer climes. Once that has been done, the vast resources of Siberia would continue to be exploited by personnel carrying out tours of duty in the north after the fashion of military tours of duty or the exploitation of the comparably inhospitable Canadian north. Siberia would be turned into a mere natural asset for exploitation, admittedly under Russian control still (as in Brzezinski's prescription), almost in the manner that Antarctica is available to all or that planetary bodies might become one day to the inhabitants of the Earth. The authors are careful to make clear that Siberia is in itself not the liability, only the manner of exploiting it is; but the message seems to be or could be understood easily as Siberia itself being the problem.

To drive their point home they have focused attention on the single most important factor of climate. The extremes of temperature are such that the costs of maintaining urban centres in those remote regions are several times greater than they would be in warmer climates farther south. These extra costs have been computed in a number of different ways, but the novel measure has been the so-called temperature per capita or the TPC. They have arrived at this figure by establishing the mean January temperature weighted by the number of persons at any one location.[7] They have calculated the extra expenses at any one spot relative to mean expenses in warmer centres and arrived at the burden these cold towns have been on the GDP. The lower the TPC, the more expensive life would be. Numerous costs have been worked out, but two figures are arresting: Siberia has an excess population of about 16 millions and these have cost about 1.5-2 per cent of GDP annually, which may imply a cumulative loss of 35-50 per cent of growth over a 15 year period assuming an average of 3 per cent per year.[8] If that burden had not been placed on Russia, the country might have been so much more prosperous. The problem is not with Siberia, since that is a given, but with a location policy which did not factor in these additional costs. Soviet central planners populated Siberia regardless of cost; however, had a market logic been allowed to run its course, these cities would not have come up in the first place; yet the resources of Siberia could still have been made available through the tour of duty system.[9]

We are thus back to the fundamentals of Cold War polemic: Soviet central planning got it all wrong, the market would have got it right, as it has in the West, and it is time to correct the mistakes of the twentieth century; central planning is coercive, the market is democratic, and Russia's reversion to democracy is her only salvation. The correction would lie in moving the surplus 16 million of the population of Siberia southward and westward, chiefly to European Russia; but the authors themselves are not certain how it could be carried out. As they have discovered, there may not be anywhere for them to go to, unless these be to refugee camps. Even if these camps were to be set up, why would anyone want to move into them and what would they do. If new towns were to be constructed and employment generated, there is no guarantee that these surplus Siberians would want to move there. When these surplus people do move out of the cold, it is from the permafrost regions to the frost belt, or from the extreme cold to the cold, to the famous Siberian towns of Irkutsk, Yakutsk, Krasnoiarsk, Omsk, Novosibirsk, Cheliabinsk, Perm, or Ekaterinburg, which are responsible in the first place for such low TPCs. By the authors' own reckoning, it would take market forces a century to relocate this surplus population out of Siberian cold enough to raise the TPC to the levels of 1926 when Soviet coerced settlement began.[10] All research suggests that they do not want to leave and that the locally elected democratic leaderships do not want to empty out these lands. Of course, the central leadership in Moscow cannot countenance any such drastic move. If the market cannot undo the mistakes of Soviet central planners, only decisive action by the central government can do so. In short, only another round of central planning can correct the mistakes of the first cycle of central planning, and only undemocratic action can set right the consequences of the initial undemocratic action.[11] Both democracy and the market seem to be irrelevant, although the exercise was undertaken to show how democracy and the market would have developed Siberia the right way but for gratuitous undemocratic non-market Soviet planning.

But there is a further implication to this line of argumentation. Not only has Russia been in error by pursuing central planning and communism, that is undemocratic socialism, it has deviated in some sense from its true European destiny by becoming the Soviet Union and even the Russian Empire. While it has corrected an important part of the error by discarding the Soviet Union, it remains mired to the extent that it retains Siberia. Siberia after all is not Europe, it is merely an appendix to Russia; and if the salvation of Russia lies in Europe, Siberia would have no place in it. The authors have been careful to deny that they are recommending the abandonment of Siberia, but the thrust of their argument pushes a reader to think of the possibility and even the probability. As they argue, if Russia should run short of manpower to exploit Siberia, where would it be found. The ominous possibility of China supplying the manpower looms, and Russians get paranoid about such suggestions. Hill and Gaddy's answer is that any Chinese presence could be contained; and should a security problem arise with China, Russia should rely on rapid action forces, special security guarantee treaties with China and the US, and make Siberia a world heritage site under UN auspices. In a sense this gives the game away. Siberia would be protected by Russia, the US and the US surrogate, the UN, jointly, when rational location policy and market forces operate. Siberia becomes a Western responsibility with Russia acting as steward to the US in those frozen wastes. This is where the discourse on the European identity of Russia comes to rest: in the twenty-first century or the post-Cold War world it implies the salvation of Russia through European levels of material prosperity and European levels of strategic subordination to US leadership. The discourse on the identity of Siberia is but one small agenda item in this Western grand strategy and painful dilemmas it poses for Russian strategic planners and thinkers. It brings the Cold War closer to conclusion.

But Europe did not always mean prosperity and defeat: for long it had meant prosperity and triumph, leadership and growth. From the early Middle Ages when the concept of Europe was devised, Europe was understood as the world of Latin Christianity bounded by the ocean, Orthodoxy, and Islam.[12] Peter in the eighteenth century arbitrarily extended the meaning of Europe to include Russia up to the Urals and even asserted primacy in Europe by assuming the imperial title and bringing himself level with the Holy Roman Emperor. Europeans may have sniffed at such a suspect reconstitution of Europe, and the Russian Orthodox Church may have dreaded their sworn enemy, the Roman Catholic Church, extending its tentacles into Russia, but the Russian nobility and secular power structures were comfortable. Thereafter, the modernization, westernization, and Europeanization of Russia were experienced as a triumphal progress for the Russian state until the first shock of the Crimean defeat in 1856. The defeats in the Napoleonic wars were humiliating and the occupation and burning of Moscow in 1812 were traumatic, but they were speedily reversed by the heady victories of Leipzig and Waterloo, by the tsar entering Paris as a liberator, and by the almost uninterrupted foreign policy successes of Nicholas I until the Crimean disaster. The Russian state recovered within a decade from even this defeat as Gorchakov, the foreign minister, repudiated important clauses of the treaty of Paris that followed the Crimean defeat, and Russia acquired a vast colonial empire in Central Asia and played an undiluted imperialist role along with the other European great powers in China and on the Pacific. The subsequent wave of industrialization until the Revolution was advertised as Russia becoming European to the marrow, even if that marrow was thoroughly cancerous by Narodnik reckoning. The defeat of the tsarist state in World War I was welcomed by the Bolsheviks as an opportunity for fulfilling the European promise of development, not through its decadent capitalism in its last and "highest" stage, but through its socialism. What some considered to be defeat, others saw as victory; and Lenin and the Bolsheviks were able to endorse the dissolution of the Russian Empire as the condition for the impending triumph of a great tradition of European culture, its socialism. In wholly symmetrical fashion, Russian reformers of the late twentieth century looked forward to the defeat of the Soviet Union in the Cold War and accepted the dissolution of the Union thereafter as once again consummating another great European tradition, this time called liberalism and capitalism. It was the antithesis of Lenin's argument, but it was congruent with his manner of argumentation. Like Lenin and his heirs, Russian perestroika and other reformers have been bitterly disillusioned, and what was imagined as a victory is now almost universally regarded a defeat and disaster. Numerous and entirely opposed traditions have since Peter's time looked upon Europe as signifying rationality, progress, and prosperity, and they have been prepared to dissolve the Russian Empire, the Soviet Union, and now perhaps even the Russian Federation to become European, however that was and is interpreted.

However, if a European commitment seemed to head toward failure without prospect of redemption, the legacy of Peter would be questioned. The first rumblings were heard by the end of Catherine II's reign when the beginning of industrialization and the ferment of the Enlightenment at the extreme end of the European continent transformed Russia into a retarded province of Europe. Russia no longer seemed to be in a position to compete on equal terms. There were insistent demands that Russia jettison her European identity and retreat into a uniquely Russian one. Generations of the most gifted intelligentsia and bureaucracy, and journalists and propagandists ceaselessly debated the question of Russia and Europe; it is the stuff of text books and university courses; it is the background to virtually every discussion about Russia; it is exhausting, tedious, and repetitive; yet it remains alive as an existential question in Russia and as a strategic lever in the West down to this day as the interventions by Brzezinski and Hill and Gaddy in post-Soviet times suggest. It penetrates every debate on strategy, politics, and economics, on history, sociology, and psychology, on law and morality, on religion, art, and music; it is the fate of Russians to debate the question and it is the fate of every student of Russia to handle the question even if he chooses to dismiss it all as exempla of Russians *in extremis* inhabiting the world of Dostoevskian liminality.

But one broad point is clear through the debates of over three centuries. As long as the Russian state, whether extant or in waiting, felt it was triumphant in Europe, that same Europe seemed to be the route to salvation; when Russia seemed to be hopelessly slipping, as the discourse on backwardness seemed to reveal from the late eighteenth century, then Europe could look like the road to perdition also. At such moments of doubt, the self-sufficiency and uniqueness of Russia would be asserted with greater conviction than before. The question of Russian identity is locked into this perennial uncertainty and ambiguity, and post-Soviet Russia is caught in one of its moments. A strategy for Siberia has been presented in the context of the identity of Russia. If Russia is European, Russia must in some sense lose Siberia. It is not a problem that would have presented itself to Peter, the supreme westernizer of all; yet to despairing Russians today, Siberia just seems to have been wrongly composed and hung as an albatross around Russia, while policy advisers like Hill and Gaddy from the West have suggested how Russia could divest herself of the Siberian encumbrance. It arises from the sense and experience of defeat in the Cold War. In such a context, the uniqueness of Russia becomes a source for strategy rather than for obfuscation; and the place for Siberia in Russia is found through Eurasian uniqueness rather than European universality.

Eurasianism is inclusive and would include Siberia in a Russian state apparently without demur; Europeanism on the other hand is exclusive and bifurcates the Russian Federation by excluding Siberia. Eurasianism was elaborated by Nikolai Trubetskoi and Georgii Vernadskii among others aftèr the multiple catastrophes of World War I, the Civil War, and Revolution, as an answer to a major defeat in Europe and seemingly by Europe.[13] As a variant of civilization theory, it identified a Eurasian civilization distinct from the European, or Romano-German as Trubetskoi termed it; it was highly polyglot and was composed of multiple elements, Orthodox, Islamic, and Buddhist; and these elements enjoyed their autonomy in a non-merging unity which he called a symphony. As a civilization it was not European; yet it was not Russian nationalist despite the preponderance of Russians or Slavs within it, and despite its embracing virtually the same territory as that of the Russian Empire. As the Russian Empire went down in defeat and irretrievable ruin, this theory provided a principle of reconstitution free of the much reviled Empire, of the highly divisive Russian nationalism, and of Bolshevik fantasies. It seemed to provide an equal and autonomous place to non Russians and non-Christians and thus to capture the vibrant polyvalency of the historical construction that went by the names of the Muscovite tsardom and the Russian Empire. Like its antecedent civilization theory, Nikolai Danilevskii's historico-cultural typology of the 1870s,[14] the Eurasianism of the twentieth century was an answer to what was experienced as a catastrophic defeat. Following a long tradition dating back to Prince Mikhail Shcherbatov in the 1780s, it traced the debility of Russia to absorption in Europe and logically enough sought to identify the entity and the principles that were autonomous of Europe. Not surprisingly, after the squalid collapse of the Soviet Union and *therefore* of Russia, Eurasianism has enjoyed an enormous revival.[15] In such a polyglot and historical construction, Siberia would effortlessly find an honoured and secure place.[16]

But there is irony here, as always in history. Eurasianism was devised to integrate the multiplicity of the territorial space of the Russian Empire when it was torn apart by competing nationalisms, and once again it is imagined as an answer to the centrifugalism of the nationalisms plaguing the same space when a supranational socialism has gone defunct. However, Siberia is safely and utterly Russian with no threat of a separatist nationalism against the Russian Federation. It does not make sense to turn to a Eurasianist doctrine to bind Siberia to Russia any more than it would have been necessary to integrate Riazan or Tula to Russia. Eurasianism in the construction of the identity of Siberia seems to be irrelevant and misplaced.

The big question should be: why should the identity of Siberia be an issue at all? It has been a part of Russia or the Russian Empire and its successor states since its conquest in the seventeenth century and its settlement by Russians. In this respect it is no different from the rest of Russia, each part of which was subjected to a Russian prince and eventually to the Great Prince of Moscow and peopled by Russians and Orthodox Christians for the most part through migration, settlement, and religious conversion. Only the timing is different in each case; and Siberia is not even the last. It entered the empire a century before the northern shores of the Black Sea and even before the crucible of modern Russia, St Petersburg. It became Russian by the same process as the rest of Russia "proper", that is, by conquest and settlement. But for Peter's cartographic and cultural intervention of drawing the European frontier at the Urals, it would have been as Russian as Great Russia or "European" Russia itself is. If Russia, as Kliuchevskii has said, has been created by migration, Siberia is Russian as much as any other province. If Russia is European, Siberia should be European; and if Russia cannot be European but must be Eurasian, in whatever meaning of the term, Siberia would be equally Eurasian.

From this we may ask the further question, why should the identity of Russia as Eurasian or European be raised in such seriousness, as if the fate of Russia depends on the answer. The challenge of European and Western industrial society has been faced from the late eighteenth century by all the world, and everywhere they have been obliged to ponder the extent to which European or western influences were transforming their societies. But none of them with the exception of Russia has been seized with the question of whether they were in fact European or not, none have been complaining as Chaadaev did that they are neither western nor eastern. Of course this manner of debating identity is a means to proposing a strategy of action, but almost identical strategies of action have been proposed elsewhere in the world without this particular problem of identity, the problem of whether they are European or not. This is uniquely Russian, and now the fate of Siberia has been entered into the dispute. It is perhaps futile to suggest that the debate and discussion on identity in this form be abandoned, for it is the medium through which Russia and her adversaries and friends in Europe and America conduct their power struggles between themselves as structures of state, with all the consequences for culture that flow from that position. Although latter-day academic research seeks to avoid these dead ends, to study Russia as composite and polyglot rather than Great Russian, as seen in the journals *Kritika* and *Ab Imperio*, American and Russian respectively, the more consciously political debates are trapped in these ancient paradigms, fed no doubt at various points by academic research also. The new interest in Siberia is firmly placed in both spheres, the innovative academic and the polemically strategic, and it is always instructive as much to observe the two lines intersect as to participate in the process.

Notes and References

1. John B. Dunlop, "Russia: In Search of an Identity?" in Ian Bremmer and Ray Taras, eds., *New States, New Politics: Building the Post-Soviet Nations* Cambridge: Cambridge University Press, 1997, pp. 28-95.
2. A. Solzhenitsyn, *Rebuilding Russia. Reflections and Tentative Proposals*, translated from the Russian by Alexis Klimoff Harvill, 1991, pp. 12-15.
3. See for example Aleksandr Kazintsev, "Nasledie SSSR. Kak im rasporiaditsia Rossiia", *Nash Sovremennik*, 1994, no. 7, pp. 150-156, here pp. 152-153.

4. In 1989, less than 5 per cent of the population of Siberia were indigenous; in 2001 in UK 7.9 per cent were from "non-white ethnic background"; in France in 2007 about 10 per cent of the population were estimated to be of Arab or African origin.
5. Zbigniew Brzezinski, "A Geostrategy for Eurasia," *Foreign Affairs*, 76:5, September/October 1997.
6. Fiona Hill, Clifford G. Gaddy, *The Siberian Curse. How Communist Planners Left Russia Out in the Cold,* Washington D.C.: Brookings Institution Press, 2003, p. 303.
7. Taken from two research papers: Tatiana Mikhailova, *The Cost of the Cold. The Legacy of Soviet Location Policy in Russian Energy Consumption, Productivity and Growth*, July 29, 2005, p. 46. (*http://people.bu.edu/tmikhail/research.html*), and Tatiana Mikhailova, *Where Russians should live: a counterfactual alternative to Soviet location policy*, Aug. 2005, (*http://people.bu.edu/tmikhail/research.html*)
8. As it would have been for America, hence so much worse for Russia, Hill and Gaddy, *The Siberian Curse,* p. 47.
9. For spirited Russian rebuttals of the thesis, see the two issues of *Problems of Economic Transition*, vol. 48, no. 11, March 2006, and vol. 49, no. 9, January 2007.
10. Hill and Gaddy, *The Siberian Curse,* pp. 130-132; by Tatiana Mikhailova's reckoning, it would take 150 years, Tatiana Mikhailova, *Where Russians should live: a counterfactual alternative to Soviet location policy*, Aug. 2005, (*http://people.bu.edu/tmikhail/research.html*), p. 51.
11. Hill and Gaddy, *The Siberian Curse,* ch. 10.
12. Marc Bloch, *Feudal Society*, Vol. 1, London: Routledge and Kegan Paul, 1962, p. xx.
13. Kniaz' N.S. Trubetskoi, *Evropa i chelovechestvo*, Sofia: Rossiisko-Bolgarskoe knigoizdatel'stvo, 1926; I.A. Isaev, ed., Puti Evrazii. Russkaia intelligentsia i sud'by Rossii, Moscow: Russkaia Kniga, 1992, pp. 347-415 which reprints the original manifesto, *Evraziistvo. Opyt sistematicheskogo izlozheniia*, Paris 1926.
14. N. Ia. Danilevskii, *Rossiia i Evropa,* Moscow: Kniga, 1991, slightly abridged from the 1871 edition.
15. Mark von Hagen, "Empires, Borderlands, and Diasporas: Eurasia as Anti-Paradigm for Post-Soviet Era," *American Historical Review*, April 2004, pp. 445-468; Stephen Kotkin, "Mongol Commonwealth? Exchange and Governance across the Post-Mongol Space," *Kritika. Explorations in Russian and Eurasian History*, New Series, Vol. 8, No. 3, Summer 2007, pp. 487-532.
16. Many groups are active and popular in Russia today, one of the more

extravagant being Alexander Dugin's Arctogaia, for details see their website *http://arctogaia.com*, and their programme in English at *http://arctogaia.com/public/eng/Program.htm.*; for a somewhat jaundiced view of their activities and their influence as a revivalist nationalism bringing together Red-Brown forces, see Charles Clover, "Dreams of the Eurasian Heartland. The Reemergencc of Geopolitics," *Foreign Affairs*, vol. 78, no. 2, March-April 1999, pp. 9-13.

2

Conceptualizing Eurasian Geopolitics: Debates and Discourses on the 'Heartland'

Anita Sengupta

We have No Choice but to Continue the Heartland Debate[1]

Concluding his influential book *What is Asia to Us? Russia's Asian Heartland Yesterday and Today*, Milan Hauner had noted "We have no choice but to continue the Heartland Debate". Originating in a presentation made by Sir Halford Mackinder to the Royal Geographical Society in 1904, this debate identified a vast geographical expanse east of the Urals as the 'pivot' of world history, control over which would determine who 'controlled' global politics. A century later the world hardly resembles the one that Mackinder wrote about. However, the geographical area that he had identified as the pivot and later heartland i.e., Eurasia, continues to be identified as the globe's central arena and Russia's Asian question continues to be conceptualized in terms of the 'heartland debate'.[2] *What is Asia to Us?* was published in 1990 at a juncture when the Eurasian space was on the verge of cataclysmic changes that would transform not just the geographical contours of the Union of Soviet Socialist Republics but also the geopolitical balance within the space. While the concept of a 'space' is more generally defined its transformation into a 'place' entails a synthesis of geographical and sociological imaginations.[3] The identification of the Eurasian region as the "heartland" assumes significance to the extent that it signifies this transition from 'space' to 'place' and symbolizes the conjunction between geographical and sociological imaginations. However, new definitions of 'place' have emerged over time and this presentation looks at some of the discourses that have conceptualized the idea of

Eurasia from a more generalized 'space' into particular 'places'. These re-conceptualizations have been impelled by transformations not just within the Eurasian space but also in global politics calling for a 'rethinking' of conventional geopolitical assumptions.[4]

This 'rethinking' in critical terms conceptualized geopolitics as a discourse that seeks to negotiate a spatial understanding of the 'reality' of global politics within the multiplicity of discourses that now dominates the global arena. While unavoidably textual it offers a spatial way of thinking that arranges different actors, elements and locations simultaneously on a global 'chessboard'. Gearoid O' Tuathail, who underlined the element of discourse in geopolitical debates, in his "Introduction" to *The Geopolitics Reader* writes:

> It (geopolitics) has a multidimensional global cachet—global both in a geographical (worldwide) and a conceptual (comprehensive and total) sense – and appears more visual than verbal, more objective and detached than subjective and ideological.[5]

Tuathail of course italicizes the word 'appears' and goes on to critique the objectivity of geopolitics in some detail in his writings on *critical* geopolitics. However, geopolitics retains its interest because it promises insights into the future direction of international affairs and the coming shape of the world political map. While this is generally accepted the point of debate centers around contentious viewpoints about the shape of the world political map and its principal actors. In its imperialistic origins geopolitical visions were entwined with imperialist strategy and dominated by rivalries between sea powers and land powers. The spatial delimitation of the global resource network and the mapping of territorial actors who would compete for control over these resources dominated traditional geopolitical approaches. This was exemplified by Mackinder and Mahan who exemplify discussions of geopolitics where the binary division of the world was essentially one for control over resources. The Cold War structures created its own geopolitical discourse and practices dominated by a bipolar division of the world and rivalry between two 'superpowers'. With the end of the Cold War and the emergence of the so called 'new world order' the relationship between geography, power and world order was transformed. For some it meant the emergence of a new geopolitical order dominated by geo-economic questions and issues, a world where globalization has affected the way in which sovereignty was traditionally conceived. "New geopolitics" however, has within itself numerous competing visions and has been defined not just in geo-economic terms but also in terms of emerging transnational problems and ecological politics. Each has produced its own discourse and concpetualizing geopolitics in the present scenario involves an understanding of these contested discourses.

While the focus of geopolitics has been transformed what remains unchanged is the necessity of understanding the historical juncture at which certain geopolitical positioning assumed significance as also the context within which it was framed. The context itself was determined by several layers of interlocking institutions that influenced the way in which geopolitical discourses emerged. Sir Halford Mackinder, for example, was one of the first Professors of Geography in the United Kingdom. His career within geography was made possible by his association with the Royal Geographical Society that served as the social gathering place and network for the ruling establishment of the British Empire. It has therefore been argued that one way to interpret his influential "Pivot paper" is as a piece of long term policy advice to the British Foreign Office and its Defence Ministry that Britain needed to urgently develop it's strategic and trading links with the British Empire in order to ward off the threats posed by continental and any future sea powers.[6] In this paper Mackinder set out the central concern of western defence policy, i.e, the fear that the landmass of Euro-Asia would be controlled by one power, which would be in a position to exercise global domination. Mackinder presented his paper in 1904, to the Royal Geographical Society. In a novel entitled *Kim* first published in 1901 Rudyard Kipling had highlighted the significance of control over the region that Mackinder identified as the 'pivot' and coined the term 'Great Game' to define a shadowy game for control between continental Russia and Britain, a receding sea power. While the novel itself is only broadly familiar to most the idea of the "Great Game" caught on as a concept and has been repeatedly used to define the present contest for control over the resources of the 'heartland' indicating a transcendence that Kipling himself had clearly underlined in his book, "When everyone is dead the Great Game is finished. Not before."[7]

This transcendence was also identified by Sir Olaf Kirkpatrice Caroe, British India's leading geopolitical thinker during the final days of the Raj. Caroe had served as foreign secretary to Britain's Government of India through out the Second World War. He was afterward Britain's last Governor General of the North West Frontier Province, which lies along the border with Afghanistan in present day Pakistan. Caroe's career spanned the transition from an era of World War to one of Cold War coinciding with the onset of decolonization and the rise of air power as an organizing conception of global strategy. Caroe carefully studied and followed these developments and emphasized underlying continuties in the pattern of world power. At stake was nothing less than global supremacy. Of course Caroe was not alone in identifying this transcendence. Lord Curzon imagined a "chessboard upon which is played out a game for global domination" and of course the imagery of a "grand chessboard" resonates even today as a metaphor.[8]

What is interesting is that Caroe, like Mackinder emphasized the permanence of geography versus the vicissitudes of empire and ideology. Caroe described a map of the world divided into "Seven Theatres of Power" – Atlantic, Europe, Central Land Mass, Indian Ocean, Africa, Pacific and America.[9] Like Mackinder he also hinted at a binary division of the global space and emphasized that it was Britain's control of the of the "Indian Ocean Theatre" that had during the 19th century worked to check Russia's absorption of the colossal "Central Land Mass Theatre".[10] The central land mass is to a large extent coterminous with Mackinder's pivot (later heartland) area. However, while Mackinder identifies the state controlling the 'heartland' as 'commanding the world' Caroe argues that as a counterpoise to Soviet and increasingly Chinese power consolidating in the Asian heartland, India would remain pivotal in the maintenance of a global balance between land and sea powers. This of course was not surprising given the context within which he was presenting his ideas and his own position within it.

It has subsequently been argued that the 'Great Game' continued to be played out just as Caroe had predicted.

> Caroe recognized the subcontinent's geospatial centrality when others typically located South Asia on the world's strategic periphery. He believed that Russian land power posed a traditional and future danger to international

> stability. But when many tended to fear an implacable enemy, Caroe imagined the long term vulnerability of the Soviet Union's multi-ethnic empire in the heartland of Asia. He foresaw the resurgence of China as a great power when conventional wisdom discounted that country's potentialities separate from external organization. Caroe warned that Afghanistan and the remote Pathan borderlands of what is today Pakistan formed a political fault zone of global significance. He anticipated the resilience of Islam in the face of communism and secularizing ideologies more generally in an era when fashions were disposed to dismiss religious motivation as a spent force. And Caroe explained the importance of the Persian Gulf in relation both to world oil production and as a base area well situated for the staging of Anglo American forces throughout the western Indian Ocean and up into Central Asia. In short even though the geopolitical vision that Caroe had articulated failed to sustain the empire it had once animated – hence our difficulty in perceiving its resilience—the Great Game continues to drive the dynamic of global power and strategic competition in Asia today and presumably tomorrow.[11]

In fact with the disintegration of the Soviet Union and the emergence of new states in the region the idea of a "new" great game was revived as a part of certain geopolitical concepts and models that had become largely defunct in the recent past. The revival of geopolitics followed by the emergence of geo-economics meant that a large part of writings on the Eurasian region once again defined it in terms of traditional geopolitical concepts. The idea of a "new" great game became a persistent one in writings that alluded to a revival of the struggle for control over the region and this revival was situated within the context of acquiring control over the "heartland". Since the 1990's the use of the term and concept of the new great game and the "heartland" overshadowed the analysis of events in Eurasia. Most of these great game writings had geopolitical references or allude to them as significant. This was as true of the post Soviet world as well as of the west.

At the end of the Cold War Russia's post communist Minister of Foreign Affairs, Andrei Kozyrev noted that the Russian administration had comprehended quite fast that geopolitics is taking the place of ideology.[12] The former Cold War blocs were falling apart and new patterns of regional fragmentation prompted politicians and their advisers to depict the world as a "grand chessboard". He argued that more recently geopolitical narratives like the "clash of civilizations" or the "axis of evil" have become the focus of attention in foreign policy circles. This resurgence of interest in geopolitics can be put down to two recent trends, one relating to real world changes which have taken place and the other to the theoretical paradigms which have been constructed as part of post modern critiques.[13] What is significant here is the extent to which these contrasting geopolitical reasoning becomes part of the real world debate and influences government policies. As globalization impacts the traditional territorial structure of the state and its interstate relations, it has to come to grips with the past geopolitical images and self locations which dictated its positions. What also requires close attention is an appreciation of the extent to which geopolitics operates in proximity to agents of real politicai power. This was reflected in the ambitions as well as the achievements of geopolitics before the war as exemplified by Friedrich Ratzel, Halford Mackinder, Alfred Mahan and others. The more recent examples of Henry Kissinger and Zbiginew Brzezinski are also indicative in this regard. Similarly, geopolitics dominates conservative nationalist discourse in Russia. Leaders of at least two highly influential political parties on the far right, Gennadii Zuganov and Vladimir Zhirinovski have both written lengthy books about geopolitics. The principal theoretician of geopolitics in Russia today, Aleksandr Dugin is an influential political consultant to conservative members of the Russian Parliament.

In the background of this general discussion of geopolitical reconceptualizations, the question of how to problematize the significance of Eurasia as a distinct geocultural space—not entirely separated from Europe but functioning as a contradistinction of the conventional paradigms of 'east' and 'west' will be attempted. Here, there remains a discomfort with both European and Asian archetypes and an attempt at cultural bridging that undermines conventional dichotomies and engages the identity of the steppe. The idea of Eurasia opened up new possibilities of imagining geographical space. The term Eurasia or *Evraziia* was used by the Eurasianists to indicate a different 'geographical world', different from both Europe and Asia. It has been argued that the Eurasianists' 'geographical world' of Eurasia can be called a mega-region. [14] The Eurasianist sometimes used the word 'continent' to refer to this mega –region but that usage was for them metaphorical rather than scientific. This conception however, problematized the word 'continent'. In this new world of Russia-Eurasia the Eurasianists declared cultural independence from both Europe and Asia. The Eurasianists strongly identified ethnic Russians with other Eastern Slavs and people of the Eurasian mega-region, Finno-Ugric, Turkic and Mongolian. Eurasianists did not however define the boundaries of Eurasia with precision and in fact their various versions of Eurasia overlapped. Still the expanse of their Eurasias roughly coincided with the boundaries of pre 1914 Russian Empire. To Eurasianists, Eurasia was separated from Asia to its South by high mountains and impenetrable deserts, to its West Eurasia were separated from Europe by what Savitsky called the 'region between the Black and the Baltic Seas'. The Eurasianists devised a series of detailed arguments to justify this as the legitimate geographical divide. A strict interpretation of this geographical scheme excluded all of Russia's territory east of the Lena River. On the other hand some regions that fall outside Russia's political borders—a large part of western China for instance—was seen as an integral part of Eurasia. Eurasianists argued that there was no discernable break across the Urals, linguistically, culturally and economically there were only continuities from the west to the east.

This continuity, for instance, has been emphasized in the political and ideological discourse of contemporary Turkey where Eurasia is considered as a region settled mainly by Turkic peoples, including Turkey, the Balkans and part of the Caucasus, the former Soviet republics of Central Asia, the region of Volga in Russia and Northern Afghanistan. Adherents of this viewpoint have included Suleyman Demirel former Turkish President but also representatives of various wings of Turkish political elites. Operating on the core principles of classical geopolitical discourses, Eurasian geopolitical theories in Turkey have arrived at various innovative conclusions. An interesting example is Ramazan Ozey's (Professor of Marmara University) writing entitled "The Theory of Centre Domination of Turks". It concludes that Anatolia is the 'World Fortress' (*Dunya kalesi* in Turkish or 'heartland' in the classical sense) and the ruler country is Anatolia. Turkey possessing this acropolis has an opportunity to take control over the regions of the "Inner Circle" (*Ic cember* in Turkish and Mackinder's Inner Crescent) According to Ozey they are the Balkans and Eurasia. As the World Fortress Turkey will govern the World (*Dis Cember* in Turkish and the Outer Crescent in Mackinder's concept).[15]

While Ozey identifies Anatolia as the 'World Fortress' or the 'heartland' various other criteria have been used to indicate centrality in contemporary writings from within the region that is today identified as the 'heartland'. Sayragul Matikeeva, for instance, argues that any part of the globe may become the 'heart' of the Pivot area, since Mackinder indicated that the central location was a relative concept. She goes on to mote that it is China that is now poised to become the new pivot by virtue of her economic domination over the traditional heartland. A political scientist and lecturer at the International Relations Department at the International University of Kyrgyzstan, in Bishkek, Matikeeva argues that China's economic advance and its persistent even if 'soft' efforts to impose its conditions on the Central Asian countries suggest that the 'heartland' might shift and that China is striving to become the 'heartland' by swallowing on the sly the current heartland by capitalizing on its political and economic instability.[16] She points to Bishkek's 'unpopular' decision to transfer 30 percent of the disputed territories in the Bedel Pass (Uzongu-Kuush) area to China as the beginning of a final territorial delimitation in favour of China. Secondly she argues that political influence is now crucial in determining the pivot and that today this influence is based on how significant a state is in terms of the international counter terrorist efforts. She notes that Mackinder was correct in pointing out that the global space was now an interconnected arena where no power could deal with threats single-handedly. This was particularly true in the present context where the threat of terror has to be dealt with on a global level. This also means that a state could become the 'heart' of the Pivot area if the geostrategic interests of its neighbours, specially of those that claim the role of a world leader are dependent on the territorial integrity of that particular state. And here of course she has Kyrgyzstan in mind as the 'heart' of the Pivot. While Matikeeva arrives at this conclusion from within a traditional geopolitical framework determined by the 'new great game' imagery, others have indicated how the concepts of 'heartland' and 'rimland' are now subject to revision.

Uzbek political scientist and Associate Professor at the National University of Uzbekistan, Farkhod Tolipov clearly suggests that while Mackinder was the first to indicate the potential power of the region as the 'heartland' the concept should now be subject to revision. He writes:

> .... the heartland and the rimland are changing in the wake of counterterrorist operation in Afghanistan. To be more precise, the geopolitical transformation of Central Asia brought about by the dissolution of the former Soviet state has only accelerated after 11 September 2001. Central Asia is very likely to become a strategically important area not "overlaid" by the heartland or the rimland as a subordinate entity but represented in them as an independent entity.[17]

Tolipov uses the terms "positive" and "negative" diversification to explain not just the economic pluralization now underway in the region but also the geopolitical pluralization that would eventually underline this transformation. He argues that the inevitable multiplication of directions for the transportation of oil, gas and other resources is matched by a similar multiplication in terms of the foreign policy orientation of the states. However, he argues that these are just visible manifestations of the forms of geopolitical transformation of Central Asia.

> ...its essence consists in the change of geopolitical code or status of the region concerned in the international system. Post Soviet Kazakhstan, Kyrgyzstan, Tajikistan, Turkmenistan and Uzbekistan, for the first time in their history are acting as independent actors in international relations. This very fact is either ignored by many researchers or even misrepresented in favour of traditional and obsolete perceptions based on consideration of these states only from the view point of which great power dominates here.
>
> In a very complicated international context the overall search for local (national) as well as what can be called "external identity"(strategic orientation) by Central Asian countries can take either positive or negative forms and meanings. I call this phenomenon positive and negative diversification. Negative diversification revitalizes the classical balance of power in international relations and the zero-sum game played between great powers usually at the expense of the Central Asian states. Positive diversification avoids the zero sum approach and is inclusive in character: it means not only the equal involvement of external powers but also, more importantly, a more coordinated policy among the Central Asian states.[18]

He also stresses the fact that the Central Asian states are themselves in search of a global orientation at present and in search for their place in the world and among civilizations. At present choices like West or East, Europe or Eurasia, America or Russia is increasingly being articulated in Central Asian debates. As a result the geopolitical situation is ambiguous for all sides and stresses that the outward orientation of the region should not obstruct and undermine its inward orientation. He notes that constructive geopolitics in the Central Asian context would mean inclusion of outside powers in Central Asian affairs and full integration of countries within the region. What such writings emphasize is a desire at posing alternatives.

These alternatives, however, assume significance to the extent that they become a part of the real world debate and influence policies. Kazakh President Nursultan Nazarbaev's idea of a "Eurasian" space, for instance, serves several political aims. In his geopolitical analysis of Eurasia he writes:

> If we look at a geographical map then it is easy to notice that there is a consecutive vertical row of countries of Eurasia from Russia in the north to India in the south (Central Asian countries, Iran, Pakistan) that does not yet link either with the east or with the west. I would call this continuous belt of countries situated along the meridian of the centre of Eurasia the 'belt of anticipation'. Despite all the differences among these countries they constitute a relatively solid group from the point of view of potential resources and possibilities of influencing not only the balance of power in Asia or Eurasia but even the geopolitical balance of the world.[19]

Nazarbaev further argues that since Russia will never be admitted as an equal member into either the European or the East Asian sphere its only viable choice is to unite the countries of the "belt of anticipation" into a new security system.

Nazarbaev's "belt of anticipation" is interesting particularly because it indicates a vertical definition of the Eurasian space that is generally visualized as a horizontal expanse. It is also significant in terms of the actual states that are included, Russia, India and the countries in between, that is the Central Asian republics, Iran and Pakistan. The silences are of course more than important. The definition excludes Afghanistan, a state that is now sought to be identified as a link within the Eurasian space. What is also significant is that this definition places Kazakhstan squarely in the centre of this particular imagined Eurasia. But then there is another dimension to Nazarbaev's Eurasia. It is also conceived of as a Union intended to promote a common economic space across the territory of the former Soviet Union. Nazarbaev was clear in pointing out that this was not meant as a restoration of the Soviet Union but as a post Soviet construct that loosely resembled the European Union.

In a sense, of course this vertical definition has precedence in a vision where a North-South linkage was conceptualized as an alternative transport route that would link Russia, Iran and India. The corridor was conceived as stretching from ports in India across the Arabian Sea to the southern Iranian port of Bandar Abbas where goods would then transit Iran and the Caspian Sea ports in the Russian sector of the Caspian. From there the route stretches along the Volga river via Moscow to northern Europe. Along with Russia, India and Iran this project was subsequently joined by Belarus, Kazakhstan, Tajikistan and Azerbaijan. More recently the Turkman President Gurbanguly Berdymukhammedov in his meetings with Iranian leaders expressed interest in the project.[20]

While each of these definitions has had their adherents what remains significant is the variety of discursive reconceptualizations, at the juncture of geographical and sociological imaginations, which has defined Eurasia. Mackinder, whose first definitions of a pivotal area in world history had been instrumental in focusing attention on Eurasia had himself indicated that the so called 'heartland' eluded precise definition and as a strategic concept was subject to changes. The criteria that he had once indicated to define a 'heartland' have subsequently been used to define other "heartlands". Mackinder had excluded half of Siberia, east and south of the Yenisi river, the so-called Lenaland, from his last and final definition.[21] However, debates about the extent of the Eurasian space has focused attention on Russian fringe areas like Siberia. In an article in *The Geographical Journal* in 1962 and then subsequently in a monograph entitle *The New Soviet Heartland* David J.M. Hooson, a British geographer argued that a new 'heartland' was emerging within the Soviet Union which in the future could well bid to become a heartland in its own right.[22] It extends from the Middle Volga to Lake Baykal. He argues that this region qualifies as the 'new' heartland as:

> The fundamental fact is that it is the repository for most of those accessible resources of energy and raw materials upon which the growth of Soviet industrial, military and political power in the world ultimately depends. This situation itself might justify the use of the word 'heartland' taking 'heart' to be the vital generating parts of a system, in this case the Soviet State. However, the recent record of this zone as an unusually powerful magnet for urban industrial population indicates that these resources are increasingly being used to build up the zone itself as well as the long dominant regions to its west. It is not only that the rates of city growth have been faster here over the last two decades than anywhere else in the country—even in the absolute terms Volga-Baykal acquired as many city dwellers as did all of European Russia on its western flank.[23]

He goes on to argue that there are two everyday figurative meanings of the word 'heart'—one as the vital generating part of a system, the other being the central or inner part of something. Hooson argues that as a unit of generalization the closely knit communist world is more meaningful toady than a unit based on physical geography or even on recurring patterns of Eurasian history which were enacted in far away strategic, economic and technological days. Within this Communist world the Volga-Baykal zone has the marks of a real continental stronghold. Siberia was thus identified as Russia's Economic 'heartland', whose exploration and development played a vital role in underpinning the Russian economy. In the post Soviet context this 'new' heartland acquired significance from the standpoint of geo-economics and emerged as the new field of study within Eurasia given its historical, economic and cultural specificities. Connectivity once again assumed central importance as has the development of inter and intra regional trade networks. New routes and in the process new partners have been sought for creating opportunities for a rethinking of traditional ways of conceptualizing partnerships within the Eurasian space.

The emergence of the 'new' heartlands brings back into focus the discursive reformulation of 'spaces' into 'places' and the conjunction between geographical and sociological imaginations that it entails. The problem of how to view the world in a meaningful perspective is a challenge that each era confronts thereby underlining

Mackinder's comment, "Every century had has its own geographical perspective". In fact every age also has conventional ways of looking at the patterns of the world and creating its own geographical stereotypes. What remains significant and debated is the problem of gaining the most meaningful perspective on the geopolitical context at any given moment since this has a profound impact on the dynamic political realities of the moment. Various alternative 'heartlands', for instance, have emerged over time and changing realities call for taking note of the possibilities that they represent.

Notes and References

1. The concluding line of Milan Hauner's, *What is Asia to us? Russia's Asian Heartland Yesterday and Today*, London: Unwin Hyman, 1990.
2. This is a debate that identifies a resource rich area connectivity to which becomes crucial in maintaining control. While Sir Halford Mackinder had identified its resources in terms of its mineral reserves and an expanding population and pointed to the dangers of a railway that would provide a new connectivity, in present terms its oil and natural gas reserves have been emphasized along with the requirement of a new connectivity in terms of pipelines.
3. For details of the argument see John A. Agnew and James S. Duncan, "Introduction" in John A. Agnew and James S. Duncan (eds) *The Power of Place: Bringing Together Geographical and Sociological Imaginations*, Boston: Unwin Hyman, 1989.
4. This 'rethinking' was influenced by the works of critical geopoliticians like Gearoid O' Tuathail whose book *Rethinking Geopolitics,* first published in 1998, emphasized the need for a new conceptualiztaion. See Gearoid O' Tuathail and Simon Dalby (eds) *Rethinking Geopolitics*, London and New York, Routledge, 1998.
5. Gearoid O' Tuathail, "Introduction: Thinking Critically About Geopolitics", in Gearoid O' Tuathail, Simon Dalby and Paul Routledge (eds) *The Geopolitics Reader*, London and New York, Routledge, 1998.
6. Brian Blouet, "The Imperial Vision of Halford Mackinder", *The Geographical Journal*, Vol. 170, No. 4, December 2004.
7. Rudyard Kipling, *Kim,* New York: Everyman's Library, originally 1901, p. 234.
8. Zbigniew Brzezinski, *The Grand Chessboard, American Primacy and Its Geostrategic Imperatives*, New York: Basic Books.
9. Olaf Caroe, "Problems of Power Confrontation in Inner Asia" *Journal of the Royal Central Asian Society*, No. 56, 1969.
10. For details and map see Peter John Brobst, *The Future of the Great*

Game, Sir Olaf Caroe, India's Independence and the Defense of Asia, Akron, Ohiio: The University of Akron Press, 2005.

11. *Brobst,* The Future of the Great Game, Sir Olaf Caroe, India's Independence and the Defense of Asia.
12. Cited from Paul Reuber, "The political representation of space after the cold war and in the new millennium", in a *Forum* on "Is there a politics to geopolitcs?" Organizing Editor: Alexander B. Murphy, in *Progress in Human Geography,* Vol. 28, No. 5, 2004.
13. See David Newman, "An informed and proactive geopolitics" in a *Forum* on "Is there a politics to geopolitcs?".
14. Ilya'Vinkovetsky, "Eurasia and its Uses: the History of An Idea and the Mental Geography of Post Soviet Space', unpublished paper presented at the 2007 Annual Soyuz Symposium on *Locating Eurasia in Postsocialist Studies: The Geopolitics of Naming, April 27-29, 2007, Princeton University.*
15. Cited from Ruben Safrastyan, "The Concept of Eurasia and Turkey's Regional Strategies", *Global Politician* 24 May 2005 web version at *www.globalpolitician.com/articledes.asp*
16. Sayragul Matikeeva, "Mackinder's Legacy: Was It A prophecy?" *Central Asia and the Caucasus* (Special Issue) 4(34), 2005.
17. Farkhod Tolipov,; "Are the heartland and the Rimland Changing in the Wake of the Operation in Afghanistan?" *Central Asia and the Caucasus,* No. 5(23) 2003.
18. Farkhod Tolipov, "The Foreign Policy Orientations of Central Asian States: Positive and Negative Diversifications" Internet article available at *src-h.slav.hokudai.ac.jp/coezi/publish/no 16_1_ses/02_tolipov.*
19. N.A. Nazarbaev, "Sniat's Evrazii 'polias vyzhidaniia', Interview in *Kazakhstanskaia Pravda,* Almaty October 21, 1995 cited from Vinkovetsky, "Eurasia and its Uses: the History of An Idea and the Mental Geography of Post Soviet Space'.
20. "Central Asia: Turkmenistan Pushing North-South Trade Corridor with Iran", *Radio Free Europe/Radio Liberty,* Wednesday, June 20, 2007.
21. Hauner, *What is Asia to us? Russia's Asian Heartland yesterday and today.*
22. David J.M. Hooson, "A New Soviet Heartland?" *The Geographical Journal,* Vol. 128, No. 1, March 1962 and published as a monograph by Van Nostrand Co, 1964.
23. Hooson, *A New Soviet Heartland?*

3

The Integration of Asiatic Russia: The Historical Experience and Today's Problems*

V.V. Alekseev

Statement of the Problem

The role of Asiatic Russia in the Eurasian continent has very strongly increased during the last hundred years. This is connected with its geopolitical location and rich natural resources and active integration. Integration has stretched from the Urals to the Pacific Ocean, which is equivalent to the total territory of many European states. Besides, the impact of neighbouring civilizations especially the Chinese one needs to be considered. As a result Russia got additional geopolitical stability, without which there could neither be the empire of the Romanovs nor the Soviet Union.

The task is to analyse on the basis of studies on historical experience, the boundaries and borderlands and significance of integration of Asiatic Russia, which is at present comprised of three fourth of our Fatherland. In this context historical experience means the series of achievements and the abilities of generations, social practices of the past, elucidation of the character of social development, knowledge-based solutions to problems of the present.

The integration of Asiatic Russia occurred in three successive stages: trade, agrarian and industrial activities. One may of course observe the interlocking of these stages even in present conditions, but each trend tends to be dominant over the rest in a specific period. The first stage coincided with the period of the primitive state, the second one with traditional agrarian society and the third one with the era of modernization. All these three stages coincided with certain levels of civilization. Let us try to map out their basic contours

---

* Translated by Susmita Bhattacharya, Fellow, MAKAIAS, Kolkata

and draw lessons from the grandiose economic projects that unfolded in the space of Asiatic Russia.

Pre-industrial Integration

Fur trading was related to the abundance of fur animals which were hunted by aboriginal people from ancient times. With the advent of the Russians fur trade spread/expanded with particular force, since it gave larger revenue to the state treasury and played an important role in foreign trade. In Siberia 7248 thousand sables were procured for 70 years of the 17th century. 85 per cent of the sable that was procured went to the aboriginal hunters and only 15 per cent went to the Russians.[1]

Intensive shooting of sables led to their complete extinction. By the end of 17th century the fur trade in Siberia fell into decay but during 18th-19th centuries was reinvigorated. Furs comprised a substantial part of revenue to the state treasury. Fur trade was a significant phase of development of its productive forces which facilitated settlements in this *krai* and accumulation of capital. In contrast to many other assimilated territories of the world, where the people were driven out from their native lands and to a considerable extent annihilated, the Siberian aborigines, as the main supplier of furs, were well preserved and performed the significant function in integrating the regions with extreme natural and climatic conditions.

Sables were considerably less in the Far East to make up for it in return such valuable animals like fur-seal and also walrus fang were highly valued not only in Russia but also far beyond its borders. In just 30 years (1744–1775) 3.21 million roubles worth of furs reached the ports of Kamchatka and Okhotsk. The Russian fur trade extended also to the American continent. The Russo-American campaign during its activities in Komanderski Islands procured 2309270 fells of fur seals which induced profit of more than 20 million roubles,[2] which was of great significance at the initial period of capital accumulation in Russia.

The whaling enterprise received a boost in which the Americans thrived. From 1850 to 1870 they collected 900 thousand barrels of fat and 10.8 million pound of whalebone/baleen only in the Okhotsky Seas for 107.4 million gold roubles.[3] Whales became extinct as fishing became an important item of revenue and significant resource of food, especially in the Okhotsk-Kamchatka region during the end of 17th and beginning of 18th centuries. During 1900-1905 9.61 million roubles[4] was the income in the main fishing industry regions of the Far East and Siberia (Pacific coats, Ob, Yenisei Amur, Lena-Kolymskii, Baikal basins and Barabinsk region).

In this way the integration of Asiatic Russia through fur trading was of fundamental importance for the country's economy. At the initial stage fur served as money backup. Furs were used to pay tributes and salaries and were also given as presents to foreign dignitaries and sovereigns and to the native and foreign subjects. Furs served as exchange commodity, against which any articles were received from abroad even precious metals like silver out of which the country's currency was minted. The average total export by fur trade of the country only through Arkhangel'sk was 8.5 per cent in 1653.[5]

Even after many years, when the number of fur-bearing animals sharply decreased, the Siberian fur continued to remain not only a priority item for revenue in the Russian exchequer but also played an important role in world trade. According to the data of World Hunting Exhibition at Vienna in 1910, it comprised 44 per cent of the worldwide procurement of furs and was estimated at 50 million roubles.[6]

Agrarian Colonization

Agrarian colonization replaced the trading stage. Farming started to develop from the 17th century owning to integration of new and more productive lands. With the advancement of the Russians beyond the Urals farming spread in Siberia and the Far East, but the ploughed fields occupied not more than one tenths of the territory. Around 80 per cent of arable land was utilized for agricultural purposes in south Siberia. By the end of 17th century almost 7 million puds of wheat were harvested per year in Siberia.

By the beginning of the 20th century 17.4 million dessiatins of land were engaged in agricultural activities. 9.4 million dessiatins (1907) of land for cultivation, 11.1 million dessiatins were utilized as hay and as pasturable lands. Along with it there were 2.8 million horses, 4.7 million cattles, 6.4 million sheep and goats, 87.1 thousand pigs.[7] In 1911 the cultivated areas of Siberia and the Far East were estimated at 6.4 million dessiatins, which was around 7 per cent of the total cultivated field of Russia.[8] After the construction of Trans-Siberian Railroad harvest and export of wheat from Siberia to the centre of the country increased every year. By 1917 harvest of crops reached 600 million puds, and according to the estimates of Pereselencheskii Board by the 1920s it was expected to reach 1 million puds. Siberia turned into the main granary of Russia. Its share in the total harvest Russian of crops before the 1917 revolution was estimated at 17 per cent.

Cattle breeding widely expanded in Siberia. In 1913, there were 30 million cattle, i.e. one fifth of total amount of entire Russia, which was only little less than that of USA during that period. Animal husbandry of Siberia assumed world wide attention. The Siberian butter industry played a significant role. In 1913, 5.1 million puds of high quality butter was exported from Siberia,[9] against which the same amount of gold was earned in the world market as the famous Siberian goldfields yielded plenty of gold of export quality.

This way, agricultural integration played a dominant role in Asiatic Russia's economy, securing outstanding results not only at the regional level, but also at the national level. It was overtaken by industry in the 20th century.

Industrial Development

Trading and agricultural integration/agrarian assimilation were followed by proto industrialization of Asiatic Russia. At first industry was not separated from farming and remained a dominant form of domestic industry. Industrial assimilation started from the Ural region. In ancient times it supplied non-ferrous metals to a vast territory from the frontline/frontier of Asia up to the Balkans. Iron smelting considerably spread in the 17th century in central Urals.

The Ural metallurgy actually flourished in the 18th century. The favourable conditions in the domestic and foreign markets contributed to its progress. The increasing demand for metal for civilian and military purposes stimulated its production in the new iron making region, while the old ones located in the European part of the country, owing to scantiness of the explored ore reserves gradually collapsed. The demand in the foreign marked gathered momentum in connection with the industrial revolution in Western Europe, especially England.

In this atmosphere Peter I initiated active construction of metallurgical plants at the Urals. The first cast iron was produced by the Kamensk and Nevyansk plants in the second half of 1701. A multiple of other plants followed. The beginning of new industrial phase of the Ural metallurgy was marked by the transition to smelting in blast furnaces replacing the primitive small furnaces. In the first half of the 18th century 71 enterprises were built in the entire Ural, 33 out of which produced ferrous metal and 38 copper. It took a leading position in mining and smelting industry in the country. In the second half of the 18th century further more than 100 enterprises were built. In 1800 7.8 million puds of cast iron and 5.3 million puds of iron was produced in the Urals. In terms of output of ferrous metal Russia held first position in the world, moving England and Sweden while the Urals contributed four fifth of the total volume of Russian cast iron and iron products. The Ural metal was of "high quality" and was also "soft" and it compared with sable fur. In fact, it became famous in the whole world undeŕ the brand "staryi sobol" or "old sable".

In the Urals gold and platinum were mined.[10] From 1867 to 1913 around 225 tons of platinum was procured. The Urals held monopoly position in the platinum mining sector. At one point of time Russian coins were minted out of platinum in anticipation of unstable exchange rate of the rouble.[11] Large volumes of precious metal were received from Siberia. In 1800, 50 thousand puds of silver came from the Altai plants and by 1900 they extracted and processed 625 million puds of iron ore, out of which 93 thousand puds of silver and more than 3 million puds of lead was smelted (80% of total Russian output).[12] In the 19th century a singe Altai mining district (*okrug*) mined silver more than England, France, Sweden, Prussia and Belgium taken together.

The "gold century" replaced the "silver" one. It also started in the Altai, but later on shifted to Eastern Siberia. By the 20th century more than 2 thousand reserves and goldmines over a total area of more than 200 thousand hectares were explored and registered. The Leno-Vitimsk *raion* held first place in terms of its output. Every year 400 puds were mined here and from 1829 to 1848, 8.7 thousand puds were extracted which comprised almost one fourth of the worldwide output during this period.[13] In hundred years (1830-1924) the total gold output from Siberia rose from 12.5 per cent to 78.1 per cent on the Russian scale.[14]

By the beginning of the 20th century still Siberia remained primarily an agrarian *krai*, despite its considerable success in industrial ventures under conditions of proto-industrialisation and the initial stage of industrial capitalism. In 1913, 99 per cent of import to its territory consisted of industrial items, and 40 per cent of her export included butter, 23 per cent other food stuffs, 19 per cent—gold and 15 per cent—furs. Similar conditions prevailed in other regions/districts of Asiatic Russia excepting the Urals. This situation mainly changed in the first one-third of the 20th century as a result of profound socio-economic reforms by the Soviet power.

It followed the policy of active modernization—a transition from traditional agrarian to industrial society. This required huge natural resources, which were concentrated for the most part in Asiatic Russia, while the main population was based in its European part. The industry started shifting to the East There was Ural-Kuznetsk project in the *krai*, the main purpose of which was to combine the coking coal of Kuzbass with the high quality Ural iron ore, and on the basis of it build the second coal and metallurgical base of the state (the first being in Ukraine). This complex already in 1933 yielded one fourth of smelted cast iron, one sixth of coke production and around one fourth of the products of basic chemistry of the country.[15] The road to intensive industrialization of Siberia was opened to solve the problems of the Ural-Kuznetsk.

It is necessary to emphasise the phase by phase changes in the technosphere of Siberia, rather to give details of industrial build-up here. Not only there were an increase in the productive capacities of heavy industry and intensive growth in the volumes of production output in the distant outlying districts like everywhere in the country, but also extensive reconstruction was done in the national economy on the basis of new technology. The pivot of this reconstruction was fundamental replacement of the sources of energy. If the industrial production from the Urals to the Pacific Ocean previously was based on hydraulic and steam power, by the end of 30s it basically switched over electrical gear, which was the most significant component of the transition to modernization and marked technological improvements in the economy.[16]

The natural course of modernization processes in Asiatic Russia was disrupted by the Second World War. More than thousand industrial enterprises were evacuated to this part from the European regions of the country occupied by the Fascists. By the autumn of

1942, 830 enterprises were shifted to the Urals and more than 400 to Siberia. On the one hand, they increased the industrial potential of the region, and on the other hand it turned into a warehouse of weapons which slowed down the industrial integration process and created unfavourable socio-economic conditions. In this atmosphere the role of Asiatic Russia in the production of armaments rose abruptly, which had significance for our fatherland during the difficult years. During 1942-1944 the Magnitogorsk metallurgical plant produced 33 per cent of cast iron, 25 per cent of steel and roll metal, 56 per cent of iron ore and 30 per cent of coke. Every second Soviet tank was covered with Magnitogorsk armour plating and every third shell was made of Magnitogorsk metal.[17] Precisely, because of the Ural-Kuzbass, by 1943 the Soviet Union surpassed Germany in production of quality metal which served as security for its victory. Aluminium production played an important role. One of the Siberian aviation factories produced 15 thousand airplanes during the War years. By comparison it may mentioned that the USA and Great Britain supplied 18 thousand airplanes to the USSR during the Second World War. The industry of Ural produced Soviet military tanks in the USSR which surpassed production of this kind of armaments for the whole of Germany.[18] In the years of the Second World War, the Urals had a share of up to 40 per cent of the total wartime production of the USSR.[19]

The post war modernization right up to the mid 80s of the 20th century was characterized by active expansion of the scales of industrial integration. Siberia entered the arena of world achievers particularly in the energy sector. Resolving the next important national-economic problem in the agenda was the Angaro-Yenisei. The first hydroelectric power station of the Angara-Yenisei cascade generated electricity in the middle of 50s. The Bratsk hydroelectric power station started in 1961 and in 1967, the Kranoyarsk. Soon they attained the targeted capacity. The Bratsk generated 4.5 million kilowatts and Krasnoyarsk 6 million kilowatts of electricity. For a long period they remained the two most powerful hydroelectric power stations of the world. The electric power engineering became a mighty catalyst of industrial assimilation of the Angaro-Yenisei region. In 1970 it had a share of 60 per cent of electric power, 33 per cent of gross industrial output, 55 per cent of saw timber, 100 per cent of cellulose of the whole of Siberia. A number of unique territorial-industrial complexes were formed here, among which there were some world famous ones, such as Bratsk-Ust-Ilim and Sayan. At the same time one should mention that along with its enormous importance the power engineering construction had sorry effect on the environment. The flow of such a mighty river as Angara had to be held back for two years to fill the Bratsk reservoir. It was included in the list of the largest man-made reservoirs of the planet. The Irkutsk dam raised the level of the biggest freshwater lake in the world Lake Baikal by almost a meter, which reconstructed the shore line for a long stretch with all the negative consequences for the inhabitants there. All this was close to geological influence on the nature.

In the second half of the 20th century the industrial assimilation of Siberia focused on oil and gas extraction whose discovery had worldwide significance. Before the eyes of the world, oil rigs, gas pumping stations were established, oil and gas pipelines were laid with amazing speed from boundless marshlands and mines of the Ob river to the heart of Europe. Within a short period, the oil production output of Siberia surpassed that of Saudi Arabia, famous in this field, and reached the level to produce one sixth of the world production of "black gold". The export of oil and other petroleum products gave the country around 200 million roubles within 10 years (1974-84) which for some time compensated for the poor performance of the Soviet economy and averted the system crisis of the USSR.[20]

In the conditions of crisis of the Soviet system, disintegration of the USSR and the consequent liberal reforms abruptly put brakes to industrial assimilation and modernization of Asiatic Russia, though it remained the prime component of Russian economy as before. The country earned from US $ 500 to 1 million in the world market for the diamond that was produced in Yakutiya. Three fourths of platinum that was produced in Norilsk metallurgical plant at Yevenkaya yielded enormous returns. Two thirds of the gold that was extracted in Yakutiya was sold abroad and yielded an average of $US 3 to 4 million per annum.[21]

Reckless exploitation of natural resources of the East, investment of earnings from there to military complexes and food provision to the population, gaps between production and demand, underestimation of vital problems of the people led to the aggravation of economic, socio-political and ecological problems primarily in the old industrial regions, where the minerals deposits were used up, labour force migrated and environment standards degraded. For instance, 22 per cent of enterprises of military/war industrial complex of Russia was concentrated in the Urals, which had become the bastion of defense industry including the atomic one. At the beginning of the 1990s, 45 per cent of industrial production personnel were engaged and almost 42 per cent of main industrial-production funds of the region were spent on these enterprises. In terms of its impact on the environment and the level of its pollution, the Ural region held second place in the country and topped the list as the most polluted region by emission of harmful industrial wastes into the atmosphere per square unit.[22] But the depressing situation could not disrupt the process of liberal reforms. In comparison to 1991 by 2002 there was a decline in the volume of industrial production of Sverdlovsk oblast' by 55.4 per cent, which was 5.7 per cent more than the average level throughout the Russian Federation.

The social problems also aggravated. Each year the social and living standard of the population declined while in 1970 the proportional production ratio between means of production and consumer items in the territory of Zapadnosibirsk (Western Siberian oil and gas complex) was 75.7 per cent and 24.3 per cent, in 1989 it was 92.2 per cent and 7.8 per cent.[23] Because of harsh natural, climatic, material and living conditions in Siberia people started abandoning the region. In the 70s and the 80s more than 6 million people, i.e. around 30 per cent of the population left the place.[24]

The disintegration of USSR and liberal reforms of the 1990s radically changed the situation in Siberia and the Far East certainly not for the better. The rapid decline of Russia's (as the legal successor of the USSR) geopolitical and economic role caused the displacement of many Siberian and the Far Eastern manufacturers/producers from the world markets, particularly in the countries of Asia-Pacific region, where the demand for Russian goods earlier was relatively higher. With the collapse of the COMECON there was a sharp fall in the export of Siberian goods to the countries united under (the Council) it, and reduction in import of products from them needed by the inhabitants of Siberia and the Far East.

In recent years the situation of Asiatic Russia has started improving, the decline in production has come to a halt and in certain sectors there been a rise. By 2003 in the Siberian Federal Okrug District the oil output increased by 39 per cent in comparison to 1990 and the gas production hiked almost by 30 times, and a growth was recorded in the capacity of the electric power stations in the Ural and Siberian

Federal Districts. A rise was recorded in gross harvest of potatoes and vegetables through all the federal districts. According to the rest of the indicators indices of 2005, the level of 1990 could not be achieved, being stagnated at 71.9 per cent and 65.4 per cent of steel that was smelted in the Ural and Siberian federal districts respectively, while the production in metallurgy in the same districts lagged behind by up to 3 per cent from the indices of the 90s. The areas under crop cultivation came down to 60.5 per cent in the Ural federal district and 42.5 per cent in the Far Eastern one, and the gross harvest of crops in these districts reduced to 64.6 per cent and 29.4 per cent respectively. The population was 96.0 per cent in the Ural federal district and 81.2 per cent in the Far East one.[25]

To sum up the economic integration of Asiatic Russia through many phases shows one a trend—it has passed through the main stages of civilizational development from the traditional to the post-industrial society. There were achievements of both national and geopolitical significance. Its contribution to the world's industrial civilization was of particular importance. At the same time the process under review was very complex and contradictory as well as uneven in time and space, sometimes excessively wasteful and socially disruptive. But ultimately it played an important role in the destiny of the country. Asiatic Russia provided our fatherland with the mighty geo-strategic safety margin and was the inexhaustible resource base of the country.

Notes and References

1. P.N. Pavlov, *Pushnoi promysel v Sibiri v XVII*, Krasnoyarsk: 1972, pp. 104-106.
2. A.T. Mandrik, *Istoriya rybinoi promyshlennosti Dal'nego Vostoka*. Vladivostok, 1994, p. 18.
3. *Ibid.*, p. 21.
4. *Ibid.*, p. 36, 42; M.A. Vinokurov, A.P. Sukhodolov, *Ekonomika Sibiri*, 1900-1928, Novosibirsk, 1996. p. 165.
5. O.N. Vilkov, "Promyslyekologiya v feodal'noi Sibiri," Izvestiya Sibirskogo otdeleniya AS USSR, Seriya istorii, arkheologii iilosofii. 1989, Vyp. 3 pp. 39-40.
6. M.A. Vinokurov, A.P. Sukhodolov, *op. cit.* p. 161.
7. *Istoriya narodnogo khozyaistva Urala (1917-1945)*, Ekterinburg, 1988, Part I, p. 22.
8. N.P. Oganovskii, *Narodnoe khozyaistvo Sibiri*. Moscow, 1921, p. 45.

9. V.K. Alekseeva, Kooperativnoe dvizhenie v Sibiri. Konets XIX, nachalo XXV. Novosibirsk, 1993, p. 41; *Sibirskii krestyanin*, 1918, No. 1.
10. Istoriya narodnogo khozyaistva Urala, p. 14.
11. V. Lukyanin, *Plotina Rossii*, Ekaterinburg, 2001, pp. 12, 24, 28, 32.
12. M.A. Vinokurov, A.P. Sukhodolov, *op. cit.*, p. 178.
13. *Ibid.*, pp. 180-181.
14. *Ibid.*, p. 187.
15. G.K. Orzhouikidze, Stat'e rechi Moscow, 1957, v. 2, p. 562.
16. For details see V.V. Alekseev, Elektrifikatsii Sibiri, Istoricheskoe issledovanie, Novosibirsk, 1973, Part I, pp. 136-139, 157-159.
17. *VELIKII PODVIG NARODA*, Chelyabinsk, 1970. p. 88.
18. *Ural V Panorama XX V*, Ekaterinburg, 2000, p. 275.
19. *Ibid.*, p. 274.
20. For details see V.V. Alekseev, V.A. Lamin, *Prometei sibirskoi nefti*; Sverdlovsk, 1989.
21. For details see. V.V. Alekseev, *Regionalizm v. Rossii*, Ekaterinburg, 1999, pp. 102-104.
22. *Ibid.*, pp. 107-111.
23. *Sibir' na poroge novogo tysyacheletiya*, Revised 2nd ed., Novosibirsk, 1999, p. 115.
24. *Ibid.*, p. 61.
25. *Regiony Rossii*, 2006, pp. 56-57, 469, 470, 513-514, 517-518, 523-524, 545-546, 556-567, 570-571.

4

Northern Asia and North America in Terms of Colonial Administration (XVII–XVIII c.)*

Denis Anan'ev

One of the most difficult and fundamental problems concerning the historiography of European colonization is the challenge of identifying the basic analytical frameworks and methodological approaches underlying this field of historical studies. Although such problems don't have simple solutions, one can identify two basic ideas that have developed over time and have been shared by researchers. The first group of historians tended to emphasize "Europeanization" of the colonies which meant the process of merely reproducing or copying trends and patterns of life that was brought from the mother country. Another group concentrated on the unique characteristics of the colonized areas which transformed the old patterns and created a new geographical, economical and cultural environment. The first approach was largely reflected among Russian historians on Siberia's colonization and their Western counterparts who studied the history of "Russian eastward expansion" in Northern Asia. The second approach is often associated with the theory of "frontier" introduced by the American historian F.J. Turner who applied it mainly to the history of North American colonization.

The history of colonization can be studied in different ways—geographical, political, economical, social, cultural etc. Each of the methodological approaches mentioned above can also be analysed independently. Thus, the comparative analysis of the history of colonial administration and political institutions in the mother country gives us a better understanding of "Europeanization" and its "progress". Almost certainly, historians favour facts and ideas about colonial administration that fit their overall concept of

* Translated by Susmita Bhattacharya, Fellow, MAKAIAS, Kolkata

colonization. In one of his articles B. Dmytryshyn reviewed the terms in which historians characterized the Russian territorial expansion in Northern Asia: "civilizing and christianizing measure", "gathering the Russian lands", "pure imperialism similar to that of the Spanish, Portuguese, French, British and Dutch colonial empires", "complicated process of annexation and settlement"[1] etc. While none of these terms can exhaustively describe the whole process of colonization, it is clear that all of them imply the key role played by the Russian state.

The first historian of Siberian colonization G.F. Mueller was also the main advocate of Russia's decisive role in the conquest and settlement of Siberia. In the XIX century this idea was supported by Russian historians who represented the so-called "state school" of Russian historiography. In their works, the history of Russia was deemed as history of permanent colonization while penetration in Siberia was only one of the aspects of this process. At the same time they were convinced about Russia as a part of European civilization, so the term "Europeanization" seemed quite appropriate. The process can be initiated by several forces—the common people, the government or the church—which determine the specific historical "forms" of colonization. Consequently, the large-scale colonization of Siberia since the end of the XVI century had been an extensive and spontaneous process, at first dominated by the common people, then—by the government.[2]

Western historians who argued about "Russia's eastward expansion" regarded this subject as an issue of current political importance and also believed that the state played the most important role in colonization of Siberia and Far East. As the British author A. Krausse noted, "The more I see of Russian statesmanship, the more I am impelled to admire it as an instance of irresistible triumph of mind over mere intelligence".[3] More recently this view has been supported by another British historian, A. Wood, who highlighted Muscovite expansion as a territorial and colonial annexure to the Russian autocratic state whose political power became apparent with the advent of the new dynasty, growth of the bureaucracy, strengthened positions of the new nobility, submission of the church to the monarchial rule, militarization and institutionalized serfdom.[4]

Even having attributed attention to the Russian state and its role in the colonization process of Northern Asia, researchers have never conducted a comprehensive analysis of the Siberian administration. In Russian historiography this problem was formulated a century ago, but still remains unsolved,[5] due to the fact that Soviet historical science had largely neglected the history of Tsarist government in general and the history of colonial administration in particular.

Western studies of Siberian administration were also few in number. Among them the most notable work was written by G.V. Lantzeff,[6] who aptly captured the basic traits of Siberian society and administration during the first century of Russian colonization: "elements of the feudal society combined with the ideas of the bureaucratic centralized monarchy". According to Lantzeff, the new elite was ready to go back to "political feudalism" but their intentions were opposed and suppressed by the *Siberian Prikaz*—the central government agency, that was created in order to control and manage the newly acquired territories.[7] A similar approach was noticed in recent works on the history of Siberian administration, although some of the authors questioned the term "colonial" as they didn't see any significant difference between the systems of local government in European and Asiatic Russia in the XVII-XVIII c.[8]

The process of centralization of the Russian state which started at the end of the XV century resulted in the expansion of power of the Grand prince of Moscow and then the Tsar of Russia all over the country. Eventually all social classes offered their services to the Tsar and the entire country was seen as his patrimonial estate. All this hindered the path of judicial development and neither private nor public laws could transform medieval traditions to the modern principles of rationalization, unification and individual contract between an employer (the state) and an employee (the government official). In Western Europe this transformation had started earlier and was facilitated by the private-ownership mentality which allowed buying and selling official positions as one's private property.

Since the end of the XVI century the key elements of local administration in Russia were provincial governors or *voevodas*. In many aspects they resembled the local rulers of the early Middle Ages, who were recruited from the privileged aristocracy and the nobility and were commissioned to control vast areas with strong traditions of self-governance.[9] One of the characteristic features of the *voevodas* was that they were provided sustenance by the local communities who gave them regular offerings in furs, meat and other produce. Over time they started to view their administrative work not as their official duty but as their moral right to improve material standards in the intervening period between military campaigns.

At the same time the *voevod* administration acted upon several bureaucratic principles. The new local governors were appointed by *Prikazy*—the bureaucratic central agencies, which paid them salaries in lump-sum and gave unified instructions or job descriptions. In their work the *voevodas* were assisted by the "professional bureaucrats."—secretaries and technical staff who received annual wages and spent their lives in public service, while the *voevodas* remained in office just for 2-3 years.

The system of *voevod* administration had been established over the whole country, including the new Siberian *uezds* (districts), and was abolished only at the end of the XVIII century. In Siberia the bureaucratic elements of this system were strengthened for the sake of closer control over the colonized territories. The smaller districts were integrated into larger political units—*razryads*—under control of the *razryadny voevod*. However, in Siberia the *voevodas* enjoyed the loose control from Moscow which led to numerous violations of law.

In the XVIII century Peter I made several attempts to reform the system of local administration and placed the *voevodas* under control of the Siberian governor, who paid them salaries and gave orders. In due course the new bureaucratic hierarchy was formed, while the *voevoda*'s authority, especially in the military sphere, was somewhat limited. However, the new administration wasn't efficient enough as the majority of the *voevodas* came from the ruling class of nobility and viewed themselves more like feudal lords than public officials.

Till the 1760's, despite vast administrative regulations, there had been no unified rules for recruitment of staff in local government. Since the end of the 1720s the local bureaucracy didn't earn regular salaries and felt free to accept bribes. This situation revived the medieval principle of making the local communities responsible for the administration's maintenance costs. In 1763 the unified official salaries were restored but they were too insufficient as the only source of income for local authorities. The state of affairs in Siberia wasn't different from that in European Russia and the first historiographical approach takes the process of Siberian colonization in the XVII-XVIII centuries as a mere extension of legal relations and political institutions that existed in the mother country.

This process in North America is comparable to the expansion of Spanish, French and British colonial possessions. In the XVII century Spain with its powerful bureaucracy was the biggest empire in the world. Its American colonies were controlled by the Council of the Indies, which appointed all higher officials. However, bureaucratic control didn't save the administration from corruption and much of the revenues from semi-feudal Latin America went to the Spanish nobility.[10]

In New France (Canada) after the various commercial companies had failed to establish their own settlements, all the territories were eventually placed under direct control of the autocratic royal regime. Huge feudal estates had been established with the assistance of a kind of serf system, without any trials by jury or elected parliaments. The new political institutions were created much later, at the end of the XVIII century, when Canadian territories fell under the control of the British Crown. However, for many decades the British government had been pursuing a much less tolerant policy in its own colonies in New England.[11]

In the XVII century the English colonies in North America enjoyed a great variety of political institutions and extensive popular rule due to the private character of colonization and the loose governmental control in the times of Revolution and Civil War in England. The property-owning settlers preserved their political rights and kept them, even though most of the colonies eventually passed from the private companies and persons to the Crown. Since 1619 there appeared colonial assemblies, which were constantly in conflict with the appointed governors and councils. The people could even impeach the governors and some colonies exercised this right virtually till the end of the colonial period. All these constitutions and laws passed by the assemblies required royal consent and only about 5 per cent of all inhabitants had the right to vote, but this scope of political rights was almost unthinkable in many other parts of the world, for example, in Northern Asia. Since the end of the XVII century the British government had made its attempts to limit the rights of the colonies. It created the specialized governmental body—Board of Trade and Plantations—and aimed at finding allies among the upper classes of the colonial society. But these attempts eventually antagonized the American people and resulted in their political separation from the mother country.

One might argue that ideas about democracy and private law came to America from Old England which already had embarked on the path of constitutional monarchy with a strong parliament so New England was destined to evolve into a representative democracy. But in southern colonies the individualism and private-owner psychology resulted in plantation economies with a "strong aristocratic atmosphere". It was also true of New Netherlands though their mother country had overthrown the absolutist rule much earlier than in England. Finally, if colonial government in New England was just a continuation of the British political system, why would there be such a fierce military clash?

In order to explain the unique variety of traits in the colonial society and its political institutions the American historian F.J. Turner introduced the theory of "frontier". He noted, that "behind institutions, behind constitutional forms and modifications, lie the vital forces that call these organs into life and shape them to meet changing conditions". Over time the American people transformed the wilderness, but the outcome was "not the old Europe", as "each tier of new States has found in the older ones material for its constitutions". The frontiersmen grew more and more independent, and at the same time the frontier promoted the formation of a "composite nationality. F.J. Turner concluded, that "the most important effect of the frontier has been in the promotion of democracy here and in Europe" as frontier is productive of individualism, "it produces antipathy to control, and particularly to any direct control; the tax-gatherer is viewed as a representative of oppression".[12]

F.J. Turner also raised the question whether his theory had limited use or could be applied to other "colonial environments" with different political and economical circumstances.[13] Several Western historians attempted to use his theory in their studies of Siberian colonization. B. Sumner, D. Treadgold, R. Pierce admitted that to some extent the phenomenon of "frontier" did exist in Siberia as well.[14] Travellers, officials and political exiles noted that Siberian peasants differed from the peasant population in European Russia, mainly because they relied less upon the authorities. The Protestant ideology brought to North America to a certain degree corresponded to the ideology of the Old believers who settled in Siberia. A "composite nationality" had also been formed as Russians mixed with the aboriginal people and settlers who had arrived to Siberia from other parts of the Russian empire.

Siberia also served as a "safety valve", welcoming the newcomers and thus decreasing social tension in central parts of European Russia. As J.A. Harrison put it, "Siberian fever of hope and acquisition grew among all elements trapped in the horrors of the civil wars of European Russia. The peasants wanted to escape from the dutches the strong of new serfdom". But the Siberian frontier also had its characteristic features, especially in terms of its administration. Defining the nobility as "the backbone of the Siberian government", J.A. Harrison pointed out that "like young men of the East India Company, they were to make their fortune if possible, but unlike the clerks and military men of that company, they had to live off the communities they managed and defended. Also unlike East India company men, they were not trying to secure a treasure house that held the accumulated wealth of millenniums of civilization".[15]

H.R. Huttenbach also believed that the lure of the Eastern frontier, offering at once social mobility as well as security, attracted the lower-ranking gentry, the *sluzhilye lyudy*, who "recognized the opportunity of self-aggrandizement and remained in a setting where they would enjoy greater status and advancement as against the more frozen social circumstances prevailing in Muscovy with its attendant conservatism".[16] C. White described "the pioneer spirit" and "an amalgam of missionary and mercenary motives" that existed in Siberia, but didn't consider the social circumstances in Asiatic Russia as being "less frozen". While in America the frontier was colonized by free settlers, in Siberia the process of colonization was under constant control of the central government, and "the existence of the frontier didn't "free up" institutions".[17] J.P. Le Donne combined the theory of the frontier with conceptions of "geographical determinism" and viewed the Russian eastward expansion as the history of Russia's fight with neighbouring "core areas" for the Eurasian "heartland" and for the control over the frontiers that separate Russia from these core areas.[18]

Although we can find similarities and overlap in the descriptions of both North American and North-Asian "frontiers" there is one important difference. While F.J. Turner took the frontier conditions as the cardinal factor to explain the American Revolution, similar factors in Siberia never led to revolution or separation of the colonies from the mother country. Siberian colonists didn't elect their parliaments and didn't pass their constitutions. Why didn't it happen? Perhaps, the frontier individualism that had promoted democracy in North America was still to a certain extent inherent to the settlers coming from Western Europe. If we find an answer to this question we might also explain why the fate of Russia's own settlements in North America—in Alaska and California so much depended on the actions of the Russian government and weren't saved solely by the pioneer spirit and frontier individualism of the Russian settlers. Undoubtedly, the role of the frontier in America shouldn't be underestimated as they truly transformed the colonial society and created a new type of political system. However it is clear that both methodological approaches mentioned above have proven to be fruitful and require further application within the broader historical context of European colonization.

Notes and References

1. Basil Dmytryshyn, "The administrative apparatus of the Russian Colony in Siberia and Northern Asia, 1581-1700", In: *The History of Sibiri: From Russian Conquest to Revolution,* A. Wood (ed.), London, New York: Routledge, 1991, p. 17.
2. Mikhail. K. Lyubavskii, *Istoricheskaya geografiya Rossii v svyazi s kolonizatsei*, Moscow: Lan', 2000; Idem, *Obzor istorii russkoi kolonizatsii s drevneishikh vremen i do XX veka*, Moscow: Moscow University Press, 1996, pp. 40-46.
3. Alexis Krausse, *The Far East: Its History and Its Question*, London: Grant Richards, 1899, p. vi.
4. Alan Wood, Introduction "The Role of Siberia in Russian History", in *The History of Siberia. From Russian Conquest to Revolution*, Alan Wood (Ed.),, New York: Routledge, 1991, p. 4.
5. Vadim A. Aleksandrov, Nikolai N. Pokrovskii, *Vlast' i obschestvo. Sibir' v XVII v.,* Novosibirsk: Nauka, 1991; Evgenii V. Vershinin, *Voeodskoe upravlenie v Sibiri (XVII v.),* Ekaterinburg, 1998; M.O. Akishin, *Rossiiskii absolyutizm i upravlenie Sibiri XVIII veka*, Moscow, Novosibirsk: Drevlekhranilische, 2003; D.A. Anan'ev, Voeodskoe *upravlenie v Sibiri XVIII veke*, Novosibirsk: ID "Sova", 2005.
6. George V. Lantzeff, *Siberia in the 17th Century. A Study of the Colonial Administration*, Berkeley & Los Angeles: University of California Press, 1943.
7. *Ibid.*, p. 200.
8. Evgenii V. Vershinin, *op. cit.*, pp. 3-25.
9. Nikolai P. Eroshkin *Istoriya gosudarstvennykh uchrezhdenii dorevolyutsionnoi Rossii,* Moscow: Vysshaya Shkola, 1983, p. 43.
10. Aleksandr E. Kudryatsev, *Ispaniya v srednue veka,* Moscow: LKI Publishing House, 2007.

11. *Konstitutsii zarubezhnykh gosudarstv*, Moscow: BEK, 1996.
12. Frederick J. Turner, "The Significance of the Frontier in American History", in *The Annual Report of the American Historical Association for 1893*, pp. 199-227.
13. Turner, "Problems in American History", In: *The Significance of Sections in American History*, New York: Henry Holt and Co., 1932, p. 19.
14. Donald W. Treadgold, "Russian Expansion in the Light of Turner's Study of American Frontier", In: *Agricultural History,* Vol. 26, № 4, pp. 147-152; George V. Lantzeff, Richard A. Pierce, *Eastward to Empire. Exploration and conquest on the Russian open frontier, to 1750*, Montreal, London: McGill-Queen's Press, 1973; Benedict H. Sumner, *A Short History of Russia*, New York: Harcourt, Brace, 1949.
15. John A. Harrison, *The Founding of the Russian Empire in Asia and America*, Coral Gables, Florida, 1971, p. 63.
16. Henry Huttenbach, "Muscovy's Conquest of Muslim Kazan and Astrachan, 1552-1556. The Conquest of the Volga: Prelude of to Empire", in M. Rywkin ed. *Russian Colonial Expansion to 1917*, London, New York: Mansell Publishing Ltd., 1988, p. 60.
17. Colin M. White, *Russia and America: the Roots of Economic Divergence*, London: Croom Helm, 1987, p. 24.
18. Andreas Kappeler, *Rossiya – mnogonatsional'naya imperiya,* Moscow: Progress-Traditsiya Publishing House, 2000, pp. 7, 35.

5

Siberia as a Part of the Russian Empire: Economic Development, State Interest and Private Capital*

A.K. Kirillov

At the beginning of the 21st century Russia like many other countries is facing the need of economic recovery. But how it should be—remains unclear. The Russian historical experience gives diverse examples. Let us try to examine them for example in Siberia, which remains as before the source of development for Russia.

The history of Russian Siberia before the start of the Soviet experiment contains at least two glaring examples of targeted development of the region. The first project began at the end of the 18th century during the era of serfdom. The essence—the development of steel industry based on the needs of the state in precious metals. The "metallurgical project" included the production of iron but (whatever the reasons for the fact) it has not proved successful in either bureaucratic or private hands. In the 20th century, Siberian iron and steel industry had to be created anew. It was precisely the "metallurgical project" that transformed the land of hunters into a hub of advanced technologies and eventually turned it into one of the main suppliers of gold and silver to the exchequer.

The second project on the development of Siberia is related to the time traditionally referred to as the period of capitalism (after the abolition of serfdom in Russia). Conventionally it can be called as "the project of Trans-Sib": precisely the construction of the Trans-Siberian Railways at the end of 20th century carried economic development to a new level. The Trans-Sib ensured the fast growth of Siberian population, development of trade and production, and thereby unleashed a new era in the history of Siberia.

* Translated by Susmita Bhattacharya, Fellow, MAKAIAS, Kolkata

Quite often Europe with its predominance of private capital is set off against Asia, where the management of the productive forces is concentrated in the state's hands. The two examples mentioned above help us to examine the role of the Russian state in comparison to private capital in Siberia as an example. A comparison of the strategies applied by the state in each of the two cases would help us to select the most successful one out of them.

The "metallurgical project" developed for a long time within the limits of two isolated localities—Nerchinsk (Trans-Baikal) and Kolyvano-Voskresensk (in due course renamed Altaic) mountainous *okrugs* (districts). The first deposits of silver were discovered by the people of Russian service class in the Nerchinsk *okrug* as early as in the 1670's. In 1689 the construction of the factories started and along with test melting the preparatory works dragged on for 15 years. The regular production of silver started in 1704. Another decade later a certain gold mixture was revealed in the Nerchinsk silver. After the bureaucratic specialists learnt to extract them, Russia got its own source of gold. The gold and silver medals, issued in honour of the termination of the Northern War, were adorned with the proud inscription: "made with our silver/made with our gold".[1]

Thus, the state capital gave the initial impetus to Siberian metallurgy. In this the bureaucratic monopoly in mining played no lesser role. But in 1719 the Berg-privilege allowed free search for ore and construction of smelting factories. Gold, silver and copper used for making coins, had to be given to the exchequer, but anybody could get the right to produce these metals. Already within a few years Akinfii Demidov, the famous owner of Urals's metallurgical factories, discovered a deposit in Altai. The first factories of Demidov in Altai started smelting copper in 1727. Its cost was kept to the level of 100-200 roubles per tonne, and Demidov sold the copper at 440 roubles per tonne.[2] Silver smelting in the Altaic ore was done for the first time in the year 1743 and gold in 1745. Owing to Demidov's factories Altai began to be considered as one of the sources of gold for the Russian exchequer.

À. Demidov died in the year 1745, and within the next two years his Altai factories were handed over under the administration of the Cabinet of Her Imperial Majesty (Kabinet HIM). In fact this was the period when they were isolated in the form of a mining district. The Cabinet that administered the factories was an administrative body that looked after the personal property of the

Empress, but as a matter of fact it can be considered as an alternative form of state administration. In this way, the first phase of private capital in the Altai mining industry was completed. While attempting to evaluate its outcome, one should take into account the distinctive support that was rendered to Demidov by the state, which provided his factories with forced work force most of whom were peasants. However that may be, one can say with certainty that Demidov's factories on the eve of their confiscation, from the commercial point of view, were profitable and alluring.

Soon after the business of Demidov the role of private capital emerged in the Nerchinsk okrug. The highest success in the field of private capital was achieved by a merchant named Mikhail Siribryakov. Starting from 1760, he discovered 17 silver deposits and started their mining. The ore of Siribryakov's mines so important for the state's Nerchinsk factories that Siribryakov was given special privileges. Generally speaking, the common rule for the mines, situated close to the Cabinet's factories in Nerchinsk, restricted the period of their private mining to 15 years. For the mines of Siribryakov an exception was made: in 1767 they were handed over completely under his ownership. The merchant was given a noble status. And what is more, he was allowed not only to mine but also to smelt the metal. The silver-smelting factory of Siribryakov started operating in 1776. The cooperation between the *okrug* administration and Siribryakov was a notable feature in the history of silver production in Nerchinsk *okrug*. Silver smelting during 1771-1775 reached up to 40 tonnes which could never be achieved either earlier to this or later on.[3]

The conflict with the leaders of Nerchinsk okrug led to the confiscation of Siribryakov's mines and factories. In a few years the production came to a standstill and consequently the merchant could no longer revive it.[4] After the death of Siribryakov his ruined factory passed into the possession of the Empress. This way in the 19th century the Siberian metallurgy came under the treasury/bureaucratic administration. But during this period economic slump already became evident both in Nerchinsk and Altai. In order to save the situation the authorities tried to bring changes in the system of administration. For a quarter of the century (since 1830 to 1855) the factories in Altai were also transferred from the jurisdiction of the Cabinet to the administration of the Ministry of Finance. But it did not help reviving the profitability of the silver-smelting business. The factories under the Cabinet were closed in the 1890's, and the very Altai okrug lost its status for mining. The last of the Nerchinsk silver smelting factories, in spite of additional capital investments, finally stopped in the year 1907. In order to maintain the mining specialisation, the okrug had to switch over to gold mining. But the decisive role in producing this metal in the Trans-Baikal region was played by the private entrepreneurs.

The exploitation of rich ores, aggravated since the emancipation of the serfs who were engaged in the process, is referred to as the cause for the collapse of Cabinet-directed and Cabinet-administered industry. However, these circumstances did not hinder prosperity of private gold industry that started from the 1830's. Already in 1826 some big merchants of Siberia had obtained the right to find and work on gold mines. Within the next few decades this right became universal. The "gold rush" began in Southern Siberia (Tomsk province), and then gradually shifted to the east as far the old ores got exhausted and new ones were discovered. In five years from 1846 to 1850 the Siberian gold-fields provided with 106 tonnes of gold—more than 80 per cent of the entire amount of gold entered into the Russian treasury during this period.[5] In 1846 gold mines were discovered in the basin of Lena (Eastern Siberia) and thus started gold mining in the most famous industrial region of Russia in the second half of the 19th century. This was the place where the joint-stock company "Lenzoto" operated. It was famous for attracting foreign capital and using most advanced technologies. The first electric railway in Russia and the first cascade of electric power stations were built on the Lena goldfields. The goldfields solidified foundations of the Soviet gold industry.

Thus, the experience of the "metallurgical project" offers two ways of interaction between private and state capital. In the Nerchinsk okrug it was the state that started it, in Altai—a private entrepreneur. But a lot was common too. By means of administrative pressure the transfer of private enterprises was transferred into the hands of the state, which was unable to cope with the task of developing them.

However the Siberian gold industry made sufficient progress and the role that was played by the state does not look simple. Strictly speaking, the private enterprises of the second half of the 19th century were not the successors of the Cabinet factories and neither the mines, nor the equipment, nor the capitals in some other form passed over to them from the latter ones. On the other hand, it was the state, which began the tradition of mining the Siberian mineral resources the state that for the first time supplied Siberia with the necessary specialists and equipment. The Cabinet *okrugs* in Siberia became the epicentres of mining business, from where the wave of "gold rush" went to the outskirts. As a "dry residue" of the "metallurgical project" the following proposition can be formulated. The state's participation played a significant role in the development of Siberian metallurgy, though business would have been impossible without private initiative. It was in fact the private entrepreneurs who consequently took the initiative of production in their hands.

The cause behind the construction of the Trans-Siberian Railway (and this is the second project that is being examined) was strategic interest. At the end of the 1950's Russia had annexed new lands in the Far East (Priamur'e) and now it was needed to make them secure for Russia in a reliable manner. The other purpose according to the Finance Minister Sergei Witte, was intensification of Russian economic influence in China, which was facing global economic and political competition. This necessitated the following two tasks: to have as many possible inhabitants in the Far East and fast means of communication between European Russia and Vladivostok. Both the tasks were fulfilled with the help of the railway. Its construction started in 1891. The high status of the undertaking was emphasised by the formation of a special Committee for Siberian Railway, personally headed by the heir to the throne, the future emperor Nikolai II.

By the 1890's the Russian state completed 50 per cent of the entire railway project. The Trans-Sib was indeed built fully at the expense of the treasury. The laying of the railway bed to the east from Chelyabinsk and to the west (so that not to commit an error against the map—to the north) from Vladivostok started in 1891. Within 5 years the steam engine already reached Eastern Siberia. A section of the Trans-Siberian main line passed through Manchuria, a province in the north-east of China. The Chinese Eastern Railway, officially registered as a private joint-stock company, was in fact fully controlled by the Russian state. It was put into regular operation in 1903 and from this period trans-continental journey by Trans-Sib became possible. The construction of the roundabout line along the Russo-Chinese border continued till the year 1916.[6]

The journey from Petrograd to Vladivostok by rail, without leaving Russia became possible just within a few months after the fall of the empire of the Romanovs. But the economic significance of the Trans-Sib was manifested much earlier. The 1890's became a period of real revolution in the Siberian trade. The wholesalers, who twice a year used to bring goods from the Nizhegorodsk fair (the main exchange centre between Siberia and European Russia), made room for fast deliverable small batch of goods. Supply to Siberia started meeting the demands of local economy in a better way.

The striking evidence of the changes made by the Trans-Sib was the Chelyabinsk tariff break.[7] Essentially that was internal customs duty resumed in 1896, within a half of the century since the abolition of all internal customs duty in Russia. The customs duty was meant for bread transported by rail from Western Siberia to European Russia, and this made bread production competitive. In spite of the Chelyabinsk break (that existed till 1913), Siberia already got qualitatively a new access to the world market as a whole and the all-Russian market in particular. This created new conditions both for agricultural and industrial production.

One of the circumstances favouring the growth of agricultural production was the peasants' resettlement in Siberia. It was the Trans-Sib that transformed modest small migratory waves to mighty flows. Chronologically this transformation is connected with the years of Peter Stolypin's premiership (1906-11). Stolypin's resettlement programme brought about 2.7 million peasants from the Urals.[8] The bulk of them settled in the south of Western Siberia, especially lucrative for the peasant households. Precisely in the beginning of the 20th century the Siberian butter obtained worldwide recognition. As early as in 1913 the Siberian butter manufacturers monopolised 60 per cent of the Russian butter market, leaving out the previous Russia leader—Volgodchina.[9] The Siberian Union of the Butter Manufacturing Artels (formed in 1907 at Kurgan) had representation in London. The foreign companies (including that from Denmark, world's largest butter exporter) used to send its representatives to western Siberia for purchasing butter directly from the producers. Omsk, Barnaul and other cities well placed on the trading paths, rapidly grew as flour milling, bread making and butter producing trade centres. Especially noteworthy was the example of Novonikolaevsk (presently Novosibirsk). The settlement of the railway bridge builders needed just two decades to turn into one of the largest cities of Siberia.

Trade required the development of the means of communication, and private railways started emerging in Siberia. One of the first cities linked by such a way to the Trans-Sib was Barnaul. The Altai Railway, built in 1910 at the expense of joint-stock capital, passed through it. Similar joint-stock railways also provided outlet to the Trans-Sib from the nearby cities (Slavgorod, Yurga, and Achinsk). The government rendered support to the railway companies, by guaranteeing the shareholders a fixed return (3% per annum),[10] which was a normal practice for the Russian railways starting from the 1860's.

One section of the railway was extended towards the agricultural markets and others had industrial importance. The demand for coal made by steam engines urged on working in the coal mines of the Far East (Suchan), of Eastern Siberia (Cheremkhovo) and of Western Siberia (Kuzbass). Kuzbass turned out to be especially lucrative, where the coal beds were combined with iron deposits. Particularly for Kuzbass mining Kol'chuginskaya railway (connecting Yurga and today's Leninsk-Kuznetskii) was constructed. It was in the hands of the company "Kopi Kuzbass" ("Kopikuz"). Constructed in the year 1912, "Kopiкuz" became a joint enterprise of the major Russian banks and the French capitalists (each of the parties received one half of the share holding).[11] The company started building up modern metallurgical and coke-chemical factories. The construction could not be completed until the end of the Revolution. But after nationalisation "Kopiкuz" became the foundation for building the giant of Soviet metallurgy Kuznetsk Metallurgical Plant and the development of Kuzbass as the centre of coal, metallurgical and chemical industries. Thus, the Trans-Sib led to all-round development of Siberia.

The two projects examined were embodied in different conditions. Freedom (or lack of freedom) of the direct producers in particular, and national economy as a whole—a situation, which could not help having an impact on the outcome of both the experiments, nonetheless, it seems possible to draw some conclusions on the basis of a comparison between both the examples.

Both the "metallurgical project" and the "Trans-Sib project" are examples of a combination of state and private initiatives each of which made its contribution to the total outcome. The only difference was in the strategy of the state, which in the first case strived for controlling the entire production process, but in the second case remained confined to the infrastructure. The attempts by the state to control production in long-term perspective turned out to be ineffective and yielded to private initiative, which, it seemed, controlled business that had decayed and brought it to a new level of development. On the other hand, the construction of economic infrastructure by the state not only gave the anticipated result (i.e. agricultural colonisation), but also stimulated the growth of other sectors of economy including modern industrial production. As a result, the "Trans-Sib project" turned out to be a striking example of successful collaboration between the state and the private capital, which jointly secured the rapid economic development of the region.

Notes and References

1. V.G. Leshkov, E.L. Bel'chenko, B.V. Guzman, *Zoloto rossiskikh nedr*, Moscow: EKOS, 2000, pp. 201-202.
2. N.I. Pavlenko, *Razvitie metallurgicheskoi promyshlennosti Rossii v pervoi polovine XVIII veka. Promyshlennaya politika i upravlenie*, Moscow: AS USSR, 1953, pp. 444-448.
3. I. Bogolyubskii, *Istoriko-statisticheskii ocherk proizvoditel'nosti Nerchinskogo okruga s 1703 po 1871 g.*, St Petersburg: Tipografiya V. Demakova, 1872, p. 8; V.G. Leshkov, E.L. Bel'chenko, B.V. Guzman, *Zoloto rossiskikh nedr*, Moscow: EKOS, 2000, p. 199.
4. V.G. Izgachev, "Chastnyi rudnyi promysel v Nerchinskom gornozavodskom okruge v XVIII v.", in *Ekonomika, upravlenie i kul'tura Sibiri XVI-XIX vv.*, Novosibirsk: Nauka, 1965, pp. 185-200.
5. V.G. Leshkov, E.L. Bel'chenko, B.V. Guzman, *Zoloto rossiskikh nedr*, Moscow: EKOS, 2000, pp. 261-262.
6. V.P. Kalinichev, *Velikii Sibirskii put'. Istoriko-ekonomicheskii ocherk*, Moscow: Transport, 1991, pp. 134-135.
7. T.M. Kitanina, "Programma ekonomicheskogo osvoeniya Severa i tarifnaya politika S.Yu.Vitte (k otsenke Chelyabinskogo tarifa)", in *Problemy krest'yanskogo zemlevladeniya i vnutrennei politiki Rossii*, Leningrad: Nauka, 1972, pp. 191-210.
8. *Rossiya. 1913 god. Statistiko-dokumental'nyi spravochnik*. St. Petersburg: Russko-Baltiiskii informatsionnyi tsentr "BLITs", 1995, p. 24.
9. A.A. Nikolaev, *Osnovnye vidy kooperatsii v Rossii: istoriko-teoreticheskii ocherk,* Novosibirsk: Institute of History of the Siberian Branch of the Russian Academy of Sciences, 2007, p. 157.
10. T.I. Batalova, "Formirovanie chastnoi zheleznodorozhnoi seti v Aziatskoi Rossii nakanune pervoi mirovoi voiny", In *Vostokovednye issledovaniya na Altae,* 3rd edition. Sbornik nauchnykh statei. Barnaul: Az Buka, 2002, p. 181.
11. O.V. Baev, *Inostrannyi kapital v promyshlennosti Kuznetskogo basseina (konets XIX –nachalo XXv.,),* Kemorovo: Kuzbassvuzizdat, 2004, p. 109.

6

Siberian Regionalists on the Place of the Region in Civilisational Development of Eurasia*

M.V. Shilovskii

Traditionally, right up to the last one-third of the 19th century, development of the Russian statehood was interpreted in the indigenous socio-political and intellectual circle as its eastward spatial expansion to the north-east corner of the Eurasian mainland. The core of this concept was briefly formulated by K.N. Leont'ev (1831-1891), which by ruling out the national limitations of the Slavophiles declared: "Russia, taken as a whole with its Asian possessions, is an entire world, which has not yet found an original style of cultural statehood".[1] In the second half of the 19th century an alternative approach developed to the problem which can conventionally be referred to as a view "From the East to the west". It was developed by the advocates of Siberian regionalism, as a system of views of certain sections of the local intelligentsia on the past, present and future of the region as a specific province within the Russian state, and also as a socio-political and cultural movement, expressing such views. It underwent a long process of evolution in the second half of the 19th century and in the 1920's developed as a concept of territorial autonomy of Siberia headed by the provincial representative body (duma), endowed with supreme authority analogous to the competence of a state in the federal system of USA. The most prominent representatives of regionalism were: A.P. Schapov (1831-1876), G.N. Potanin (1835-1920), N.Ì. Yadrinstev (1842-1894), S.S. Shashkov, À.V. Àdriànîv, I.I. Serebrennikov, N.N. Koz'min and others.

Regionalism as a concept was formalized during statutes regarding Siberian colonies and special interpretation of the process of its

* Translated by Susmita Bhattacharya, Fellow, MAKAIAS, Kolkata

assimilation (colonisation). While studying the past of the region, its ideologues tried to find out the reasons behind serious lag of Siberia in comparison to the former colonies of the European states which too were colonised roughly at the same time (17th century) and where the population predominantly consisted of the people from the mother country. In the opinion of G.N. Potanin and Yadrintsev, the settlement and development of productive forces of the territory was solely connected with the initiative by the people, and precisely, by the most enterprising and freedom-loving elements among them. The free people's colonisation coupled with the natural resources of Siberia laid a solid base for the fast development of not only the region but also the whole of Russia. G.N. Potanin sagaciously remarked: "The Russian people laid the new foundations here for continuing their own life. To remarked: "To think of future Siberia as populated as European Russia is at present, then one cannot help thinking that the centre of gravity of the Russian state should be shifted to it".[2] But recognition of Siberia's potential did not result in the development of the productive forces of the region, enhancing the well being of the people because it was being transformed into an economic colony by the government as methods of "penal" (exile), colonisation and inefficient administration were exercised by the corrupt officials.

Nonetheless, for G.N. Potanin, Siberia was a special country and the Siberians—special people. And in this context "Siberia is (was) not only better than Russia, but even better than the other colonies of the European peoples".[3] In his opinion the absence of nobility, detachment from the great Russian traditions, individualism in the rural sphere, dispersion of the land owner community and *Tabula rasa* in the sphere of land use management, being a land of numerous cultural races, different physical conditions, different climate, different nature,[4] were in fact factors which caused the transition of local '*sotsium*' into a new qualitative state—the community of the region. Siberia should not repeat the matrix of development of the European states and USA. After attaining their level the region would move further. That should be the role of Siberia not only for "the general life of our common fatherland of Russia... but also for the world-wide importance of our homeland".[5]

G.N. Potanin and N.M. Yadrintsev had personal knowledge and experience about the people and lands of Central Asia. Grigorii Nikolaevich completed four large-scale expeditions (in the years 1876-77, 1879-80, 1884-86, 1892-93) and a number of journeys to

Mongolia, Altai, Tuva, the northern and central China and Tibet. In the summer of 1889 the expedition led by N.M. Yadrintsev followed the trails of Potanin and discovered the ruins of Karakorum (Khara-Khorina), the capital of the state of Chingizids in Mongolia.[6] But it was not the only event that made sensation in scholarly circles. Yadrintsev and his fellow travellers discovered stone steles of Bil'ge-Kagan and Kiul'-Tegin with parallel inscriptions in Chinese and ancient Turkish (orkhon runic) languages. Being deciphered by the Dutch linguist V. Thomsen (1893) and the texts marked on the steles of Karakorum read by the Turkologist V.V. Radlov (1894) facilitated knowledge about many tribes and people of Central Asia. G.N. Potanin's associate D.A. Clements characterised his research style the following manner: "In his expeditions he not only thought of what he would bring along home but also what he himself would carry to the distant lands. In this sense he was a genuine apostle of civilisation and humanity".[7]

The conceptual base of G.N. Potanin's numerous works was his conviction about the influence of natural and climatic factors on the evolution of separate people and also his assumption about a single source of epic heritage of Europe and Asia. Finding himself in the upper reaches of the Irtysh in Chinese territory in March 1877 he wrote: "Of course, this place, where we live, is the real homeland for a man. The first cult emerged here ... The rivers here were regarded by the first men as mother's bosoms and they saw their fathers in the mountain summits. Now I believe that the paradise of Adam and Eve was situated in the upper reaches of Irtysh, on the banks of which I was born".[8] Even at the base of the evangelical story about Christ, in his opinion, "lies the Central Asian shaman legend", and "Christianity originated in southern Siberia or northern Mongolia".[9] Potanin concretised his hypothesis in 1896 as he conveyed his ideas to V.G. Korolenko: "May be, you are interested to listen my view on the origin of the legend about Christ. I have come to the conviction that various incidents related to this legend were prominent among the shamans of Central Asia, the hordes and from there they spread to the west, along the northern side of the Caspian Sea, then came to southern Russia before Palestine and that Ossetic Christianity has not been distorted but has retained the original form of Christianity".[10]

In the perceptions of Grigorii Nikolaevich a single source—the legend of the creation of the world of the Central Asian (horde) origin served as the initial base for the eastern and medieval European epics. "On a steamer in the Indian Ocean", he informs D.A. Clements on 23 January 1894, "I have prepared articles on the similarities between Iliad-Odyssey and Geser (and Apollo with Ar'ya Balo, Hercules with Irkyl, Argyl and others), closeness of the novels on the cup of St. Gr [aalya] with the Mongolian legends and many other proximities. To sum up my observations—before Buddhism [there was] the cult of Ar'ya-Balo in Central Asia, which spread to the west not only to southern Russia, but also up to the distant Celtic west".[11]

My hero passionately also calls for exploring character of the people of Central Asia: The ignorance of the scholars about the steppe people is hampering the development of this subject. Our Aryan arrogance, false historical perspective...and timidity of thought enslaved by the routine views and routine beliefs have prevented correct views on the role of these barbarians and the history of the spiritual-cultural adoption".[12]

The views of G.N. Potanin highlight the unique relations between Europe and Asia that are reiterated in contemporary academic circles. In the opinion of Yu. V. Popkov, E.A. Tyugasheva, Kh. Tsoohuu and Kh. Tsedevà: "... it is possible to talk about distinguishing yet another specific constant of the Eurasian civilisation—the European orientation in the migratory processes. The mathematical expression of the given constant is Asia-Europe vector. It is understood that in the history of Eurasia the migratory processes proceeded to all possible directions. These vectors of migrations—the Indo-European, Indo-Iranian and Indo-Chinese mainly oriented towards India, had a peripheral character and did not determine the civilisational process in the continent.[13]

À.P. Schàpov on the other hand was discreet about the geopolitical, anthropological and ethno-mental peculiarities of the Eurasian civilisational space.[14] He was the first to conclude that the Siberian people were an offshoot of the Slavonic tribe.[15] His views were reiterated by N.M. Yadrintsev who categorically stated that under the influence of the aliens and natural-climatic conditions "a new ethnographic type is taking shape in the East". A Siberian "considers himself a Russian but looks at a Russian migrant as a person absolutely alien and doubts his Russian nationality".[16]

Being well informed about the state of affairs in Siberia and Central Asia, N.M. Yadrintsev linked Siberia's future with its access to the west.[17] In this process he assigned Siberia the role of a corridor, through which the interaction between the two civilisations would take place. In 1892 the ideologue of regionalism predicted: "The European civilisation, scientific discoveries and industrial progress would be carried out at the centre of Asia and the Asian people, famous for ancient civilisations, perhaps, would again become the arena of international rivalry after which the Russian possessions will have a new role and new tasks; it should be prepared for that. Would the British power be stable in India in view of 200 millions of indigenous population? With growing sense of autonomy, would the Europeans retain their colonies in Asia? The future will tell but the north of Asia and Siberia, occupied by the Slavonic tribes, in view of weak proportion of the alien population may count on more stable and secure existence. Isolated by oceans in the north and the east, enclosed by mountain ranges and deserts in the south with non-belligerent China in the neighbourhood, it can count on a peaceful and safe existence for a long time to come. Its destiny may be peaceful non-military development, cultural growth, peaceful progress, enhancement of prosperity, acquisition of knowledge side by side with enlightenment and civilisation. Thus, there may be an envious future ahead the country if only we give enough attention to it, if we study it, concentrate our concern on its non-military peaceful development and realise its world-wide importance".[18]

Notes and References

1. K.N. Leont'ev, *Collected Works*, v. 5, Moscow, 1912, p. 419.
2. G.N. Potanin, "Zametki o Zapadnoi Sibiri", *Russkoe Slovo*, 1860, no. 9: p. 196.
3. Cited in G.I. Pelikh, *Istoricheskaya kontseptsiya G.N. Potanina*, Tomsk: Izdatel'stvo Tomskogo Universiteta (Tomsk State University Press) 2006, p. 118.
4. GAOO (State Archive of the Orlov Oblast), f. 3, op. 15, d. 18753, l. 10.
5. G.I. Pelikh, *op. cit.*, p. 63.
6. M.V. Shilovskii, "K voprosu ob otkrytii Karakoruma", in *Sibir' i Tsentral'naya Aziya: problemy regional'nykh svyazei*, part 2, Tomsk, 2000, pp. 12-13.
7. D.A. Klements, "G.N. Potanin (1905)", *Literaturnoe Nasledstvo Sibiri*, Novosibirsk, 1986, vol. 7, p. 274.
8. Pis'ma G.N. Potanina, Irkutsk, 1989, v. 3, p. 91.
9. G.N. Potanin, "Proiskhozhdenie Khrista", *Sibir'skie Ogni*, 1926, no. 4, p. 121; *Pis'ma G.N. Potanina*, v. 3, p. 166.

10. *Pis'ma G.N. Potanina*, Irkutsk, 1990, v. 4, p. 295.
11. *Pis'ma G.N. Potanina,* Irkutsk, v. 4, p. 243.
12. G.N. Potanin, *Vostochnye motivy v srednekovom evropeiskoi epose*, Moscow, 1899, p. 856.
13. Yu. V. Popkov, E.A. Tyugashev, Kh. Tsoohuu, Kh. Tsedev, "Evraziiskaya tsivilizatsionnaya obshnost' narodov: tsennosti i konstanty razvitiya", *Gumanitarnye nauki v Sibiri*, Novosibirsk, 2007, no. 3, p. 94.
14. A.V. Sveshnikov, "Evraziistvo i oblastnichestvo (k voprosu o sopostavlenii dvukh techenii russkoi obschestvenno-politicheskoi mysli)", *Stepnoi krai Evrazii: istoriko-kutur'nye vzaimodeistviya i sovremennost'. Tezisy dokladov i soobschenii v Mezhdunarodnoi nauchnoi konferentsii*, Omsk, 2007, p. 130.
15. A. Schapov, "Istoriko-geograficheskie i etnologicheskie zametki o sibirskom naselenii", *Izvestiya Sibirskogo Otdela IRGO*, Irkutsk, 1873, v. 3, no. 5. pp. 250, 253, 261.
16. N.M. Yadrintsev, "Russkaya narodnost' na Vostoke", *Delo, 1875, no. 4,* pp. 170, 177. N.M. Yadrintsev, 'Russkaia narodnost' na vostoke', *Delo*, 1875, 14, pp. 170, 177.
17. N.M. Yadrintsev, "Puteshestviya na verkhov'ya Orkhona i k razvalinam Karakoruma", *Izvestiya IRGO*, St Petersburg, 1890, v. 26, part 1, p. 271; Yadrintsev, *Sibir' kak koloniya*, St Petersburg, 1882, p, 120.
18. N.M. Yadrintsev, *Sibir' kak koloniya*, 2nd edition (1892), Novosibirsk, 2003, pp. 40-41.

7

Siberian Studies: Re-examining a Distant Domain

Suchandana Chatterjee

Introduction

Siberia, stereotypically defined as wilderness, and redefined as dynamic and self-assertive, is a fresh discursive site for Eurasian studies' specialists. There are a range of perspectives that look at Siberia not only as Russia's resource frontier but also as a self-assertive unit with Turko-Mongol intertwined histories, community identities and sensitivities of a heterogeneous population. These perspectives deal with Russia's presence in Asia, the web of relationships between Russia and her borderlands and internal dynamics of those borderlands. Siberian researchers are attentive to the fatherland's history and have analysed Russia's Asiatic policies in the 19th and 20th centuries.[1] Siberia also tends to be the reference point for Inner Asian studies' specialists who are of the opinion that the nomads' steppe empire extended to Chinese Hunnic dominions in Siberia's eastern borderlands long before the Russians' entry to the region. The Chinese interregnum in the Far East, evidence of sinicization in the agricultural oases of Priamure, Okhotsk seaboard, Kamachatka, Chukotka, Sakhalin and the Kurile Islands along with Yakutia, Transbaikalia and Manchuria have created interest in the character of local authority in the Yenisei basin east of Lake Baikal that was inhabited by Hunnic tribes as early as the 12th century.

The new gaze of area specialists has extended beyond the study of Siberia's potential as Russia's 'extractive frontier' that attracted fur-traders, missionaries, migrants, colonists and intellectuals to a space that had acquired a certain artistic image. The image of Siberia as an exotic landscape that was portrayed by 19th century Russian painters and exhibitionists and the panorama of a huge Eurasian landmass experienced by travelers on 'a virtual voyage' of the Trans-Siberian railroad became a subject of analysis.[2] Recounting 'the new ways in Russian literature', Geoffrey Hosking refers to the contemplative mood of village prose writers like Valentin Rasputin and Vasily Shukshin.[3] Ideas that have also gained ground are cultural perceptions about Siberia and its environment reflected in the Sibiriaks' imagining of a cultural landscape and their expressions about 'freedom' and 'people's will' and community consciousness that is not stereotypically Russian, but looks backward to links with the Cossacks, Turco-Tatars, Mongols, Uyghurs, nomad Kazakhs and 'peripheral Islam'.

There is a revocation of the image of Siberia's 'human environment' that otherwise cannot be explained by such binaries as settled and nomad, the taiga and the steppe, the hunter and the pastoralist. Indigenous communities (Yakuts, Buryat Mongols, Telengit Altaians and the Chukchis) and community traditions were fringe areas in terms of research and were subsumed within the overall fabric of development that was showcased by the Soviets, but are recently being addressed by sociological and ethno-historical studies with a fresh perspective about 'indigeneity'.[4]

A genre of writings has reviewed regionalism as a phenomenon in Siberia, tracing the genesis of *oblastnichestvo* in the 19th century and recounting milestones in the development of *oblastnichestvo* as a movement for autonomists in the 20th century.[5] Discussions also revolve round how the Siberian movement was both adaptive and belligerent, adding emphasis on disparities between the Eastern hypothesis of the *oblastniki* and autonomy agendas of the Bashkirs and the Tatars.[6]

Juxtaposed to these historical issues is a category of writings that portray Siberia's contemporary situation—as the new hub of Eurasian geopolitics, referring to projects that are specific to Siberian regional units like Tyumen and Altai and initiatives that have gained ground in the wake of the Siberian accord (1990) and have extended the scope of debate about the viability of Siberian alternatives. These alternatives and initiatives are assessed in terms of Siberia's 'contiguity' with her Asian borderlands e.g. Mongolia, Xinjiang or Ust Kamen in western Kazakhstan. The Far Eastern reserves of energy and gas have led to wide speculations about energy games between Russia, China and Japan. Siberia's role in the state economy of the Russian Federation is being assessed and the Sino-Japanese 'scramble for colonies' in the Far East is a subject that has impacted on the broader discourse of energy projects in Northeast Asia. The discourse about security has directed attention towards Siberia's maritime territory in the Far East[7] and the spotlight has shifted to the Amur region in debates about land and water borders in the Russian Far East. Critical views about regional projects have shifted attention to other debates about transnationality, diaspora and migration.[8] The present essay deals with diverse research trends that have broadened the canvas of Siberian 'studies'.

From Colonial Hangover to 'Living' History

Siberia's landmass, straddling over 4000 miles of steppe, grasslands, mountains, forests and lakes has been an enigma for scholars who have tried to map Siberia's history primarily through the lens of Russia's contacts with her southern or eastern borderlands. In the past century, Siberia's history was written as a grand political narrative of Muscovite princes' Asiatic ventures east and south of the Urals, with descriptions of military encounters of Muscovite Russia vis-a-vis their Tatar vassals (and the exaction of tributes from them) that brought the entire stretch of Golden Horde territory (divided into independent khanates of Crimea, Astrakhan, Kazan, Nogai and Siberia) under Russian subjugation, direction or control. 'Historical studies' of Siberia revolved round details of invasion and conquest in south Russia and western borderlands, the encounters of the Cossack warrior Yermak Timofeevich with Siberian Tatar khans and the ignominous defeat of his Siberian adversary Kuchum Khan, settlement policies of A.N. Kulomzin (1838-1924) and development projects (e.g. railroad projects of the 19th century) that transformed the region. In connection with Russia's military expansion in Siberia the image of a military frontier and the military abilities of Cossack battalions led by legendary figures like Yermak got strengthened. Russia's 'discovery' of Siberia, highlighting the military exploits of the Cossack armies, the subjugation of Siberian khans and the occupation of their territory, the voluntary submission of the *korennie lyudi* and the transformation of Siberia through gigantic railway ventures became the central themes of the narratives.

These narratives were also based on a progression of events and highlighted 'discovery' as 'development' that began with Russian contacts in the 16th century and culminated in the military reconfiguration of a territory through a network of *streltsy* and *voevodas*. Contestations heralding the victory of Yermak and the defeat of Kuchum Khan became milestones in the military expeditions of Muscovite princes. A brigand like Yermak became a legend for his military pursuits whereas memories of Kuchum Khan as the lone Siberian khan, resolutely fighting the Russians for 16 years to restore his Siberian khanate (a process that began with his refusal to pay tribute to the conquering forces) faded into oblivion. Yermak succeeds and Kuchum fails, this is the basic theme of the narratives on the campaign. On the one hand, Yermak's campaign is remembered more as a private Cossack affair because it was not engineered from Moscow. On the other hand, the campaign seems to be a continuation of Russia's policy of conquest and control—Moscow was using her 'pioneers' to control the routes of Russian advance into the region bordering the steppe. Yermak must have been one of Moscow's trusted pioneers who tried, to the best of his abilities, to subjugate the Siberian Tatars on the Tobol-Irtysh-Ob basin.[9]

In connection with the Cossack component of Russian imperial history, the evolution of the Cossacks as a community that was integral to Russia for more than 400 years and whose members emigrated to the west during the 1950's and the 1960's is being re-examined. Their reflections are poignant memories of a warrior class and a service community that has diasporic contacts in the west. As warriors on horseback they became an asset for the Muscovite princes and the source of strength for the White forces of Ataman Dutov during the Russian Civil War. The Cossack community was associated not only with military activism but also with missionary activities and entrepreneurship and traversed the entire territory from the west to the east of the Urals. They are currently trying to reaffirm themselves through worldwide community links. This zeal of re-establishing community links is reflected in publications like *Entsiklopedia Kazachestva* (Moscow, 2007),[10] which is based on the writings of two emigrant writers A.E. Skrilov and G.V. Gubarev. *Kazachestvo* also entails an assessment of the Cossack phenomenon by historians.[11] Ipso-facto analysis suggests that the Cossacks were not maniacal warriors—the subjugators of the Siberian khans and adjuncts of the imperial Russian forces, but a community of believers, intellectuals and businessmen with worldwide contacts—an idea that is being disseminated through their community journals and newspapers.

Siberia's potential as a resource region that was explored by Tsarist colonists, military adventurers and fur trappers brought to light a network of social contacts largely initiated by individual entrepreneurs and missionaries in Altai and Sakha. Merchant families like the Vinokhurovs and the Stakheevs for example, gained considerable social status because they established widespread contacts through their entrepreneurial ventures. Notwithstanding Moscow's merchant families like the Stroganovs and the Morozovs that became the backbone of the Tsarist autocracy in the 16th century,[12] provincial merchants of Irkutsk, Tomsk and Barnaul exercised significant local control through their monopolies over vodka, fur and gold and also through inter-community exchange with Bukharan merchants. Some gold merchants seemed to collaborate with foreign investors and were called 'Siberian Americans'. Some merchants, e.g. those in Tomsk and Irkutsk became engaged in philanthropic activities, particularly in the field of education.[13] Guild merchants of Siberia became the caucus of a commercial bourgeoisie that thrived in Siberian cities like Irkutsk, Tomsk, Tyumen, Krasnoyarsk, Barnaul, Minusinsk in the pre-1917 period.

The Siberian profile was highlighted as the visual transformation of Siberia appealed to scholars in many ways. The transformation began with the construction of the Trans-Siberian railroad that became a major theme of the discourse on development. Scholars have not only dwelt upon how the Railroad symbolised power game of Russian authorities, technological advancement and land connectivity,[14] but also how it virtually impacted on the intellectuals' imagining of a neglected landscape. The Trans-Siberian Railroad became the metaphor of life—in the poet's imagination, there was a 'tree-train' on the railroad that was not a mere machine that rumbled and roared, but symbolised a living organism—it was a tree of life for the people of Russia as it changed their way of life.[15]

Gradually, the colonial hangover lapsed and historians started delving into other important components of the region's history e.g. Russia's southern and eastern 'frontier' that was regarded not as the periphery of an expanding Russian Empire but as proactive zone with extensive Central Asian or Turkic community contacts. The focus shifted to graded perceptions of history and the region was considered to have evolved from a post-Mongolian unstable political dispensation of warring tribes to an independent Siberian khanate on the banks of River Irtysh and its tributary Tobol, rendered weak by imperial Russian forces in the 16th century and subsequently developed as a military bastion and resource frontier of imperial Russia. Attention shifted also to ethno-cultural evidence about a Chinese pre-history that dated back to the 7th century A.D. The influence of China's Hunnic military confederation and tribal culture on the Sibiriaks as far as the Yenisei region followed by the establishment of the nomadic Turkic *kaganate* in Transbaikalia and Altai-Yenisei region have been taken into account. Stories of struggle between Turkic khanates of Kazan, Nogai (Kazakh) and the Mongol horde (Kalmyks and the Kipchaks) were interwoven into an account of the establishment of an independent Siberian khanate on the banks of River Irtysh—an account that tends to have as much relevance as the saga of imperial 'discovery'. The Chinese dominions on the Amur and Ussuri sections were raided first by the Mongols from the Northeast and then by the Russians who closed on to Chinese territory in the Far East (beyond River Amur, all the way to the Sea of Japan). The Russo-Chinese negotiations were supplanted by a feeling of hostility as Russians tried to extend their hegemony in transit trade upto Ussuri territory, an issue that has been addressed by Japanese scholars in their symposium volumes.[16]

The graded perceptions about Siberia's history also point to an interesting feature: 'human phenomena in the interregional arena'—an aspect that inspires interest in textual readings, e.g. the memoirs of Indian scholar traveller Rahula Sankrityayana and the Russian painter Nicholas Roerich. Roerich's metaphorical interpretations about the Altaian landscape,[17] his identification of the Altai as the real-life location of the land of the Shambhala, fabled in Buddhist mythology about Altai as the heart of Asia and his canvas of paintings immortalizing his Central Asiatic expeditions of the 1920's and Sankrityayana's retrospection about dispersed groups and communities of the Turko-Mongol civilization[18] highlight diffused cultures and 'living history' of the Siberian people. Recent reappraisals of what Sankrityayana and Roerich thought or wrote reflect the tendency to go beyond the mainframe of Russian or Slavic studies and emphasise the community setting and sometimes its entirely different esoteric aspect.[19]

These studies often disseminate ideas about an idyllic landscape-about the Siberian domain that focus on Siberia as dynamic and not tranquil. *Oblastnichestvo* was a major component of this Siberian domain that came under scrutiny in the post-Soviet years. Though primarily associated with the regional patriots of Russia of the late 19th century, *oblastnichestvo* came to be linked with the conscience of other groups with differing loyalties. Regional concerns about educational reform, popularization of the regional press and increasing historical and anthropological knowledge of Russia's peripheries were on the ascendance and the classification of *oblastnichestvo* within the single rubric of autonomy became cliche. It had manifold properties and recent studies indicate the 'fluctuations' in the *oblastniki*'s proposals over a span of 50 years. The heterogeneity of the concept came to full view during the post-revolutionary ardour of the SR's (social revolutionaries) and their adherents who propounded programmes that were very dissimilar from Yadrintsev's or Potanin's original concept of Siberia's autonomous development. The dichotomous centre-periphery relations that was the pivotal issue in Yadrintsev's treatise *Sibir' kak koloniya* was somewhat redefined-20th century proponents of Siberian regionalism were preoccupied with ideas about a federative structure in Russia. Claims of distinction and authority by the *oblastniki* who demanded 'self-administration and economic management as the Russian local councils' (*zemstva*)[20] became restricted in scope. Critics have denounced the ambiguities that surfaced in the 20th century and sealed the fate of *oblastnichestvo* as a political formula. The regional alternative posited by the *oblastniki* soon lost ground because of the limited scope of *zemstva* activity in the local arena, particularly among the Buryats.

The critique has added a new dimension to the form and content of *oblastnichestvo*. It not only has enriched the literature about *oblastnichestvo* but also has raised questions about the hypothesis of *oblastnichestvo* as an autonomous movement with political ambitions only. The salience of cultural specificities of the East, the projection of the 'Eastern hypothesis' by the *oblastniki* and the emphasis on the Eastern folklorist influence on the west are some features of this re-examination.[21]

Frontier Research

Reappraisal of Siberia also makes us attentive about Siberia's links with her neighbourhood. Scholars engaged in a 'rediscovery' of Russia in Asia[22] and the linkages between Russia and its Asian borderlands have focussed on a new dimension about frontiers—not as peripheries or the outer domain of an expansionist empire but as provinces and regions with experiences of development and contact with metropolitan centres like Moscow and St. Petersburg. The focus is also on the frontier mentalite of the Volga Tatars, Bashkirs, Kazakhs and the Siberians who were the autochthonous people of the Russian Empire and have retained a distinct socio-political culture. Attention is on the individual roles that 'frontiers' played as integral components of an expansionist empire. On the one hand they emerged as a competitive force vis-à-vis the colonial settlers. But they also have specificities that make them distinct from one another. Besides, they had economic, social and cultural contacts with each other. Andreas Kappeler revives Owen Lattimore's paradigm of 'frontier zones' by referring to Russia's dynamic southern and eastern borderlands (comprising of Kazakhs, Kalmyks and Tatars of the Golden Horde or the Nogai tribe) and describes how the steppe frontier of Russia evolved since the 16th century from an 'extractive frontier'[23] in western Siberia close to the Urals (where exploitation took place) to a 'settlement frontier' beyond the Urals and south Siberia (where Cossacks were inducted into Russian military service).[24]

Kappeler's view about the settlement of Russian peasants as a novel experiment is juxtaposed to William Sunderland's critique of a settlement policy that created difficulties for Russian settlers and peasant communities as they relocated to new settings, i.e. the agricultural settlements in Siberia and the northern Kazakh steppe in the 1890's in the wake of the settlement policy of Kulomzin.[25] Settlement became a sentimental issue for the Russian peasants—peasant reflections indicate contrasting images of the frontier—utopian freedom on the one hand where peasants got away from the world of feudal lords and a more ambivalent vision in which the frontier was associated with infidels and bandits like Yermak. Settlement-related information as communicated through peasant scouts or settlers themselves have acquired relevance as a source depicting peasant resettlement experience. So, there were impressions about fertile lands near Irkutsk where wheat grew in plenty and abundance of berries in the Yenisei province. To these were contrasting images about things that were beastly and inhuman, such as stories of wild Kazakh nomads who 'swept down from the huge mountains, kidnapped unsuspecting peasants etc.'[26] Overall, these images of the frontier reflected a mindset of the peasant who moved to the unknown frontier.

Frontier encounters, emanating from a sense of distance or isolation from the settler communities, tend to be the dominant theme of writings that deal with Russian colonial developments in the Eurasian steppe. There are examples of cultural encounter too as indigenous people experienced and encountered the everyday reality of colonial rule. Differences that arose between imperial legislation and native custom are also interesting features of the discourse on frontier encounters. Colonial land legislation at the beginning of the 20th century and arbitrary methods of determining *izlishki* (excess or free land) in the steppe that was distributed among Russian settlers and deprived nomads of their ownership rights was criticised by Kazakh scholars. Late 19th century statistical investigations reveal the miscalculations of colonial administrators regarding *aul* property and *aul*-dominated land relations in the Kazakh steppe which signified the imminent threat of loss of pastures.[27]

Another interesting subject of frontier research is the nomadic cultures of the south, particularly the Kazakhs and the Volga Tatars. The 'modernization' paradigm of the 1990' brought to prominence a large volume of literature on the Tatars and the Bashkirs. The emphasis was not only on the Tatars' conceptualization of history and tradition, but also on the Tatar biographical genre in the Volga-Ural region. Bibliographical studies on research trends in modern Central Eurasian studies have drawn our attention to varying interpretations about cultural renaissance, intellectual history of the Tatars, proliferation of a Tatar 'economic elite' in the suburbs of Kazan, dissemination patterns and Islamic institutional structures in late imperial Russia (and many more which is outside the scope of this paper).[28] Quite clearly, studies have been concerned with Tatar intellectualism and Islamic renewal of the Tatars in and around Kazan. What is less conspicuous is research about communities in Siberia that may have been influenced by the Tatar formula but also displaying an indigeneity that is unique.

Resonances: Indigeneity

Compared to the Central Asians, Siberia's Muslim people and Turkic communities have remained a fringe subject though they belong to the same Turko-Mongol stock as the Central Asians and have experienced similar historical processes that have integrated communities and have also dispersed them. Due to the heterogeneous content of the population, the results of research on Siberian communities are fragmentary. Yet one cannot possibly ignore the new reach of studies, extending beyond Kazan and touching Omsk. The Kazan approach highlighting the supranational activism of the Volga Tatars and the dissemination of Tatar literature is juxtaposed to the Omsk variant which highlights popular culture. Recent studies go beyond the stereotypical framework of ethnogenesis of the people of Siberia and genealogies of tribes and the distribution of various Mongolian or Turkic tribes. The new focus is on an examination of 'peripheral issues' like Islamic practices in the steppe or what Allen Frank has described as 'Kazakh religiosity',[29] the aspect of 'indigeneity' and cultural representations of tradition (story-telling and music) among various indigenous groups of Siberia like the Khakass and the Mansis. The renewal of interest in rituals like the *telengit* or the *Ak Jan* and the distinctive features of these ritualistic traditions[30] have unfolded Siberian ethnography as a 're-internationalized field'.[31] The field that was considered to be 'closed and tranquil' to researchers between 1930 and 1980 became popular as interest was aroused in a range of subjects like ethno-history, the 'ethics' of Siberia, the high-handedness of the local elite, ambiguities of survival, nomadic dispensation in the steppe and reflections on the nomadic way of life—topics that are analysed by Russia's Institute of Ethnography and specialized centres and faculties of the Academy of Sciences, Oriental Studies Institutes and Siberian scholar groups and the western academia who are engaged in field-based research as well as archival research in the repositories of Irkutsk, Tomsk, Omsk and Novosibirsk.[32]

Interest about Siberia however, continues to be limited. Glaring revelations by voices from within have indicated the limited academic environment in Siberian centres like Barnaul where scholars hardly gave attention to Siberia's relations with her Turkic neighbours.[33] The subject of Islam and Muslim communities in Siberia were restricted to the Volga-Ural phenomenon whereby the bias is about the powerful synergy of the Tatars, their confessional and ethnic categories, the institutional jurisdiction of the *muftiyats* or spiritual assemblies of Ufa and Orenburg and their concord with Russian imperial or Soviet authorities-a subject of analysis by scholars in

Japan.[34] There was hardly any analysis of any other Muslim community in Siberia that might have not followed the same pattern of absorption by imperialists or the Soviets. There is also a possibility that the patterns of relationship did not match. The *korennye lyudi* certainly did not share the experience of the Volga Tatars who became the beneficiaries of reform that was introduced in the sphere of education (universal primary education) or government (local self government or *zemstva*).[35] Revisionists are strongly critical of the 'monochromatic picture' about Siberian provincial cities like Ulan Ude that were portrayed as passive recipients of policies determined by Moscow. The growing popularity of Buddhism in Ulan Ude strongly reflects the new cultural space which is not determined by Russian contact but by the "Buryatness".[36]

Dissenting voices are reflected elsewhere. Speaking about ethnic processes among the Turkic population of the West Siberian plain, Nikolai Tomilov and his group of collaborators in Omsk and Novosibirsk have stressed on the independent development of diaspora groups among Siberian Tatars, strongly disapproving the view of Kazan historians that Volga and Ural Tatars had a cultural influence on the Siberian Tatars as late as the 19th and the 20th centuries. Tomilov's viewpoint is very similar to that of the Irkutsk-based historian Igor Naumov. The latter is of the opinion that Siberia has a millennia-old fascinating history that was more close to the Mongol than it was to the Russian.[37] In these regions, there was a combination of sedentary economy of the Kyrgyz and Uighur tribes as well as nomadic pastoralism of the Golden Horde and the Mongols who were successors of the Yenisei Kyrgyz. Supra-tribal projects as Burkhanism constructed images of a new faith that would combat the hegemonic control of the Tsar. Burkhanism progressed from a soul-searching mission to a political alternative (expressed through their demands of a Karakorum-Altaian Soviet District in 1918)—an idea of congregation round a White Faith leader who represented the 17th century Oirot confederation.[38]

Another interesting feature of revisionist writings is their focus on stratified or 'layered' responses. While conducting fieldwork studies, the Siberian research group of Max Planck became very attentive to the youth of Siberia who were somewhat detached from the overall structure of formal education, creative art and even sport activity. The alienation of the young people from the elders' decisions, say, about land use turned them into recipients of traditional knowledge and failed to transform them as protagonists of cultural revival (*vozhrozhdenie)*. Though considered to be the agent of change in Soviet society (through *komsomols)* they yielded to collective interests rather than individual ones. The new-age studies' group in Halle began concentrating on youth responses rather than collectivism and community participation. The new emphasis on Siberia's youth seems to have broken new ground in Siberian anthropology.[39]

Reappraisal

Culture and development thus became the new discursive sites for mapping Siberia as a domain. Sentiments of the present influenced the style of new writing—for some the reality of Siberia was gloom and darkness. For others, it represented development and transformation. Trained in the 'youth prose' tradition of the 1950's, village prose writers like Shukshin, Rasputin and Astafev disseminated feelings about their Siberian homeland that was experiencing transformation. The images of Siberia as *volia* (free will)', as a pastoral, uncorrupted, spiritual landscape and a place of unrestricted space and complete individual freedom were getting appreciated.[40] Others like Antonina Kortayeva were ecstatic about the new opportunities for people from remote northern regions like Yakutia.[41] The Swedish traveller Nansen's predictions about Siberia evolving as 'a land of the future' proved to be true—the region was visually transformed by construction projects as the Trans-Siberian Railroad. Siberia became a space that was not wilderness per se, or a space that was disconnected from Russia but had scope for inter-ethnic communication among various Asiatic natives like Dersu Uzala. What gained attention is not the hostile environment of Siberia where bandits and raiders and Soviet daredevils left their mark but the century-old Siberia of angry rivers, icy cliffs and frozen deserts that symbolised Siberian identity and a Siberian landscape that is also part of the Eurasian steppe. These are 'plebeian' images of Siberia with the dominant view of Siberia as the 'ecological paradise'—a sharp contrast to the exiles' reflections about 'hell'. Like their 19th century mentors who wrote about their experiences in Siberian cities like Irkutsk recounting the joyful and enchanting atmosphere that was different from the gloomy world of the Russian capital of St. Petersburg,[42] a brave new generation of writers like Valentin Rasputin, also an Irkutsk writer, wrote about their homeland and disseminated to the world the all pervading myth of Siberia as a threatened paradise.

Yet, reality was often more harsh than imagined. Rasputin and village prose writers of the 1950's wrote about the problems Siberia encountered in the Soviet period—social displacement and ecological degradation, concentrating on the lost reserves and the beauty of the Angara river and Lake Baikal. Lake Baikal was transformed into a large reservoir and Irkutsk's huge dam projects were calamitous for the Siberian environment. Siberia's defacement bothered sentimental writers like Rasputin-he not only wanted to undo what the Soviets had done but was also keen to project Siberia in terms of its own history and reveal the Siberians' links with nature.[43] It is this sentiment that is the most talked-about affair in Siberia today—reflected in the yesteryears of socialist realism and continuing as a literary trend among the post-Soviet generation of writers. Such varying impressions of change have reconfigured the format of Siberian studies.

Notes and References

1. Issues specific to Tsarist reorganization of Siberia and Soviet strategies of control are being critically assessed. Examples of this trend are: M.V. Shilovskiy, 'Agrarnaia reforma P.A. Stolypina I Sibir'. K 100 letyu ukaza ot 9 Noyabrya 1906 god', *Gumanitarnye Nauki v Sibiri*, No. 2, 2006; V.I. Shishkin, 'Politika sovetskoi vlasti po otnosheniyu k povstantsom Zapadnoi Sibiri v 1921 god', *Gumanitarnye Nauki v Sibiri*, No. 2, 2006.
2. Claudia Weiss, 'Representing the Empire: The Meaning of Siberia for Russian Imperial Identity', *Nationalities Papers* 35, No. 3 (July 2007): 439.
3. Geoffrey Hosking, 'The twentieth century: in search of new ways, 1953-80', in Charles A. Moser edited *The Cambridge History of Russian Literature*, Cambridge: Cambridge University Press, 1989.
4. Indigeneity as tradition is a strong component of sociological studies pursued by Max Planck Institute and Hokkaido's Slavic Research Centre. Sociologists and historians in Barnaul, Novosibirsk and Tomsk have also raised pertinent questions about Siberia as a component of Asiatic Russia.
5. N.N. Ablazhei, *Sibirs'koe oblastnichestvo v emigratsii*, Novosibirsk: Institute of Archaeology and Ethnography RAN, 2003.
6. Writings depicting 20th century activism of the Sibiriaks highlight autonomy as the motivating factor behind collaboration between

oblastniki and anti-Bolshevik Kazakh and Bashkir activists. Despite such attempts, there were inherent problems in the Siberian autonomy movements—there were regional peculiarities and centrifugal tendencies that became the crux of conflicts and debates among the Sibiriaks during the Civil War period.

7. There has been growing concern about Russians' 'human security', especially economic security and in Khabarovsk and Vladivostok, negative views and complaints about Chinese migrants who are said to have earned a better living than local residents have gained ground. Such apprehensions also existed in the past.
8. Some examples are V.I. Dyatlov ed. *Migranty I Diaspory na vostoke Rossii: Praktiki vzaimodeistviya s obshestvom I gosudarstvom*, Moscow-Irkutsk: Natalis, 2007; Galina Vitkovskaya, "Does Chinese Emigration Endanger Russian Security?", *Carnegie Endowment Briefing Papers* 1, Issue 8 (August 1999); Elizabeth Wishnick, "Chinese Migration to the Russian Far East: A Human Security Dilemma", *gsti.miis.edu/CEAS-PUB/200209/Wishnick.pdf*.
9. The chronicles are analysed by Terence Armstrong in her introduction to *Yermak's campaign of Siberia: A selection of documents translated from Russian by Tatiana Minorsky and David Wileman*, London: The Hakluyt Society, 1975: 1-33. Selected descriptions from the Stroganov chronicle (pp. 47-52) also provide information about the unequal encounter. Not only were Kuchum's men unable with their arrows and spears to destroy the Cossacks who were armed with small shot-guns and fortress guns, but also were deserted by 'friends' like the Ostyak prince. His favourite, his own son Mametkul, was badly wounded in the battle.
10. *Entsiklopedia Kazachestva*, collection of articles by G.V. Guvarev and A.E. Skrilov, compiled by O.O. Antropov, Moscow: Veche, 2007.
11. V.V. Alexeev edited *Istoriya kazakchestva Aziatskoi Rossii*, 3 volumes, Ekaterinburg: UrO RAN, 1995.
12. Prince Ivan's patronage of merchant families signified the depth of imperial control.
13. According to Barnaul-based historian Vladimir Boyko, the guild merchants of Tomsk actively participated in the establishment of the University of Tomsk.
14. Steven G. Marks, *Road to power: The Trans-Siberian Railroad and the colonization of Asian Russia*, Ithaca: Cornell University Press, 1991.
15. Anindita Banerjee, "The Trans-Siberian Railroad and Russia's Asia-Literature, Geopolitics, Philosophy of History", *Clio* 1-2, No. 34 (2004-2005): 30.
16. Iwashita Akihiro ed. *Siberia and the Russian Far East in the 21st Century: Partners in Community of Asia*, 2 vols., Sapporo: Slavic Research Centre, 2005; Iwashita Akihiro ed. *Eager Eyes Fixed on*

Eurasia, Russia and its eastern edge, Vol. 2, Sapporo: Slavic Research Centre, 2007.

17. Nicholas Roerich, *Altai-Himalaya: A Travel Diary,* New Delhi: Book Faith India, 1996.
18. Rahula Sankrityayana, *Meri Jeevan Yatra* (translated into Bengali as *Amar Jibon Jatra,* edited by Satish Mitra and Saikat Rakshit, Rahula Sankrityayana Birth Centenary Committee, 1995, 5 vols).
19. Letters of Nicholas Roerich in *Peterburgskii Rerikhovskii Sbornik, Vypusk 1-5,* 1998-2002 gody. Website: *http://www.spbu.ru/Science/Centers/RoerichCenter/SCREENS.*
20. Dina A. Amanzhalova, "The movement for Siberian regional and national autonomy in the early 1920's", *Sibirica* 3, No. 1, 2003:92.
21. Elena Kovalaschina, "The historical and cultural ideals of the Siberian *oblastnichestvo*", *Sibirica,* 6, Issue 2 (Autumn 2007).
22. Stephen Kotkin and David Wolff eds *Rediscovering Russia in Asia: Siberia and the Russian Far East,* Armonk, New York: M.E. Sharpe, 1995.
23. 'Extractive' in terms of the mining and extractive industries like gold, non-ferrous metals, coal, salt etc.
24. N.I. Nikitin. 'Voennosluzhilie lyudi: osvonie Sibiri v XVII veke', *Istoriya SSSR,* 1980, No. 2.
25. Steven G. Marks, 'Conquering the Great East: Kulomzin, Peasant Resettlement and the creation of modern Siberia', in Stephen Kotkin and David Wolff eds *Rediscovering Russia in Asia: Siberia and the Russian Far East,* Armonk: M.E. Sharpe, 1995.
26. Willard Sunderland, "Peasant pioneering: Russian peasant settlers describe colonization and the eastern frontier, 1880's-1910", *Journal of Social History,* (Summer 2001).
27. An account deals with the image of nomadic customs like *barimta* as 'crime' among imperial legislators who tried to administer and control the steppe during the 1820's. Virginia Martin, "Barimta: Nomadic Custom, Imperial Crime", Danel R. Brower and Edward J. Lazzerini eds. *Russia's Orient: Imperial_Borderlands and Peoples, 1700-1917,* Bloomington: Indiana University Press, 1997; Gulnar Kendirbai, 'The struggle for land on the Kazak steppe at the beginning of the twentieth century', in Gabriele Rasuly Paleczek and Julia Katschnig eds. *Central Asia on Display, Proceedings of the VII Conference of the European Society for Central Asian Studies,* Lit Verlag, Wien 2004.
28. Marsel Farakhshatov and Christian Noack, "Research trends in studies on the history of Islam and Muslim peoples (Bashkirs, Volga and Siberian Tatars), conducted in European Russia and Siberia ca. 1985-2000", in Stephane A. Dudoignon and Komatsu Hisao eds. *Research Trends in Modern Central Eurasian Studies (18th-20th centuries): A selective and critical bibliography of works published between 1985 and 2000,* Part I,

Tokyo: The Toyo Bunko, 2003. Part II of the same volume (published in 2006) is resource-rich, containing categorized information on modern Central Eurasian studies, echoing both western and non-western voices about Central Eurasian history, linguistics, sociology, anthropology, religion and politics.

29. Allen Frank, *Muslim religious institutions in imperial Russia, The Islamic world of Novouzensk District and the Kazakh Inner Horde, 1780-1910*, Brill: Leiden, 2001. Other aspects of religiosity have also been examined by Frank in 'Varieties of Islam in Inner Asia, the case of the Baraba Tatars, 1740-1917', *Cahiers du Monde russe*, Avril-Septembre 2000: 41/2-3.
30. The *Ak Jan* is a religious trend that was dissimilar from the Altaian shamanic "core" religious tradition. Andrei Vinogrodov, *Ak Jan in the context of Altai religious tradition,* Ph.D. thesis submitted to the College of Graduate Studies and Research, University of Saskatchewan, 2003; Agnieszka E. Halemba, *The Telengits of Southern Siberia: Landscape, religion and knowledge in motion*, London: Routledge, 2006.
31. Patty Gray, Nikolai Vakhtin and Peter Schweitzer, "Who owns Siberian ethnography? A critical assessment of a re-internationalized field", *Sibirica,* 3, No. 2, (October 2003).
32. There is an appreciation of the nomad way of life, bringing into full view their adaptation to the outer world. The nomad, in their view was not only a shepherd, a wanderer or a looter, but also a bard, an orator and a minstrel. One can see a remarkable growth of interest in steppe music and tales of love, mysticism of steppe rituals etc. Case studies portray not only the inner world of the nomad but also explore the world outlook of some communities like the Telengits of Altai. *Ak jan* and *Altai jan* represent purity of the soul and the *Ak Jan* movement upholds the principle of harmonious existence between human beings and nature.
33. Vladimir Boyko, "The Barnaul School of Central Asian Studies: A brief Review of Scientific research in Barnaul concerning Central Asian politics and international relation", *CESR* 1, No. 2, (Spring 2002).
35. Naganawa Norihiro, "Maktab or school? Introduction of universal primary education among the Volga-Ural Muslims"; Norihiro, "Molding the Muslim community through the Tsarist Administration: Mahalla under the jurisdiction of the Orenburg Mohammedan Spiritual Assembly after 1905", *Acta Slavica Iaponica* 23, (2005): 101-123.
36. Robert Montgomery, Review of *History of urbanization of a Siberian City: Ulan Ude,* by Balzhan Zhimbiev. *CESR* 2, No. 3, (Fall 2003).
37. Igor Naumov, *The History of Siberia*, London: Routledge, 2006.
38. Andrei Znamenski, "Power of Myth: Popular ethnonationalism and nationality building in Mountain Altai, 1904-1922", *Acta Slavica Iaponica* 22, (2005).
39. Joachim Otto Habeck, "Introduction: growing research on youth in

Siberia" (Special Issue "Youth in Siberia"), *Sibirica,* 4, No. 1, (April 2004).

40. As depicted by Archpriest Avvakum Petrovich (1620-1682) in *The Life Written by Himself.* Bruce T. Holl, "Avvakum and the Genesis of Siberian Literature", in Galya Diment and Yuri Slezkine eds. *Between Heaven and Hell: The Myth of Siberia in Russian Culture*, New York: St. Martin's Press, 1993.
41. Antonina Kortayeva, *Ivan Ivanovich*, Moscow: Foreign Language Publishing House, 1952.
42. Galya Diment, "Exiled *from* Siberia: The construction of Siberian Experience by early Nineteenth century Irkutsk Writers", in Galya Diment and Yuri Slezkine eds. *Between Heaven and Hell: The Myth of Siberia in Russian Culture*, New York: St. Martin's Press, (1993): 60.
43. Chapters 3 and 4 in Valentin Rasputin, *Siberia, Siberia*, Illinois: Northwestern University Press, 1996.

8

Islam in Siberia: Historical and Anthropological Aspects

Stéphane A. Dudoignon

Despite the recent enrichment of existing bibliography, Siberian Islam continues to be given a specific, essentially peripheral status in both Siberian and Islamic studies. In the last three decades, however, Siberian Islam has gradually become a more complete asset of both history and social sciences thanks to the parallel, mostly unrelated endeavours of several schools of research—amongst which the schools of Omsk in Russia and of Bloomington in the USA. Recently, occasional collaborations and cross-critical echoes to works by researchers from these respective schools have undoubtedly created new dynamics, paving the way for a novel intermingling of disciplines and even perhaps, to some extent, to philosophies of research. Already far from the colonial and Soviet ethnography that, used to study peoples for classifying them into fixed categories, the innovative combination of historical and anthropological approaches that has been developing since the late 1980s has cast new light on the successive impact of modern state policies, and on conversion narratives on collective identities. Being the first who gathered authors on Siberian Islam from these varied horizons (in a multilingual volume published in Paris in 2000, largely echoed by A.G. Seleznev in his *Sibisrkii islam*, 2004), I would like in this short synthetic and necessarily provisional paper to sketch a state of the field and the perspectives aroused by these recent discoveries and reappraisals, and to evoke the roles played respectively by at least the two aforementioned schools of research in this renewal.

The University of Omsk and the Omsk Subsidiary of the Siberian Institute of History, Philology, and Philosophy of the Academy of

Sciences of the Federation of Russian must be credited with a significant spadework on the ethnic history of Siberia. The more productive teaching of the School of Omsk—let's call it like that—results from a close association of anthropology and history: For decades, ethnographers of Siberia have been endeavouring to use a wide range of written sources for resituating inside varied durations particularly fluid phenomena of community building observed during the twentieth century. In parallel, more recent works by Bloomington-based researchers have been oriented towards the analysis of the place and functions of conversion to Islam, and of conversion narratives, in different processes of community construction. This combination of approaches at least allows us nowadays to tackle the important issue of the variations of the content of community identities among the Turkic-speaking Islamic-background populations of Siberia in a period of time comprised between the late seventeenth century and the present.

Why such an interest for this outlying region of the world of Islam? Because since the beginning of its long process of conversion to Islam in the fourteenth century Siberia has been a melting pot of the most various economies and cultures of Inner Eurasia—from sedentary Transoxiana and Altishahr, from nomadic Turkic and Mongol steppes, and from imperial, then Soviet Russia, without omitting more anciently settled Siberian communities. Since the first Russian conquest of the mid-seventeenth century, Siberian Islam has been confronted with a durable European colonisation, accompanied since the nineteenth century with the demographic dominance of Slavic and Orthodox Christian-background populations. For all these reasons it has seemed to us that Siberian Islam, though of a limited demographic significance, and for this reason ignored for long by historians and social scientists, offers a particularly interesting case of borderland Islam.

The Institutions

The School of Omsk (V.G. Malinovski, N.A. Tomilov, S.N. Korusenko, A.G. Seleznev) has brought decisive contributions to the recent evolution of the "ethnic history" of the Turkic speaking populations of Western Siberia, especially in the form of subtle analyses of the highly problematic ethnicity of 'Siberian Tatars'. Though a considerable amount of the studies emanating from the

School of Omsk partake to ethnography, one must underline the great attention shown by a majority of its authors in evolutions on the long and middle durations. As a matter of fact, the chronological framework of these studies is commonly extended from the sixteenth to the early twenty-first century, with a particular interest in the consequences of the more and more massive migrations from European Russia at the turn of the nineteenth and twentieth centuries. In their studies of different ethnic groups the authors take into account not only economic and social factors, but also the complex history of the modes of auto-denomination and the processes of mutual opposition between the different communities. So doing, most authors manage to escape from the ethnic essentialism that is more commonly diffused in purely synchronic ethnographic studies (and is dominant, for instance, in Central Asian studies).

It is true that contemporary research is served by the availability of relatively abundant and diverse written sources, among which can be found the first Russian censes (*revizii*) realised at more or less regular intervals since the first years of the eighteenth century. Of course, the often simplistic taxonomies used in this kind of documents could have exerted a negative influence on the perceptions and representations of nowadays researchers. However, the study of these documents has often been combined with that of other sources, collected by the numerous ethnographic expeditions undertaken by the Universities of Omsk and Tomsk since the late 1960s.

Among the significant contributions of these researches can be distinguished the following ones: a more qualified perception of the demographic evolutions (in particular the discovery of a natural growth bend of the Turkic-speaking populations of Western Siberia in the nineteenth and twentieth centuries, correcting the received idea of an overall depopulation process); a subtler measure of the varying degree of the acculturation of the Muslim-background communities of Siberia; a better account of the role played by city planning and migrations linked with the Russian colonisation of the second half of the nineteenth century. Many leading figureheads of the School of Omsk, beginning with its leader N.A. Tomilov, insist on the essentially composite character of the categories used by Russian ethnography. Such is the case of the famous Siberian "Bukharans" among whom Tomilov has been detecting the presence of Uighurs, Kazakhs, Turkmens, and rather numerous Karakalpaks. Analogous considerations have been indeed applied to numerically more significant groups, beginning with that of the 'Volga & Urals Tatars'.

'Ethnic History' and the Impact of State Policy

The reconstruction of genealogies on the basis of late-nineteenth—early-twentieth-century censes (*revizii*), compared with more recent field data, has for instance permitted comparative studies of the development of ethnicity in the two main groups of the Middle-Irtysh Tatars—*i.e.*, on the one hand the Kurdal & Sargat Tatars and, on the other hand, the Tara Tatars, according to the migratory history of these two groups in the eighteenth and nineteenth centuries. The researchers of the School of Omsk have been particularly interested in variations that have been introduced in both groups' communal identity by the change in the composition of each—for instance by the much larger part of 'Bukharans' originating from Central Asia in the latter's case. This set of studies reveals that the Tara Tatars have preserved a more precise memory of the varied geographical origin of their ancestors, in particular of those coming from the Volga-Urals region, and of those pertaining to the more ancient but still prestigious group of the 'Bukharans'. These patiently reconstructed genealogies offer a highly significant contribution to the study of the development of symbolic identity among Turkic-speaking Muslim communities of Western Siberia. In this case, genealogical history definitely appears as a needed auxiliary to the study of the ethnic composition and of the complex ethnicity of the mixed Turkic-speaking Muslim populations of a region like the shores of the Middle-Irtysh River.

With the ethnic historians of the School of Omsk, we also question acculturation phenomena, in particular of the Siberian Tatars with Turkic-speaking populations of the Volga & Urals region who arrived to Siberia in the course of the late nineteenth and early twentieth centuries. Researchers insist in particular on the *very relative* homogeneity of the early-twentieth-century 'Tatar' culture, and on strong differences of perceptions between 'Siberian' and 'Volga' Tatars. On this point, the Omsk School of ethnography is clearly opposed to its counterpart of Kazan, west of the Urals. Indeed the latter's spokespersons have been permanently stressing, especially since the end of the Soviet period, an unobtainable unity of the Volga Tatars, disseminated on a discontinuous territory extended from

Poland to Manchuria. A primary issue at stake here in the content to be given to the concepts. Russia's ethnographers in general, and in particular Tatar historians and ethnographers of Western Siberia use to take 'popular' culture as the main if not exclusive object of their research. This postulate brings them to an overvaluation of remainders of pre-Islamic religious practices, or the influence of regional and local ecosystems on vernacular 'popular' cultures. And when they speak of learned cultures, it is for underlying the relations of the Turkic-speaking Muslims of Western Siberia with their coreligionists from Central Asia or from the Urals region. Conversely, the specialists of demographic history from Kazan tend to focus on late-nineteenth and early-twentieth-century reform and modernisation movements, and to insist on the intellectual influx from the Middle-Volga region towards the outermost bounds of Siberia, so stressing the cultural unity of the 'Tatar world'.

An epistemological parenthesis may be opened here: The ethnographical approach partake of a taxonomic intention and brings the authors to an underlining of differences; the historical approach focusing on intellectual milieus—which is that of a majority of Western scholars, relying on written sources and less familiar with regional fieldwork—brings the latter to overvalue interregional connections, exchanges, and acculturation phenomena, getting closer on these points to the relatively remote observers of the School of Kazan. For this set of reasons, it is particularly important that the observed or studied phenomena be quantified, and their dimension be tested, for a more precise evaluation of the role of Siberia as a centre of endogenous cultures or a periphery *par excellence* of the world of Islam.

The Memory of Conversion

Islam as a vector of communal identity has been tackled by the School of Bloomington, for instance in the exceptional and illustrative case of Baraba Tatars—a community relatively homogenous from an ethnic viewpoint, but divided from the mid-eighteenth century onwards by the divergent strategic choice by its members of conversion to Islam or to Orthodox Christianity. A prominent representative of the School of Bloomington, A.J. Frank, has been basing his argument on a particularly rich vernacular tradition of legendary conversion narratives. At the same time, he has been exploiting the narratives let by Volga Tatar travellers and missionaries of Islam, who arrived in large numbers in the Baraba Steppe at the turn of the nineteenth and twentieth centuries, and who played a crucial role in the 're-Islamicisation' of Baraba Tatars. This questioning of non-vernacular Islamic sources has allowed the historian to reconstruct the negative, derogatory vision of local, Siberian Islam shared by these early-twentieth-century newcomers from the urbanised areas of the Middle-Volga region, who were to play a key cultural role in a time when the Baraba Steppe was extracted from its isolation by the mass-migration eastwards of the peasants from Russia, and by the multiplication of communication routes.

In Siberia as well as in the whole Inner Eurasia the modern (re)-Islamicisation process has been described from several viewpoints. This diversity of perspectives raises the issue of the indications of the adoption of Islam of such or such community—a key issue for the dating of conversion, which is itself a key issue of the history and anthropology of Islamic-background societies and communities of Inner Eurasia. Russian sources (and a number of modern, notably Western studies that continue to be inspired by them) generally insist on the 'survivals (*relikty*)' of pre-Islamic practices till the last third of the eighteenth century as far as Baraba Tatars are concerned. In fact, it seems that the Islamic cult was well-spread among the latter in the mid-eighteenth century. At this date, Baraba Tatars modified their political status: Whence a minority of them, in quest of Russian protection against steppe nomads, opted for the conversion for Orthodox Christianity, a majority chose to be attached through conversion to Islam to the Tara Tatars, one of the most privileged non-Christian communities of the Russian Empire—in particular to the 'Bukharan' *'ulama* of the Middle-Irtysh River who were behind their conversion. Becoming at the same time subjects of the Russian Empire and members of the *umma*, the Barabas could reasonably hope for taking profit of varied fiscal exemptions as well as of efficient protection against the raids of the Kazakhs and other nomadic peoples coming from the south.

In the case of the Baraba Tatars, we observe a community converting to Islam and preserving, if not reinforcing its inner cohesion in the aftermath of conversion—even if can be denoted the presence of Baraba Muslims well before the overall adoption of Russia's citizenship by the whole community, and even if we must admit that significant change occurred in the steppe well before the arrival of Volga Tatars at the turn of the nineteenth and twentieth centuries. The research describes well this opposition of two cultures and two religious traditions, the Volga Tatars considering the Barabas Muslims who had fallen again into "savagery (*wahshaniyya*)" or even into *jahiliyya* (the state of ignorance anterior to conversion). From their own viewpoint, however, late nineteenth-century Barabas naturally considered themselves as having *always* been Muslim, estimating that they simply had become 'better Muslims' thanks to the Islamic influence coming from European Russia. The cross-study of sources implemented by the School of Bloomington reveals a different vision of conversion by different protagonists and narrators inside the *umma*. This perspective allows us to question and to qualify the Russian, Christian vision of the things, still prevailing today in a number of publications, which perceives conversion and the transition to Islam as an abrupt and one-to-one passage from paganism to Islam. The case of the Baraba Tatars usefully warns us against quick and superficial distinctions between 'real' and 'superficial' conversion to Islam and, more generally, against the categories of the 'Islamic' and the 'pre-Islamic' as they were prevailing till recently in the ethnographic literature on Inner Eurasian Islam.

Conclusion

The paradigmatic cases of the Kurdal & Sargat Tatars on the one hand and of the Baraba Tatars on the other provide ample suggestion that Siberia appears as a promising field from the viewpoints of heuristic methods and epistemological experimentations—for instance on the central question of colonisation vs. civilisation (in the Siberian case, a modern Slavic-dominated mass-migration eastward having unexpectedly resulted in a re-Islamicisation process, notably enriched by the influence of the ideas locally developed by Russian Populist intelligentsia). In particular, their discovery and study by researchers of the Schools of Omsk in Russia and Bloomington in the USA perfectly correspond with a substantial rapprochement between history and social sciences that has been sketched and called for by leading historians since the 1980s (see notably the French medievalist Georges Duby in his testament *L'histoire continue*, 1989).

9

Rasputin's *The Fire* and Perestroika

Rashmi Doraiswamy

Rasputin's *Pozhar* (The Fire/1985), Astafiev's *Pechalny Detektiv* (The Sad Detective, 1986) and Aitmatov's *Plakha* (The Executioner's Block/1986) are called the 'Three Ps of Perestroika'. All three works were written in the Asian part of the Eurasian landmass that was the Soviet Union. That these works were emblematic of the last period of the Soviet Union's history, is testimony to the cultural arrival of the periphery, even as the Soviet Union had begun its dissolution politically and economically. It would be probably more correct to call the periphery the non-centre. The Asiatic part of the Soviet Union was too large to be a marginal periphery! Siberia, in particular, has had a paradoxical dual identity: although geographically it is part of Asia, it has been considered to be more an extension of the European west of the Soviet Union. The Transcaucasus and Central Asian Republics have always been clearly identified as 'Asia', as distinct from Siberia, which lies to the North. Religious, ethnic and other historical factors, no doubt, contributed to this variance of the cultural imaginary from geographical reality.

The Fire and *The Sad Detective* are novellas; *The Executioner's Block* is a novel. All three works deal with important political and social questions relevant to debates around perestroika. Rasputin was one of the leading village prose writers who emerged in the '70s in the Soviet literary scene. Astafiev too was a village prose writer who also wrote about the Second World War. Aitmatov wrote about, among other things, the Second World War and the countryside and later even science fiction. While all three writers engaged significantly with the problematic of rural Soviet Union, they also dealt with themes that were set in semi-urban, urban areas. In the case of Aitmatov, he did not exclusively set his works at a given point in his career in the village. He set his short stories and novellas in all kinds of locations, which is probably why he was never classified as a 'village prose' writer, as the others were. What all three writers share in addition is a sensibility that moves beyond realism into myths and legends.

Village prose was, in fact, breaking new ground in Soviet literature from the sixties onwards. Many consider this prose to have been a parallel current to dissident literature in its ignoring of the canon of socialist realism. Its mode of being was, however, very different from that of dissident literature. It neither loudly proclaimed its opposition to the political order nor did it question the tenets of socialist realism, by going into the realm of modernism. The authors of village prose delved into the life of people who lived in the village, who tilled the land, whose lives were deeply bound up with the ecological systems. Solzhenitsyn called the writers '*nravstvenniki*' ('ethicists'). They drew on mytho-poetic traditions, the spiritual life of the people and traditions of realism. The countryside featured in the works of nineteenth century realist fiction in Russia, but there was a difference in the new village prose. According to Edward Brown, "... in the second half of this century a number of writers, some of them close to peasant life, attempted to give us an account of that life from the inside. Nineteenth-century studies of the peasant, in contrast, were written for the most part by intellectuals who observed them from an aesthetic distance".[1]

The oppositional stance to the official canon that is implied by several critics writing on village prose, may not present the entire picture. Brown, for instance, insists that: "Sinyavsky has pointed out that it is a gross oversimplification to treat uncensored and censored Russian literature as distinct entities, one free to tell the truth, the other not.... The situation in Russian literature is actually more interesting than that. The very existence of uncensored literature has, Sinyavsky believes, obliged the government from time to time to make concessions, to allow certain talented writers a measure of autonomy. And uncensored literature, widely read in the Soviet community, has had a measureable influence on certain authors, encouraging them to undertake risky and even heretofore forbidden themes. This practice may partially explain the publication and wide readership of Rasputin, Trifonov, Shukshin, the novels of Okudzhava, and many other things".[2] Village prose writers, it is possible, did not really draw on dissident or underground literature for inspiration, style or theme as much as it is made out to be by critics such as Brown, for most of them were deeply grounded in realism. They did away with stereotypic characters and offered to Soviet literature a gallery of new characters from the countryside. What they focused on was '*narodnost*' rather than on '*klassovost*' and '*partiinost*' which constituted the three important principles of socialist realism. According to Leiderman and Lipovetsky "Following the democratic traditions of Russian literature which connects the concept of the aesthetic ideal with the people, the creators of 'village prose' also see the people as carriers of the ideal, but as carriers specially of ethical values, those which grow not on the basis of class ideology and speculative social doctrines, but on the soil of life, experience, work on the land, direct contact with nature.... And this was new and fresh in comparison to the ideal of socialist realism. 'The simple, Soviet man' lost the epithet 'Soviet', his image began to be defined not by ideological, but by cultural coordinates – through the land, nature, family cares, the foundations of the way of life in the village".[3] They underline the fact that it was this prose that addressed the 'deficit of spirituality'[4] that Soviet life suffered from.

The Russian gaze on Siberia underwent many subtle changes over the centuries. It was initially viewed as an Asiatic colony, conquered from the Golden Horde in the sixteenth and seventeenth centuries. Later, Siberia became the place of exile. Vera Tolz points out that "The very concept of internal exile, established in Moscovy in the sixteenth century, dramatically symbolized the inequality of Russia's different areas. Remote areas of the empire, for instance, Siberia, acquired the status of a prison, and it became a punishment to send people charged with various offences to live there".[5] In the nineteenth century, the Decembrists, who served their sentences in the East, presented Siberia in a totally different light: "They emphasized that because Siberia did not know the institution of serfdom, it was much freer than European Russia, and therefore could offer the Russians a place of escape and salvation. The Decembrists' glorification of the progressive qualities of Siberia was further developed by Alexander Herzen. During his exile in London from the late 1840s onwards, Herzen turned from a belief in the need to Europeanise Russia to a search for 'indigenous roots; in the hope of achieving Russia's political transformation. Whereas European Russia symbolized the autocratic oppression of Nicholas I, Siberia became the genuine Russia of unspoiled people".[6]

Siberia had found representation in literature since the XIX century as the place of exile and camps. The village prose writers gave Siberia a different presence on the literary scene, portraying its villages and countryside 'from the inside'. According to Julian Laychuk, "Siberia, a vast land noted as much for its inaccessibility and remoteness as for the as for the richness of its abundant national resources was, along with the isolated and traditional Vologda region in the northwest (which served as the locale for the works of such talented village-prose writers as Vasily Belov and Fyodor Abramov), a location which had experienced the intrusion of the central authorities least. As a result, the traditions and ways of the people had survived the Soviet experiment in whole or in part, and the region served as a microcosm for studying the effects and changes wrought by the planners after they had finally penetrated these areas".[7] It is of interest to note that several of the village prose writers are from Siberia: Vasily Belov, Shukshin, Valentin Rasputin and Viktor Astafiev. While Brown and Laychuk state that the context for this prose was the unofficial, uncensored, dissident literature and the remoteness of time and space that allowed Siberia to remain somewhat cut-off from Soviet intervention, I would argue that the context that village prose 'arrived' in was different. Village prose writers not only 'freed' Siberia from an Europeanised gaze, but also rejoined links with the Slavophilian tradition of Russian thought and Tolstoyan beliefs in their faith in the peasant and the Russian *obshina*. It was this sense of the village community that was foregrounded once again in the twentieth century by the village prose writers. Realism was the preferred mode of representation, and it was the Russian-Soviet encounter that produced a literary language and movement that served as a marker of cultural identity, even as it linked up with movements from Russia's past. It was the dynamics of the Russia-Siberia relationship that created the possibility of a literary movement from the periphery that could capture the cultural imagination of the entire Soviet space.

The style that writers such as Fyodor Abramov, Vasily Shukshin, Valentin Rasputin and Viktor Astafiev developed as village prose writers, served them as and when they moved on to other themes and locales. Valentin Rasputin, who began as a village prose writer, moved on to semi-urban and urban themes after 1975. His *The Fire* is set in Sosnovka, a semi-urban settlement, whose inhabitants have moved here after their native lands have been submerged under water due to the construction of dams and hydroelectric projects. The nostalgia for the village community remained in his writings even after the village prose period. Mikkelson and Winchell point out that "His most cherished themes are the earth as a unified ecosystem. Including soil, air, water, plants, animals, humans, and spirits, all of which are subtly and inextricably interwoven and interdependent; a nation's history as a unified and unbreakable continuum made up of past, present, and future generations, all of which are connected by a common place of birth and by the same cultural and ethical traditions; the psychological motivation of individuals, whether ostracized or accepted by society; the clash between modern and traditional mores, especially as it affects the earth, one's sense of historical roots, and one's behaviour during a crisis; the perils and ecstasies of solitude and introspection; and the harshness of Soviet law, particularly when applied arbitrarily and without regard for mitigating circumstances".[8]

II

> "Disorder all around you is one thing, and disorder inside you is quite another"[9]

The Fire is a novella that takes up themes whose scale would be more suited to the novelistic form: migration, the setting up of new townships, shifts in generational values, the destruction of the environment. It is to Rasputin's credit that his novella measures up to the ambitious themes he takes up to elaborate. In Sosnovka, the warehouses catch fire. The warehouses housed foodstuffs worth hundred thousand roubles, candy, crates of canned goods and of vodka, sugar, *pelmeni*, sausage rings, butter, fish, barrels of oil, flour; household items such as scythes, saucepans, crockery, fancy Japanese clothes that people came all the way from Irkutsk to buy. The town had never seen such a major fire in all the years of its existence. The fire is real in the material destruction it causes; it is metaphoric in the burning down of humanistic values that Rasputin sees as the bane of the then contemporary Soviet society. It is also symbolic of the anger and despair that rages in the heart of the main protagonist, Ivan Petrovich.

The Fire is the logical sequence and sequel to the village prose novella, *Farewell to Matyora*. It is the story of what happens when the village is no more. The township Sosnovka is set up by people who have left their villages. Ivan Petrovich has left Yegorovka because it was flooded due to the hydroelectric project set up. This displacement is difficult for him to come to terms with, all the more so, because he realizes that the place he and his wife have moved to, is a temporary township, and that they will be forced to move from here as well when they have finished cutting down all the forest in the surrounding taiga. The people do not let their roots go down deep enough here and it is this that affects the nature of the relations between the people as well as the very topography of the township. Rasputin, through his main protagonist moans the loss of the sense of community that had existed in Yegorovka. "Your homeland was your homeland, nobody could deny it. There every stone had foreseen and awaited you even before you were born and there with each new spring every blade of grass brought you something from bygone days either as a warning or for support. There everything kept a quiet ancestral eye on you".[10] The arbitrariness of the new town is reflected in everything, in the nursery school and recreation centres that were present in the diagrams of the towns, but absent in actuality; in the fact that people here did not care to grow greens around their home, and in the fact that very little replanting was done in place of the hectares and hectares of trees that were being cut down. In particular, cutting down of trees to meet quotas, without replenishing the land, seemed to have eaten into the moral fibre of a community that was anyway held only loosely together. "If you didn't replant your quota, they'd bawl you out a little; if you didn't cut your quota of timber, they'd tan your hide".[11]

More and more people were needed to meet quotas. People came in in spring and autumn when more work had to be done. These temporary hands had their own lifestyles and work ethics that were different from the generation of Ivan Petrovich. The better among them went about their work joylessly: "In more recent years a special breed has appeared, made up of people who aren't totally worthless or lost for good, who are after something other than money in their endless migrations and who readily and easily squander what money falls their way, seemingly driven by a fanatic rejection of and indifference to absolutely everything. Such a person accepts no help for himself and won't offer it to anyone else. He goes through the motions of living in an abbreviated way, having no family, no friends, and no attachments, and he acts as if it's a burden, as if he's serving out his life like a prison term".[12] They were yet others who banded together like gangs: "There had always been drunks, of course – when hadn't there been drunks in Holy Russia? But to huddle in a circle, to grow into an unconcealed force that feared nothing and was ashamed of nothing, with its own ataman and council exercising power – such a thing had never happened before. This was something we have accomplished all by ourselves".[13] The younger crowd that came to the town, behaved like goons with scant respect for the people who lived in Sosnovka or their values.

It was the new work scenario, the changing mindset of the people of his own generation who began to adopt and adapt to the new values, and the realization that he could not cope with it anymore that had driven Ivan Petrovich to hand in his resignation: "For Ivan Petrovich, going to work had gotten to be like going off to hard labour".[14] The fire brings all the townspeople together to one spot, with each of them acting according to their own moral vision: some trying to help in putting out the fire and saving the goods in the warehouse; others making the most of the opportunity to cart off and steal goods; some trying to indulge in both, a little bit of help and a little bit of private profit. Rasputin underlines the primitive instinct that comes to fore in man in moments of crises. Ivan Petrovich wonders why man only shouts loudly when going to battle and not when sowing seeds or harvesting. At the end of a long night of the fire, Uncle Misha Khampo and one of the 'roughnecks', Sonya die in an embrace. Khampo is beaten to death by the roughnecks for trying to stop Sonya from stealing.

The conflagration, the author seems to say, was almost waiting to happen. The warehouses were built with no planning or foresight and if one caught fire, all would burn. In this hastily put together town, the burning down of warehouses was the last thing on their minds. As Rasputin puts it laconically, when fleeing from water (the flooded Yegorovka), who thinks about fire? The dry-goods warehouses could still have been saved if there had been a fire-truck: "But about two years ago the only hook-and-ladder for the whole logging operation had been cannibalized for spare parts, so it existed only on paper".[15]

The major theme of Rasputin's works has been as Gillespie has pointed out "... the human response to crisis, and the exploration of bonds that tie the individual to the community".[16] The fire exposes the relationship the townspeople have towards one another, and to the material goods that belong to the State; it also exposes all the misinformation that the administration had spread and blunders it had committed: all the food items that never reached the canteens, the Ural motorcycle that had been hidden, the items on inventories that had disappeared....

III

> "We've stood up to foreign enemies in the past and we'd do it again; the enemy among us, like the thief among us, is more frightening"[17]

Why was *The Fire* seen as one of the 'three 'P's of perestroika? According to David Gillespie, "In 1985 the publication of *Pozhar* (*The Fire*) was greeted with some caution, as it seemed a particularly nihilistic tale of death, wholesale destruction and moral and social decay.... We learn that people are indifferent to their new home, they have no feeling for the land, they are uprooted, dislocated and demoralized.... The impression we get of the population, with few exceptions, is of a thoroughly debased people that has lost all vestiges of its humanity, culture or traditions".[18] Had it been only a nihilistic tale, it is likely that Rasputin would have been subjected to political criticism. The work is not merely a descriptive account of the 'moral and social decay'. It offers an analysis of this decay and places the blame squarely on bureaucratism, on the building of socialism on quantitative rather than qualitative ideals, on laws that did not take into account of the everyday life of Soviet citizens, and the rift between what existed on paper, and life as it was actually lived: "Quotas, you say? Quotas?! We'd be better off without them! We'd be better off setting up different quotas – not just for cubic meters of timber but for souls, too! So we could keep track of how many souls have been lost, have gone over to the Devil, and how many are left!"[19] What is the meaning of prosperity, the story asks, when the distinction between good and evil is blurred, and one feels homeless and lost?

The focus of this tale is on the 'enemy within', the corruption in their life which extended from small acts by people who were not basically corrupt, to those who had made it a way of life. From here on to stealing, intimidation by brute force and killing, was but a small step. Ivan Petrovich is shocked to find out that peace-time deaths due to drunken brawls, drowning, freezing, accidents at the workplace and killings equaled war-time deaths in number.

The story was published at a time when glasnost and perestroika were becoming key words of the political lexicon of the leaders of the Soviet Union. Although Mikhail Gorbachev had used these terms as early as 1984, it was only after he became General Secretary of the Party in 1985 that these terms were actually given grounding in official policies. From then to 1991 when the Soviet Union collapsed, the word 'perestroika' took on many meanings. The first period of perestroika saw the critique of Soviet work culture by the Party leadership, which was seen as one of the factors leading to economic stagnation. Culture, as it had often happened in Russia in the past, had prepared the ground for political processes and writers had, in the present instance, cleared the way for perestroika. *The Fire* which had laid bare the workings of a 'command' work culture that had lost all human face, almost foresaw the critique of Soviet life that the 'political and economic perestroika from above' envisaged. Bureaucratism, alcoholism, criminality – these were the themes of *The Fire* as well as the issues raised by Gorbachev for a restructuring of the economic, political and social life of the Soviet Union. At the Party Conference in 1988 it was stated that "Social life as a whole had become 'straightjacketed' by governmental controls of various kinds, and ordinary working people had become 'alienated' from public ownership and management. It was this 'ossified system of government, with its command-and-pressure mechanism' that was now the main obstacle to perestroika".[20] The novella was thus not only timely, but prophetic. It upheld the conscience and consciousness of an ordinary worker, who protested at the way his contemporaries had begun to accept all that came 'from above' without a question: "Ivan Petrovich's resentment was not against the roughnecks – what else could you expect from them?! – but against his own folks, who'd grown accustomed to all this and simply looked the other way, believing that any change was always for the better".[21]

The range of issues touched upon by Rasputin in this novella is almost novelistic. Using the event of the fire, he delineates an entire spectrum of characters who populate the logging town of Sosnovka. The lead protagonist is a 'positive hero' of socialist realism in the make-up of ethical universe. He has, however, reached a point of no-return in his disgust and despair over the existing order and wishes to remove himself from it. The end of the novella is an open one:

Ivan Petrovich has handed in his resignation, he had only a week of working to do; he has also considered shifting to his son's town with his wife, because things seemed better there. After the fire, however, we see him walking off alone into the taiga, and it is not clear if he is planning to return. His friend, Afonya, who has also come from Yegorovka after the flooding, insists they must stay on in Sosnovka as a signpost of the values of their generation, even if it is ephemeral as putting up a sign on water to show where Yegorovka had once existed. Whether Ivan Petrovich returns or not, what is clear is his complete disjunction from the state of affairs as they exist in Sosnovka. There is no revolutionary optimism here, but a deep pessimism at being out of step with the times.

What makes *The Fire* an exceptional novella is not just the range of issues raised, but the realisation of a social and historical time, of imparting a sense of its unfolding, of its inexorable and irreversible march, in which people like Ivan Petrovich are going to find themselves out of alignment. This non-alignment is not just social, but has touched the very core of the protagonist's being: "You and they. You are the ruler, carrying in your body a kingdom with all its cities and hamlets, all its institutions and means of communication, all its vices and glory. And they are what form the secret life of your world. You and they are both a single entity and entirely separate. .... And you and they are separate when discord arises and when the realm that belongs to you refuses to obey you".[22] Rasputin has, in the space of the novella, not merely provided a social canvas against which the conflagration takes place, but also portrayed the processes by which a human being becomes out of sync with his environment. Rasputin has created a cartographic metaphor that encapsulates not just Sosnovka, but Ivan Petrovich's internal being as well: the disorder of various parts not coexisting in harmony is not just in the town, but within oneself. *The Fire*, in fact, moves beyond a disjunctive state of being; it points to a state of homelessness that is ontological: "And he never felt at home anywhere. Not in his native land – what wasn't flooded had been emptied out by logging, with neither concern nor regard for this land. Inside him there was total pandemonium, like in a smashed-up overturned wagon. And if there is no refuge in either the one place or the other, there won't be any in the middle either, no matter how hard you try".[23] It is in this sense of not being at home anywhere that the first rumblings of a new thematic of literature, beyond the framework of socialist realism, can be sensed.

This notion of homelessness, first depicted in *The Fire*, is stretched to its limit in Aitmatov's *The Mark of Cassandra* (1995): Filofei, the lead protagonist, does not feel at home on this Earth itself, and chooses to commit suicide in Space.[24]

The Fire is, without doubt, one of the most accomplished works of Rasputin's literary career.[25] This is despite the fact that the structure of the novella is conventional, its parts alternating between the protagonist's flashbacks and the catastrophic event in the present. Its importance lies in the fact that it almost achieves a sense of novelistic time within the space of the novella. It is nostalgic for the sense of community, a belief that forms the core of the author's belief. In an interview, Rasputin discusses the different kinds of stratification that Soviet society faced: 'vertical' in terms of the people and the bureaucracy and bureaucratic apparatus on top. Of the other stratification, he says: "But the most disturbing stratification is in the horizontal aspect. Today it is hard to speak of the people as being a whole, united by a common goal.... As never before we are showing ourselves to be a people eager to demonstrate its difference: in age, nationality, culture, taste and profession. The people was always united and inspired by concern for the land as birthplace, a provider, as something eternal. When this concern weakened it was inevitable that the ties among the people would weaken as well".[26] *The Fire* is work that deals with both the 'vertical' and 'horizontal' stratifications of Soviet society. It is the everyday experience of these stratifications, that make Ivan Petrovich feel 'hollow; "Not too long ago he'd been a real man, you see—now only the shell of a man remained".[27]

The novella, while it has this nostalgic longing for a lost community in its veins, sets out in detail all the contemporary ills of Soviet society, through the destiny of its very ordinary and simple lead protagonist, and the history of the logging town, Sosnovka. If XIX century Russian realist fiction charted the fates of 'accidental families', *The Fire* is the story of an 'accidental township': "This was a bleak and untidy town, neither a city nor a village. It was more like a camp site, as if the residents, migrating from place to place, had stopped to wait out a storm and to rest up and had simply gotten stuck. ... Meanwhile, children were born and grew up and were now raising children of their own".[28]

In his views on literature, however, Rasputin shows himself to be a realist, without any sentimentalism. In a reply to Elisabeth Rich on whether the movement of village prose is over, he says: "It's over. Finished. There is a post-village prose, however. By 'post' I mean remnants in which former village inhabitants return (to the countryside) as they would to a summer cottage or return with nostalgia and memories of the years when they lived there.... It is interesting with respect to its language and feeling, but it does not deal with any real any real problems. All of that is gone already. It is a return to a burned-out home".[29]

Rasputin was elected to the Congress of People's Deputies along with other writers such as Chingiz Aitmatov and Evgeny Yevtushenko in 1989. In the eighties he had successfully campaigned to stop the project of diverting the waters of northern and Siberian rivers. *The Fire* belongs to this period of active social intervention. In the nineties, after the fall of the Soviet Union, Rasputin espoused political agendas that reflected on his stature as a writer: "An extremely gifted writer whose novels were major successes in the 1970s, Rasputin has witnessed the total collapse of the school of 'village prose' of which he was the most prominent member. An Orthodox Christian, and as he calls himself, a cultural nationalist, he has lost status as a writer, political figure, and leader of opinion".[30] Whatever the subsequent literary career of Rasputin, the issues raised in *The Fire* dovetailed with the agenda of perestroika, and were successful in portraying the ills that Soviet society suffered from then.

Notes and References

1. Edward J Brown, *Russian Literature Since the Revolution*, USA: Harvard University Press, 1982, p. 293.
2. *Ibid*., pp. 292-293.
3. N.L. Leiderman and M.N. Lipovetsky, *Sovremennaya Russkaya Literatura* (Contemporary Russian Literature), Vol. 2, Moscow: URSS, 2001, p. 55.
4. *Ibid*., p. 54.
5. Vera Tolz, *Russia*, London: Arnold, 2001, p. 179.
6. *Ibid*., pp. 163-164.
7. Julian Laychuk, 'Conflicts in the Soviet Countryside in the Novellas of Valentin Rasputin', *Rocky Mountain Review of Language and Literature*, Vol. 47, No. 1/2 (1993): 11-30, p. 13.
8. Gerald Mikkelson and Margaret Winchell, 'Introduction', *Siberia on Fire*, Dekalb: Northern Illinois University Press, 1989, pp. xvii-xviii.
9. Valentin Rasputin, 'The Fire' in *Siberia on Fire*, trans. by Gerald

Mikkelson and Margaret Winchell, Dekalb: Northern Illinois University Press, 1989, p. 130.

10. *Ibid.*, p. 116.
11. *Ibid.*, p. 122.
12. *Ibid.*, p. 124.
13. *Ibid.*, p. 123.
14. *Ibid.*, p. 139.
15. *Ibid.*, p. 120.
16. David Gillespie, 'Valentin Grigor'evich Rasputin 1937—' in *Reference Guide to Russian Literature*, Neil Cornwell, (ed.), Chicago: Fitzroy Dearborn Publishers, 1998, p. 690.
17. Valentin Rasputin, 'The Fire' in *Siberia on Fire*, trans. by Gerald Mikkelson and Margaret Winchell, Dekalb: Northern Illinois University Press, 1989, p. 138.
18. David Gillespie, 'Valentin Grigor'evich Rasputin 1937—' in *Reference Guide to Russian Literature*, Neil Cornwell, (ed.), Chicago: Fitzroy Dearborn Publishers, 1998, p. 689.
19. Valentin Rasputin, 'The Fire' in *Siberia on Fire*, trans. by Gerald Mikkelson and Margaret Winchell, Dekalb: Northern Illinois University Press, 1989, p. 126.
20. Stephen White, *Gorbachev in Power*, Cambridge Soviet Paperbacks, Great Britain: CUP, 1990, p. 25.
21. Valentin Rasputin, 'The Fire' in *Siberia on Fire*, trans. by Gerald Mikkelson and Margaret Winchell, Dekalb: Northern Illinois University Press, 1989, p. 142.
22. *Ibid.*, p. 131.
23. *Ibid.*, p. 152.
24. See the chapter 'Ethics in the time of Dystopia' in my book *The Post-Soviet Condition: Chingiz Aitmatov in the '90s*, New Delhi: Aakar, 2005, for a discussion on the difference between postcolonial and postsocialist notions of homelessness.
25. Some critics believe that after the 1970s, Rasputin's work has been going downhill. For instance: "Valentin Rasputin is best known as a writer for the four novellas (*posvesti*) on rural themes published between 1967 and 1976. His writing subsequently, both fiction and non-fiction, has deteriorated aesthetically, and in the mid-90s bears all the hallmarks of embittered tendentiousness". David Gillespie, 'Valentin Grigor'evich Rasputin 1937—' in *Reference Guide to Russian Literature*, Neil Cornwell, (ed.) Fitzroy Dearborn publishers, Chicago 1998, p. 688.
26. 'According to Conscience', Interview with Valentin Rasputin, Elvina Shugaeva, *Literaturnaya Gazeta*, 1 January 1988, in Vladimir Mezhenkov, Eva Skelley (eds.), *Perestroika in Action: Soviet Scene 1988,*

A Collection of Press Articles and Interviews, London: Collets, 1988, pp. 350-351.

27. Valentin Rasputin, 'The Fire' in *Siberia on Fire*, trans. by Gerald Mikkelson and Margaret Winchell, Dekalb: Northern Illinois University Press, 1989, p. 106.
28. *Ibid.*, p. 109.
29. Laura Weeks and Elisabeth Rich, 'Russian Literature After Perestroika' in *South Central Review*, Vol. 12, No. 3/4, (Autumn—Winter 1995): 45-69, p. 46.
30. Deming Brown, 'The Russian Literary Climate: Summer 1994' in *South Central Review*, Vol. 12, No. 3/4, (Autumn-Winter, 1995): pp. 146-152, p. 152.

10

The Siberian Republic of Tuva: Linkages with Mongolia

Sharad K. Soni

Last year the Siberian Republic of Tuva was much in news as it was chosen out of 88 Russian regions by the Russian President Vladimir Putin to host Monaco Prince Albert II for a 3-day holiday.[1] The fact that Tuva's importance lies in its cultural richness and natural beauty must have attracted Putin to spend holidays with his guest there. Covering an area of 170,500 sq. kilometers, Tuva, formerly known as Tannu Tuva is located in the geographical "center" of Asia where the Siberian and Central Asian landscapes congregate, i.e., in the south-eastern Siberia in the region of the Enisei (also spelled Yenesei) river. Moreover, the whole area is separated from Mongolia by the Tannu Ola range and from Russia by the Sayan range of mountains. Otherwise known as Uryankhai,[2] whose indigenous inhabitants are connected with the Mongols, is now the smallest and most remote republic of the Russian Federation, situated at a distance of 1,000 kilometers south of the Siberian super city of Krasnoyarsk. It has a population of just a little more than 300,000 with 90,000 people alone are staying in the capital Kyzyl formerly known as Belotsarsk. From the eighteenth century onwards due to its strategic location of being in the zone of Sino-Russian rivalry, Tuva emerged as a geo-political entity, which finally came under Moscow's ambit in 1944.[3] The background story of Tuva's incorporation in to former USSR reflects the whole history of Sino-Russian/Soviet rivalry for dominating the Mongolian borderlands. And this rivalry always prevented attempts of unification of Tuva with Mongolia on the basis of their ethnic and cultural links, in which Russia succeeded in outweighing Chinese claims over Tuva.[4] However, in the post-Soviet period, the revival of Buddhism in Siberia has provided significant opportunity for Tuva to relink itself with the Buddhist world in Asia particularly with Mongolia, which in turn could contribute positively towards enhancing Russia's stake in Asia.

It is in this context that this paper seeks to analyze Tuva's linkages with Mongolia and Russia in retrospect and various circumstances leading to incorporation of Tuva into former USSR. It also highlights Buddhist factor in Tuva-Mongolia relations, besides exploring the prospects of linkages between Siberian Buddhist republics and other Buddhist nations in Asia.

Tuva in Retrospect

Historically speaking, the Tuvans of Turkic Uryankhai-Tuva developed from ancient indigenous tribes and some groups such as Tugiu-Turks, Uyghurs and Kirghizs besides absorbing some Mongolian tribes who came to be Turkicised.[5] This Turkic influence on native Tuvans in addition to the geographical and religious considerations became the basis of claims made by Russian scholars that the Tuvans are different from Mongols in their origin, culture and language, i.e., they are Siberian and Turkic-oriented, hence somehow closer to Russia than to Mongolia.[6] Western scholar like Rupen too agrees to this point of view when he says, "There clearly exists some genuine basis for distinguishing Tuvans and Mongols." [7] But at the same time he argues that "the former [Tuvans] do display far greater Turkic influence, yet it is also true that Western Mongols, the Oirats, differ from the predominant Khalkha Mongols in many of the same characteristics that differentiate Tuvans from Khalkhas." According to him, "some Tuvans are 'very Mongols,' while other are 'very Turkic,' so they could be described as constituting an ethnic and cultural bridge between Central Asian Turkic and Central Asian Mongol group."

The territory of Tuva remained under Mongol control from thirteenth to the first quarter of eighteenth centuries. It was an industrial and raw material base for the Mongol army under Chinggis Khan and his successors, which carried out campaigns to the west. Though Chinese sovereignty over Tuva was recognized by Russia in 1728 Kiakhta Treaty,[8] the area had formally come under the Manchu-Chinese Qing rule in 1757 and a year later it had been administratively attached to Outer Mongolia (now known as simply

Mongolia) under Sain Noyan Khan *aimak* (province).[9] Since then, throughout the eighteenth, nineteenth and early twentieth centuries, the area remained a Qing dependency not only politically but to some extent economically as well.[10] It was only in 1911 when a liberation movement provided Mongolia an opportunity to declare its independence from the Qing rule, Tuva too found itself outside the Manchu sphere. However, what is striking to note here is that although Tuva was under Qing control for almost 150 years, the latter "never exercised close control there."[11] Instead, it were Russian settlers who entered the territory during the middle of the nineteenth century, most of them for trade purposes, ultimately played significant role in deciding Tuva's future. The issue of their protection from Chinese traders often invited concerns of the Russian Government, which took a political shape.

Increasing Russian settlement in Tuva region particularly since 1910 owes much to the foresightedness of Tsar Nicholas II who, in 1908, had acknowledged Tuva as an area, which "may become very useful for Russia in the future."[12] Tuva's geo-political importance, thus, was one of the key reasons for encouraging Russian settlement in the area and as time went on, more and more Russians including merchants and farmers crossed the border. Consequently, the number of Russian settlers increased considerably so much so that the figure rose from 2,100 in 1910 to 8,200 in 1916, which further grew constantly to reach the figure of almost 12,000 in 1944.[13] Moreover, nonexistence of any permanent Chinese settlement in Tuva also smoothen the progress of Russian settlement as Rupen notes down that "the Manchu administrative system operated indirectly through Tuvan and Mongol agents, whereas Russian control was more direct and straightforward."[14] This apparently helped prevent Chinese ambitions in that area.

Since Tuva was known to be rich in natural resources especially minerals, the activities of mineral explorers also gave way to the Russian penetration in this area. The motivation for Russian penetration was that Tuva was "an extremely valuable colonisable territory with fertile soil, good pastures and rich mineral deposits, above all gold."[15] Many Russian merchants, who came to Tuva in search for gold, returned with such considerable amounts of gold that "Russian government agencies began to be interested in the natural resources of the region."[16] In fact, Russians were the first to do business in Tuva.[17] Since 1867 when the first Russian merchants came and established three trading stations in Tuva, there had been sharp increase in their business as well as their penetration. By 1890s, almost the whole Tuvan territory seemed to have been covered with Russian trading stations.[18] These commercial activities further continued in the Soviet period as well mainly due to the fact that Tuva's richness in natural resources had shaped the area largely as "economic necessity to the Russian centre."[19]

The beginning of twentieth century witnessed new developments on the political front due to the circumstances of the day. Encouraged by the permanent Russian settlement Tsarist Russia became interested in adding Tuva to its territory. The first attempt in this direction was made in November 1911 after the Mongols of Outer Mongolia proclaimed their autonomy following the success of their liberation movement against the Manchu-Qing rule.[20] But the Tsarist government decided to follow the policy of what Morgen Mongush describes as "peaceful penetration".[21] After the Autonomous government of Outer Mongolia was established in Urga, Jebtsun Damba Khutukhtu, the Urga living Buddha whose area of control bordered Tuva, tried to encourage Tuvans for joining the new state. Moreover, since the Mongols considered Tuva as legitimately falling within their own territory, they wanted the area to be incorporated in Autonomous Mongolia. At that point in time, most of the native Tuvans too, desired for the same, which is evidenced by the fact that in 1912, even a Tuvan *amby-noyon* (feudal lord) Gombodorji applied to the Urga government for inclusion of Tuva in latter's territory.[22] Despite the fact that his application was accepted without any delay and soon he was made Urga's official representative,[23] he, on the other hand, came under the influence of Russian forward policy in Tuva. The Russian policy with regard to Tuva can be understood by a statement of the Imperial Council of Ministers issued in 1913. The statement stressed that the Russian recognition of the autonomy of Mongolia as per the Treaty of October 21, 1912 [old style] and the departure of Chinese officials not only from Mongolia but also from Uryanghai [Tuva], placed the issue of Russian government's relation with the latter in a new direction.[24] It further said:

> The proclamation of the Republíc in China and Mongolian independence, and the departure of the Chinese officials who had been responsible for Uryanghai from Ulyasutai has as a consequence put an end to the departure of

> Uryanghai on China; also Khalkha [Outer Mongolia], now first entered into political life, can not claim this land. Therefore, His Majesty suggests to Minister Sazonov that Russian policy concerning Uryanghai should take the direction of fixing this land in Russian interests.[25]

And in fact, as recorded in the third edition of the *Great Soviet Encyclopedia*, "in 1912-13 many big landowners and officials repeatedly appealed to the Russian tsar to incorporate Tuva in to the Russian empire."[26] Gombodorji, however, made a request to the Russian government in St. Petersberg through a letter dated October 26, 1913 for the establishment of a Russian protectorate, an idea which was originally advocated by Sazonov. After prolonged discussion, the idea was accepted by the Russian cabinet and on April 5,1914, a Russian protectorate over Tuva was announced. But Sazonov was calculated so much so that he declared that in exchange of getting Russian protection "the Uryanghais [Tuvans] must first of all give up the right of external relations and must pledge themselves to form connections with their neighbours only through the official stationed in the territory by the Governor-General of Irkutsk."[27] A few months later in July 1914, an instruction was communicated to Gombodorji by a Russian border Commissioner, Zererin saying, "Your duty is to maintain no relations of any kind with foreign states, including Mongolia...."[28] Gombodorji immediately agreed to abide by the instruction. Tuva, henceforth, remained under Russian protection until 1917 when the Russian Revolution overthrew Tsarism. However, during this period, neither Chinese nor Mongolians stayed away of the Tuvan affair. They repeatedly argued that Tuva was an integral part of Outer Mongolia but nothing substantial they could achieve due to the success of diplomatic maneuvering on the part of Tsarist Russia.

At that time Russian policy towards Outer Mongolia and Tuva differed in its nature. According to Dallin, "the old Russian governments strove to achieve 'independence' and 'autonomy' for Mongolia, whereas Tuva was to be subjected to direct control by Russia."[29] Nevertheless, the Revolution of 1917 in Russia changed the scene at least for the time being and these tendencies were no more in sight. The course of events in both Tuva and Mongolia from 1918 onwards was similar, as their territories became a battleground due to the civil war between Red and White Russians.

It was only in 1921 when White Russian troops, who had overrun Mongolia and Tuva, suffered a heavy defeat at the hand of the Red Army that the Soviet period in Tuva's history began. The first step that the Soviet government had taken was to abolish Russian protectorate "forever" and proclaim Tuva's independence.[30] In fact, it was at the first Congress of the Representatives of the Tuvan *Khosuns*, which took place from August 13 to 16, 1921, that the declaration of Tuva's independence and sovereignty as well as the first draft Constitution were adopted.[31] Subsequently, a Tuvan government was formed and on September 9, 1921, the RSFSR declared that "it did not consider Tuva to be Russian."[32] Tuva, thus, was recognized by Soviet Russia in the same year and just a little over one and half months after Mongolia became a People's Republic.

Pan-Mongolist Movement and Tuva's Fate

After the establishment of the Tuvan People's Republic (TPR) a Tuvan People's Revolutionary Party (TPRP) was formed on October 29, 1921. The TPRP issued its first manifesto to the people of Tuva on December 20, 1921.[33] Significantly, the party soon became pro-Soviet in the same manner as was the case with the Mongolian People's Revolutionary Party (MPRP) that ruled Mongolia. Three successive Tuvan Constitutions were also drafted in 1922, 1924 and 1926. But it was the third Constitution which was adopted on the Soviet model and was finally confirmed by the Fourth Great *Khural* on November 24, 1926.[34]

It is, however, to be noted that although Tuva proclaimed its independence, its desire to unite with Mongolia was not dead. There existed a tendency to participate in the movements for Pan-Mongolism. Tuva constituted one of the territories to be included in the unified state. In fact, Pan-Mongolism represented the desire of indigenous Mongols to have a united state based on the model of the Empire of Genghis Khan. This concept was so deep rooted that it called for reunification of all the Mongols wherever they were as well as all the Mongolian areas into a single "Greater Mongolian state." The idea of creating such a state that would essentially be a Pan-Mongolian in nature, primarily focussed on including territories comprising of not only Outer and Inner Mongolia as well as Buryat and Tuva regions of Siberia but also the territories of Tibetans, the Kyrgyzs and Kalmyks, thereby stretching the whole area from the

Caspian Sea to Lake Baikal. However, Pan-Mongolism could not grow into a movement for a single unified state against the desire of the native Mongols whose region was now separated in different areas by different powers.

The key factor behind this denial was the geopolitical importance of Mongolian areas, which attracted various powers mainly Russia, China and Japan to establish their hegemony over there. In doing so these powers exploited the concept of Pan-Mongolism in various situations for their own benefit and the Mongols were left with nothing but a dead desire of having a Pan-Mongolian state. Tuvans were also discouraged and forced to remain separate from Mongolia despite their continuous urge for unity. In early 1920s, Donduk, the Tuvan Prime Minister explained: "The Tuvinian people is small, poor and backward in the cultural aspect. That is why it must be united with Mongolia."[35] Even in 1924, the Tuvan people went to the extreme by declaring their "affiliation" with Outer Mongolia.[36] But they received a setback when Soviet troops were sent to suppress the revolt successfully.

Nevertheless, the events that followed were of vital importance in the history of Tuva-Mongolia linkages. The issue of Tuva's union with Mongolia was again placed on the agenda at a Tuvan Great *Khural* session in 1924. But soon after in July 1924, three-sided talks among Mongolia, Russia and Tuva in Kyzyl ended with "the *de facto* recognition of the country".[37] Yet, in August 1924, the matter of Mongolia-Tuva unity was placed at the Third Congress of the MPRP. During its deliberations it became clear that the Mongol side wanted to include Tuvan territory into the Mongolian People's Republic. Almost all the Mongols were unanimous on the question of Tuva despite objection made by Soviet representative A.N. Vasiliev at the Congress. He made it clear that the Russians would not allow Mongols to regain Tuva. In the end, the Congress adopted a resolution seeking for a mixed Russian-Mongolian Commission to settle the question of Tuva. Moscow agreed to send the mixed Commission and finally Mongolia's aspirations were met on only one point. A very small sector of the Tuvan territory called, Darkhat was given to Outer Mongolia.[38] This was how Mongols and Tuvans were prevented from uniting themselves. But Mongolian side did not stop to lay claim over Tuva. For instance, a Mongol leader, Amor is said to have told the MPR's First Great *Khural* held in November 1924 that "Uryankhai [Tuva] was part of Mongolia."[39] At the Fourth

MPRP Congress held during September-October 1925, the Comintern representative, Amagaev was of the opinion that "... up to this time the so-called 'Uryankhai question' has not been resolved. Perhaps Mongolia will require the union of the Uryankhai people with it."[40]

However, nothing substantial could be achieved and in July 1926, Soviet diplomatic initiatives resulted into the signing of a treaty of friendship between the Tuva People's Republic and the Mongolian People's Republic. By this agreement Tuva was recognised as a fully equal and independent sovereign state, entirely separate from the Mongolian People's Republic. One month later, another treaty of friendship was signed between Tuva and the Soviet Union which was modelled on the Soviet-Mongolian agreement of November 5, 1921.[41] The agreement among other things included "reciprocal recognition of independence and exchange of representatives." Thereafter Soviet influence over Tuva remained undisturbed and what followed next was the beginning of a period of "Sovietization" of Tuvan politics, economy and culture. The Sovietization drive in Tuva lasted from 1929 to 1933,[42] which not only kept Tuva separate from Mongolia but also isolated it from the outside political influences. Every Tuvan leader who tried to advocate Tuva-Mongolia unity was declared to be "pro-Chinese" and a "traitor". Peter Tang attributes Moscow's success in Tuva in the following way:[43] Firstly, China was used to keep foreign powers out of Outer Mongolia as a whole. Secondly, Outer Mongolian "independence" was used to oust China and lastly, Tuvan "independence" was used to prevent Pan-Mongolist moves for unity.

Significantly, Soviet policy in Tuva met with a positive response from the Tuvan leader Solchak Toka who became the General Secretary of the Central Committee of the TPRP in 1932. In fact, the government of Tuva headed by Toka sought to integrate Tuva into the Soviet Union thrice, first in 1939, second in 1941 and the last in 1943.[44] But due to Soviet engagement in the Second World War, their petitions received a delayed response. On August 17, 1944, a special session of the Little *Khural* of the TPR met and signed a petition addressed to the Moscow government requesting for the incorporation of Tuva into the USSR. The request was approved on October 11, 1944 by the Presidium of the Supreme Soviet of the USSR and two days later Tuva was officially declared to have become an autonomous *oblast* of the Russian Socialist Federated Soviet

Republic (RSFSR).[45] This was announced on November 1, 1944 at the Eighth Extraordinary session of the Little *Khural* in the Tuvan capital Kyzyl.[46] Later on by a decree issued on October 9, 1961 at the Presidium of the Supreme Soviet of RSFSR, Tuva's status of autonomous *oblast* had been transferred to autonomous republic known as Tuva ASSR.

After the collapse of the former Soviet Union, Tuva retained its autonomy in 1993 as a Republic within the Russian Federation. The same year witnessed the adoption of a new Tuvan constitution, the first post-perestroika constitution, which was written under Yeltsin's slogan "Take as much sovereignty as you can swallow!".[47] The 1993 constitution created a parliament that became responsible for foreign policy as well. The latest constitution, the ninth in its history since the first one came in to existence in 1921, was adopted at an All-Republican Referendum on May 6, 2001. This document has become the guiding principles for Tuva's domestic and external affairs. However, following key points are to be kept in mind while highlighting Tuva's linkages with Mongolia: The Tuvans are a Turkic speaking people with Mongol influences and are mainly adherents to *Tibetan Buddhism,* combined with native Shamanism. This factor has been playing a major role in strengthening the Tuva-Mongolia linkages. The other factor which contributes to the growth of people to people contacts between Tuva and Mongolia is Tuvan ethnic minority itself, which outside Tuva, concentrates mainly in northwestern Mongolia.

Buddhist Factor in Tuva-Mongolia Relations

Tuva is one of the three Buddhist Republics of the Russian Federation, the other two being Buryatia and Kalmykia. While Tuva and Buryatiya are in the Siberian region, Kalmykia is situated in the Volga river region and has the distinction of being the only Buddhist republic in Europe. The official religion of Tuvans is Lamaism or Tibetan Buddhism or more precisely the Mahayana form of Buddhism, though Shamanism continues to exist as a traditional belief. However, what is significant to note here is that there is no rivalry between the followers of Buddhism and Shamanism in Tuva as the two beliefs co-exist together for a very long time now. It has been revealed that Lamas often advise people to go to Shamans and Shamans, in turn, go to Buddhist temples to offer prayers there. In the philosophical tone "the fundamental values of both Shamanism and Buddhism depend on the principle of respect for nature, and they say it doesn't matter who you go to as long as you live in harmony with the world and yourself."[48]

The credit for providing the Tuvan tribes with the first knowledge of Buddhism goes to the Uyghurs, a Turkic language tribe who in the beginning of the tenth century experienced some influence of Buddhism from Sogdiana and China.[49] Initially, the Uyghurs translated Buddhist texts from Sogdian and Chinese, but later on a sizeable amount of translation work was made from Tibetan texts, which ultimately led to the dominance of Tibetan influence on Uyghur Buddhism.[50] The influence of Buddhism among Uyghurs at that time has been considered as part of the first wave of Buddhism spreading in Mongolia, Tuva and Buryatia, though several researchers are of the opinion that it did not last long.[51] It was, in fact, during the period of Great Mongol Empire, especially during the reign of Khubilai Khan, the founder of Mongol Yuan dynasty (1260 AD-1368 AD) that the larger wave of Buddhism made its entry to Mongolia from Tibet.[52] Significantly, Tibetan Buddhism was well accepted even by the Turkic language tribes of the Great Mongol Empire.

Historical records suggest that Khubilai preferred Buddhism as a neutral and more universal religion while compared to other religions known to him. Having converted himself to Buddhism as far back as in 1242 AD, Khubilai rewarded this religion by placing a Tibetan Buddhist monk the Phags-Pa Lama Lodoijalsan as the "State Preceptor" (*kuo shih*).[53] On the basis of Tibetan writings, the Phags-Pa Lama developed a Mongolian alphabet and used it for translating Buddhist texts in to Mongolian.[54] Besides, from the Phags-Pa Lama Khubilai accepted the concept of a ruling duality in which two spheres—the sacred and the secular, operated co-terminously.[55] Though the concept of the dual principle ended with the downfall of the Yuan dynasty, its ideal was preserved in both Mongol and Tibetan literature.

So far as Tuva is concerned, by the eighteenth century Tibetan Buddhism travelled from Mongolia had already made its considerable impact on the Tuvan society. Evidently, the first monastery in the Tuvan territory was built in 1772 followed by another, the largest one in 1773, which strengthened the influence of Buddhism on the Tuvan society.[56] Like Mongolia and Buryatia, it was mainly the

Gelugpa tradition of Buddhism that was prevalent in Tuva. All this helped strengthen spiritual contacts not only between Tuva and Mongolia but between Tuva and Tibet also. It has been revealed that prior to the 1921 revolution 22 Buddhist monastic complexes with 4,000 lamas were active in Tuva, which more or less remained intact until 1930s when a general religious decline was witnessed.[57] Moreover, due to the separation of religion from the State, all Buddhist monasteries gradually became inactive and finally ceased to exist. During the period between 1940 and 1990 no monastery was opened in Tuva, nor were there legally practicing lamas, which resulted in a complete loss of Buddhist tradition in the Tuvan society, though it remained confined within the individual families.[58]

It was only in the early 1990s under the influence of Gorbachev's policy of *glasnost* and *perestroika* that the revival of traditional culture and religious belief began to be witnessed in the Russian Federation territories of Kalmykia, Buryatia and Tuva. As a result, in the post-1990 period, 17 Buddhist prayer houses (*dugan*) and a Buddhist monastery (*khure*) have been built in Tuva, where 44 Buddhist lamas and novices offer their services.[59] Besides, Buddhist literature and its translation too have played a tremendous role in making a positive impact on the socio-religious life of the Tuvans, especially after the Dalai Lama visited Tuva in 1992. It is evident from the fact that "not only works by specialists on Buddhism but also Buddhist works themselves, published in Russian, have become popular in Tuva."[60] Of late, the Tuvan Scientific Research Institute of Language, Literature and History has taken initiative to translate the Buddhist works in to local Tuvan language as well. This will obviously endow the rural populace of Tuva with deeper understanding of Buddhist teachings in general and gradual restoration of Buddhism in particular much after it faced destruction in the 1930s. Today most of Tuva's urban and rural population can be seen visiting Buddhist temples and performing rituals and celebrations there, besides reading Buddhist literature and wearing Buddhist symbols as part of their socio-religious life.[61] The popularity of Buddhism in Tuva is also evident from the fact that in 2006, the biggest-ever Buddhist mantra has been sanctified in this tiny Siberian republic itself.[62] The mantra was written in white colour on a huge stone of a mountain in the vicinity of the capital Kyzyl.

The revival of Buddhism not only in Tuva but also in Buryatiya and Kalmykia has a political aspect too because it involves the Sino-

Russian relations as well. As it happens in the case of Mongolia the Chinese side repeatedly speaks against the visit of Dalai Lama to these Buddhist regions of the Russian Federation. Yet at the same time, there is also a strong recognition of the political advantages of Buddhism. It links the Siberian people to the world of other Buddhist nations, especially neighbouring Mongolia, which would really broaden the opportunities of support coming from abroad to the three Buddhist Republics, particularly in their spiritual integration. Buddhism is thus seen as a unifying force, which is usually presented in contrast to Shamanism that is seen as too diverse and uncontrollable to become the religion of a nation-state.[63] Besides, the Buddhist factor provides ample scope for Tuva-Mongolia cooperation in diverse areas, not to talk of mineral exploration in both areas for which Russia has shown keen interest in recent times. In order to make people-to-people contact between Tuva and Mongolia, last year in March 2007, a Tuva-Mongolia Friendship Society known as *Naiyral* was established in Kyzyl, which aims at re-establishing cultural, economic and artistic ties between the two sides.[64]

To conclude, Tuva's incorporation into former USSR strengthened Moscow's hand in the Siberian region, which touches the border with Mongolia thus keeping aside other powers in particular China from exerting any influence in the region. It was more so because Tuva had traditionally been regarded as part of Outer Mongolia and hence the Chinese made their claims. For Mongolia, both the downfall of Buryats as well as Tuva's incorporation into the USSR proved to be a major set back in its aspirations of a Pan-Mongolian state which never came into being. However, the Buddhist factor in Tuva-Mongolia relations in particular and Russia-Mongolia relations in general may prove to be politically advantageous. This factor can play a bigger role in ensuring the safety of Siberia from any potential threat from the outside world. For Buddhism provides an excellent opportunity for the Siberian people to remain connected with the people of other Buddhist nations in Asia.

Notes and References

1. "Putin Chose Tuva as a Holiday Place for his Honourable Guest" ***http://en.tuvaonline.ru/2007/08/16/1946_putin-in-tuva.html***

2. Uryankhai, which means "distant forest people", came to be known as Tannu Tuva (Tangno Toba) since 1921 when it was proclaimed as an "independent republic" under Soviet influence. A bit later its official name became Tuvinian People's Republic (TPR). In 1944, it was absorbed into former USSR as an autonomous Oblast. After the collapse of the USSR in 1991 it became the Republic of Tuva within the Russian Federation.
3. For more details on Soviet take over of Tuva, see Sharad K. Soni, *Mongolia-Russia Relations: Kiakhta to Vladivostok*, Delhi: Shipra Publications, 2002, pp. 73-80.
4. Robert A. Rupen, "The Absorption of Tuva," in *The Anatomy of Communist Takeovers*, edited by T.T. Hammond, New Haven: Yale University Press, 1975, p. 145. The Chinese claims was inspired by the assumption that so long as Mongolia remained under formal Chinese rule during Qing dynasty, Tuva being a part of one of the provinces of Mongolia thus belonged to China.
5. *Great Soviet Encyclopedia*, vol. 26, 1977, p. 523.
6. For more details, see Rupen (1975), *op. cit.*, pp. 153-157.
7. *Ibid.*, p. 154.
8. Peter S.H. Tang, "Sino-Soviet Territorial Disputes: Past and Present," *Russian Review* 28, No. 4 (1969), p. 406.
9. Robert A. Rupen, *Mongols of the Twentieth Century*, Bloomington: Indiana University Press, 1964, p. 74.
10. *Ibid.*
11. Robert A. Rupen, "Mongolian Nationalism: Part I," *Journal of Royal Central Asian Society.*45 (1959), p. 163.
12. *Ibid.*
13. Rupen (1975), *op. cit.*, p. 150.
14. *Ibid.*, p. 159.
15. Toomas Alatalu, "Tuva—A State Reawakens", *Soviet Studies.*44, No. 5 (1992), p. 882.
16. David J. Dallin, *The Rise of Russia in Asia*, London: The World Affairs Book Club, 1950, p. 138.
17. *Ibid.*, p. 137.
18. Peter S.H. Tang, *Russian and Soviet Policy in Manchuria and Outer Mongolia, 1911-1931*, Durham NC: Duke University Press, 1959, pp. 403-404.
19. Albert L. Weeks, *The Other Side of Co-existence: An Analysis of Russian Foreign Policy*, New York: Pitman Publishing Co., 1970, p. 43.
20. See Morgen Mongush, "The Annexation of Tannu Tuva and the Formation of Tuva ASSR," *Central Asian Survey*,12, No. 1 (1993), p. 81.
21. *Ibid.*
22. Rupen (1964), *op. cit.*, p. 75.

23. *Ibid.*
24. See Rupen (1975), *op. cit.*, pp. 159-160.
25. Cited in *Ibid.*
26. *Bol'shaya Sovetskaya Entsiklopediya* (Great Soviet Encyclopedia), 3rd ed., vol. 29, Moscow, 1977, p. 284, cited in Alatalu, *op. cit.*, p. 882.
27. Cited in Tang (1959), *op. cit.*, p. 410.
28. *Ibid.*
29. Dallin, *op. cit.*, p. 84-85.
30. *Ibid.*, p. 85.
31. Cited in Mongush, *op. cit.*, p. 82. In fact, it was on August 14, 1921 that the Tannu Tuva People's Republic was proclaimed. Later on, in 1926 the word Tannu, meaning *taiga*, was dropped to remain just as Tuva People's Republic, see Alatalu, *op. cit.*, p. 883.
32. Cited in Rupen (1964), *op. cit.*, p. 189.
33. Xenia J. Eudin and Robert C. North, *Soviet Russia and the Far East*, Stanford: Stanford University Press, 1957, p. 259.
34. *Ibid.*, p. 258.
35. Rupen (1975), *op. cit.*
36. G.M. Friters, *Outer Mongolia and Its International Position*, Baltimore: The John Hopkins Press, 1949, p. 130.
37. Alatalu, *op. cit.*, p. 884.
38. Friters, *op. cit.*, p. 131.
39. Cited in Rupen (1964), *op. cit.*, p. 189.
40. *Ibid.*
41. See Robert M. Slussar and Jan F. Triska, *A Calendar of Soviet Treaties, 1917-1957*, Stanford: Stanford University Press, 1959, p. 57.
42. William B. Ballis, "Soviet Russia's Asiatic Frontier Technique: Tannu Tuva," *Pacific Affairs,* 14 (March 1941), pp. 91-96.
43. Tang (1959), *op. cit.*, p. 419.
44. Mongush, *op. cit.*, p. 83.
45. *Ibid.*
46. *Ibid.*
47. "Tuva celebrates Constitution Day," *http://en.tuvaonline.ru/2007/05/06/constitution-day.html*
48. "Russia close-up: Shamans and Lamas Buddy Buddy in Tyva", *http://en.tuvaonline.ru/2007/09/09/0330_shamans.html*
49. See Marina Mongush and Mergen Mongush, "A Preliminary Study on the Cultural Ties between Tuva and Tibet: The History and the Present," *The Tibet Journal*, 24, No. 1 (Summer 1999), p. 93.
50. *Ibid.*
51. *Istoria Tuvy* (History of Tuva: Summary in Russian), Moscow, 1964, p. 106, cited in *Ibid.*
52. For an insight into socio-political and cultural developments within the domains of the Yuan dynastic rule, see Sharad K Soni, "Mongol Yuan Dynasty and Its Legacy", In *Statehood of Nomads: History and*

Tradition, edited by B. Enkhtuvshin, Ulaanbaatar: International Institute for the Study of Nomadic Civilizations, 2007, pp. 35-40.

53. For more on Khubilai's religious policy and his relationship with Phags-Pa Lama, see Sh. Bira, "Qubilai Qa'an and Phags-Pa Bla-ma," in *The Mongol Empire and its Legacy*, edited by Reuven Amitai-Preiss and David O. Morgan, Leiden: Brill, 1999, pp. 240-249.
54. The Phags-Pa Lama basically devised a square script, which contained 44 letters to be used in the Mongolian language. The square script could also be used to write in Sanskrit, Tibetan and Turkish languages, see Sharad K. Soni, *Mongolia-China Relations: Modern and Contemporary Times*, New Delhi: Pentagon Press, 2006, p. 7.
55. While Khubilai himself retained the task of ruling the secular sphere, the position of ruler of the sacred sphere was given to the Phags-Pa Lama. See Larry Williams Moses, *The Political Role of Mongol Buddhism*, Bloomington: Indiana University, 1977, p. 78.
56. In 1772, the first Buddhist monastic complexes were built in the Tesgol *kozhuun* of Tuva, which is now divided into Erzin, Tes-Khem and Tandyn *kozhuuns*. The *kozhuun* is the biggest administrative unit of Tuva. For more detailed description of various Buddhist monasteries built in Tuva, see Marina Mongush and Mergen Mongush, *op. cit.*, pp. 94-95.
57. *Ibid.*, p. 95.
58. *Ibid.*
59. "General Information on Tuva: History, Economy, Resources, Art," *http://en.tuvaonline.ru/2006/10/08/general-information-on-tuva-history-economy-resources-art.html*;
60. Marina Mongush and Mergen Mongush, *op. cit.*, p. 97.
61. *Ibid.*, p. 100.
62. "Buddhist Mantra on a Mountain in Tuva Sanctified," *http://en.tuvaonline.ru/2006/09/15/buddist-mantra-on-a-mountain-in-tuva-sanctified.html*;
63. See Roberte Hamayon, "Shamanism in Siberia: From Partnership in Supernature to Counter-Power in Society," in *Shamanism, History and the State*, edited by Caroline Humphrey and Nicholas Thomas, Ann Arbor: University of Michigan Press, 1994.
64. "Tuva-Mongolia Friendship Society Established in Tuva," *http://en.tuvaonline.ru/2007/03/13/mongol-links.html*

11

Buryatia and Russia: Interaction and Linkages

K. Warikoo

Covering an area of 3,51,000 sq. kms. and situated in the southern part of East Siberia to the southeast of Baikal Lake, the Republic of Buryatia has its borders touching Mongolia in the south, the Republic of Tuva in the southwest, the Irkutsk oblast in the northwest and the Chita oblast in the east. The major part (about 60 per cent of coastline) of the 636 kms. long Baikal Lake, the deepest freshwater lake in the world, falls within the territory of Buryatia. Buryats, Evenks and Soyots constitute the main indigenous nationalities, besides Russians, Ukrainians and other nationalities. By the year 2002, the population of Buryatia had crossed one million, with Russians and Buryats constituting over 68 and 28 per cent respectively.

Zabaikalye (Trans-Baikalia) has been integral part of the historical and cultural process in Eurasia since early times. The world famous Lake Baikal which is situated in the centre of Asia, has been the main attraction for Russian visitors and explorers. With an area of over 31,500 sq kms, Lake Baikal contains 22 per cent of world's fresh water resources and a reservoir of diverse flora and fauna. It was a Cossack explorer, Kurbatlvanov, who in 1643 AD, along with a group of Cossacks and traders travelled up to the western coast of Baikal Lake and wrote about the Baikal, its fauna and the rivers flowing into it. In 1675 AD, a Russian statesman and scientist, Nikolai Gevrilovich Spafariy travelled to Siberia and Baikal. His travel account namely, *Travels of a Russian Ambassador N. Spafariy through Siberia to Nerchinsk and the Borders of China* provided rich geographical and other information about Siberia. It remained the main source of information about Buryatia for Russians. Another

Russian scientist who visited the Baikal and wrote about it was D.G. Messerschmidt. The Russian Academy of Sciences started intensive study of Siberia in 1725 AD. Scientific expeditions led by Gmelin, P.S. Pallasa (1731-72), I.G. Gregori and others travelled to Baikal and wrote about it. A hydrographic expedition led by K. Drizhenko, which worked in Baikal during the period 1896-1902, prepared a detailed atlas of Baikal's depths. The Russians also used the Buryat name *Baigaal* for the famous lake, later replacing the typical Buryat 'g' sound by traditional Russian language 'k' and turning its name into 'Baikal.'

It was in the 17th century that major part of Buryat territory was incorporated in the Russian empire. Thus a vast territory on both sides of the Baikal got separated from the Mongolian world and the socio-political system of Mongols. With the result, the dominant ethnic group in this area, who were Mongolian speaking tribes, clans and sub-groups, got isolated from the original ethnic Mongolians. This was followed by the settlement of Russian officials, Cossack fighters, farmers, artisans and traders. The detachments of Cossacks led by G. Lavtsov and O. Vasiliev arrived in Buryatia in 17th century. In 1666 AD, Russian Cossacks built a wooden fortress on the bank of the Uda River, which turned into a large city namely Verkhneudinsk and later became the capital city of Buryatia under the new name of Ulan-Ude. Kiakhata outpost was built in 1728 AD and the border with China was established. The Nerchinsk Treaty of 1689 and Kiakhta Treaty of 1728 formalised the incorporation of Buryat territory into Russia. The joining of Transbaikalia with Russia was followed by the settlement of Russians in the newly acquired lands. The Russian settlers in Transbaikalia included Cossacks who guarded the frontiers with China and Mongolia, peasants who came to escape the oppression by their landlords in mainland Russia, state peasants forcibly settled in the vacant lands, and Old Believers (*Semeyskii*) who were exiled to this region since 1760s. From the late 18th and early 19th centuries, Transbaikalia received a large number of exiled people from Russia. The Russian immigrants who settled along the main rivers such as Selenga, Urda, Irkut and Djida, started agriculture and animal husbandry practices in these fertile lands. These migrants, prisoners and political dissidents such as the Decembrists who were deported to Siberia including Buryatia, influenced the local society and life in various ways. The peasants, prisoners and exiles gave impetus to agriculture and trade in southern Siberia, particularly alongside the rivers and in the centres of economic and industrial activity. The Russian settlers also introduced Christianity (both Greek Orthodoxy and the Old Believer Christianity) in Buryatia where Shamanism was predominant among the local population of Buryats and Evenks. Whereas the Tsarist Russian government followed Greek Orthodoxy, a section of Russian Christians (Old Believers) who did not accept the reforms of patriarch Nibon migrated to Russia. The Decembrists built their landed estates, studied the Buryat language and opened health centres and schools in the region. On the whole, the Russian Christian settlers, political exiles, traders and farmers did contribute to the culture and educational system in Buryatia.

After joining Russia, the new ethno-national identity of Buryats shaped up in the evolving historico-political situation. The Russian two-headed eagle, the Christian Cross, White State Flags and name of Tsar-Emperor became part of the symbols of Buryatia. The growing inter-ethnic social and cultural relationship including mixed marriages, a new class of assimilated Russian-Buryat families came into being. Interestingly, many Buryats played a positive role in the development of culture and self-identity of Buryats. For instance, A. Shapov and A. Bobrovnikov became prominent Russian scientists and public figures. Galsan Gomboev became a professor at the University of Kazan in mid-nineteenth century. The Tsarist government supported the University of St. Petersburgh, Imperial Academy of Sciences and the Russian Committee for the Study of Central and Eastern Asia, in their efforts to promote the academic pursuits of Buryat intellectuals like Jamtsarano (1880-1940), Rinchino (1885-1937), Baradin (1878-1937) and Tsybikov (1873-1930). Agvan Dordjiev even persuaded the Tsarist administration to build a Buddhist temple in St. Petersburgh, which contributed to a greater understanding of Buddhism in Russia.

Though the Tsarist government had its own system of administration in Zabaikalye, local administration remained in the hands of Buryat nobles. Traditional caravan routes connecting Russia to the Far East as well as the construction of the Trans-Siberian railway that crossed the territory of Zabaikalye contributed to the economic development of the region during the 18th and 19th centuries. The settlement of Russian peasants, missionary work of Orthodox Christians, the presence of Cossacks and widespread usage of Russian language, led to the Russification of this area. With the introduction of Russian language, culture and education, a new powerful class of Buryat intellectuals came into existence and they wielded considerable influence in Russian politics particularly in its dealings with Mongolia and Tibet. Russia employed several Buryats as their emissaries in Outer Mongolia and Tibet. Many Buddhist Lamas from Buryatia became influential at the Tsarist Russian courts of Alexander III and Nicholas II, mainly through the efforts of one Badmaev, Buryat physician and practitioner of Tibetan medicine at the court. In a memorial submitted to Alexander III in 1893, Badmaev advocated active Russian policy towards Mongolia and Tibet. Buryat Lama Agvan Dordjiev (1853-1938), who had acquired some influence over the Dalai Lama XIII at Lhasa in early 20th century, was received by Tsar Nicholas II in October 1900 and July 1901. Dordjiev even proposed to the Tsar that Russia should proclaim to be the champion of Asia and the defender of Buddhism. The October Revolution of 1917 led to further integration of Zabaikalye with Soviet Russia. The Buryat-Mongol Autonomous Soviet Socialist Republic was established in the year 1923. However, in the year 1936 the official name of Buryatia became Buryat Autonomous Soviet Socialist Republic, after dropping the term 'Mongol'. On 27 March 1991, the Republic was named as the Republic of Buryatia of the Russian Federation.

Notwithstanding their Russian education and training, Buryat intellectuals played key role in retaining the Buryat traditions and culture while modernising themselves. In this process of syncretisation, as a result of application of Russian science, technology, language, literature and culture in the traditional nomadic society of Buryatia, the indigenous Buryats retained their local tradition and ethos adjusting themselves to the new wave of dominant Russian and later Soviet cultural and political influence. Even though the use of Russian language became widespread amongst the Buryats, they retained the indigenous Mongolian characteristics, nomadic lifestyle, Buddhist and Shamanist religion and traditions, Tibetan language, Buryat history and folklore. Dorji Banzarov (1822-1855) who was a distinguished scholar of Mongolian culture and history, has been a symbol of Buryat identity both in Transbaikalia and North Baikal (Irkutsk). Today, cultural, religious and social traditions of different peoples in Buryatia are closely interwoven forming a unique pattern of peaceful coexistence. The Russian element in Buryatia's culture is represented by Russian literature, opera and ballet, drama, cinema, musical performances, circus, cultural centres and clubs, which are now an integral part of the social and cultural life of Buryatia.

The Russian culture in Buryatia has been preserved and promoted through the efforts of the *Semeyskii* (Old Believers), who were the original Russian settlers. The *Semeyskii* settled in various parts of Siberia including Buryatia, following their resistance to the reforms introduced by Patriarch Nibon of the Russian Orthodox Church and the Tsar during and after the second half of 17th century. Those Russians who did not accept these reforms, migrated to Siberia to save themselves from government oppression. Thus a large number of *Semeyskii* from Russia, Byelorussia and Ukraine settled in Siberia after 1750s. This also resulted in the building of churches in the Russian architectural style. One of the first such Russian churches was built in Verkhneudinsk (Ulan Ude) in early 18th century. During the period 1860-1865, hotels and trade centres were built in main towns of Siberia. The famous Russian artists and public figures—Roerich and his son played an important role in promoting mutual understanding between Russia and the people of Trans-Baikal through their outstanding art.

It were the Russian masters who introduced several modern musical systems in the traditional folk music of Buryatia. Both the Russian and Buryat composers worked together to create innovative composition of new Buryat national style. As such Russian musical system had a strong influence over the local Buryat music particularly after 1930s. P.M. Berlinsky (1900-1976), who was an outstanding Russian musician, composer, pianist, conductor and researcher, contributed a lot to the development of music, drama and theatre in Buryatia. He trained singers, musicians—mostly from Buryatia, and created the first ever manual on *Piano Playing* in the Buryatia Republic. Another Russian master V.I. Moroshkin (1909-1942), contributed to the musical culture of Buryatia. Professor M.P. Frolov (1892-1944) visited Buryatia to study local musical folklore and he trained local musicians. Frolov created a first national Buryat opera *Enkhe-Bulat-bator*, based on an ancient Buryat epic, but employing the technique of the Russian classical opera. First *Dekada* (ten days) of Buryat-Mongol art in Moscow was held in October 1940, where the local music, drama, orchestra and other performances were held. In the post-World War period, some more works based on Buryat themes were created by the Russian masters *U prodnozhya sayan*

(At the foot of the Sayan Mountain) by S.N. Ryauzov (1905-1983) and opera *Na Baikale* (At the Baikal) by L.K. Knipper (1898-1975). During the late 1950s, both the Russian and Buryat composers created new composition of operas like *Krasaviya Angara* (Angara the Beauty) by N. Baladano and other ballet. This opera has been very popular both in and outside Buryatia. One can see that both the Russian composers and musicians and their Buryat counterparts have thus created a harmony, rather a fusion of traditional Buryat music and folklore along with the Russian music.

The art and culture of Buryatia has been projected in various parts of Russia through the activities of Buryat State Philharmonic Society, Art Museum, and State Circus of Buryatia, East Siberia Academy of Culture and Arts (ESAC&A). The ESAC&A has been playing an outstanding role in the process of cultural and educational development in Eastern Siberia including Buryatia, by imparting training to specialists in the field of culture, professional artists and scholars. This Academy promotes interaction of two cultures—of the East of Buryatia, Chita, Irkutsk, Tuva etc, and that of West—the Russian Culture. To quote its Rector, R.I. Pshenichnikova, this Academy is "supposed to be reorganised into Eurasian University of Culture and Arts in future."

Russian traveller, Przhevalsky, writer N. Chernyshevsky, Academicians Obruchev, Efremov, Okladinov, V. Kostetsky and others contributed to develop an understanding of the social and cultural life of the Buryats among the Russians. To quote a Buryat philosopher, Z. Morohoeva, "many centuries long co-existence of Buryats with Russia and their adaptation to other culture, created new opportunities for the development of Buryat culture. The Buryat personality adopted a lot from European rationality via Russian culture. The Russian classical culture of the 19th century, enormously supplied an educated Buryat person with high spirituality, having given him access to masterpieces of music, painting, literature and ballet."

Russian Orthodoxy and Old Believers' Orthodoxy had come to Buryatia in the 17th and 18th centuries. The existence of Russian churches, chapels and prayer houses in many villages testifies to the spread of Christianity in Buryatia. Both the Indo-Buddhist, Mongolian and Russian-European cultures and Shamanism, Buddhism and Christianity have played their role in the formation and development of Buryat culture through history. Due to its unique geographical location (being situated on the borders of Russia, Mongolia and China) and historico-cultural development, Buryatia and Buryats present a unique synthesis of both the culture of the East through Buddhism and Mongolian language and culture and that of the West through the medium of Russian language and culture.

Inhabitants of the Republic have strong ties with Buryat ethnic groups in other cities in the Russian Federation. Buryat Culture Societies are registered in Moscow, St. Petersburg, Kiev and Irkutsk. In July 1991, the Buddhists of the Buryatia Republic celebrated the 250th anniversary of official recognition of Buddhism in Russia. Today, the Republic is the centre of Buddhism in Russia, Ivolginsky *datsan* (monastery), being located in Buryatia. The Republic has been rightfully considered as one of the popular cultural centres of East Siberia. The glorious traditions and cultural activities of the Republic are preserved and promoted through the existence and functioning of theatres, ballets and dances. Both the indigenous Asian values, culture and ethos and the European religion and culture of Russia, have integrated and evolved into a unique synthesis of both these cultures.

12

Siberia: India's New Cultural Imperatives

P. Stobdan

As the world celebrates the Buddha's 2550th birth anniversary, a NATO air strike recently killed the erstwhile Taliban Governor, Maulavi Mohammed Islam Mohammadi, who in March 2001 supervised the military destruction of the 5th century statutes of Buddha *Virocana* and *Sakyamuni* in Central Afghanistan. This probably not the way the Buddha would have sought retribution. The reasons why the Taliban had blown up the colossal Buddhas probably may have been numerous—one of them perhaps included the act of provocation by Osama Bin Laden and his symbolic 'rehearsal' for 9/11. The militia used artillery, anti-aircraft guns and rockets to blow up the Buddha. The phenomena though had caused worldwide horror and outrage then—it was intrinsically not outside the Buddha's own concept of "impermanence" that in the path of progress both destruction and growth go together.

Despite such acts of vandalism aimed at foci of historicity, the Buddha nature and its wisdom is ushering a speedy comeback on the world stage to meet the challenges of 21st century. The Buddha's 2500 old doctrine once transcended the deserts of Egypt to Islands of Japan and from the Indonesian archipelago to Siberian settlements, had to make a retreat from such a vast area including its birthplace during the last several centuries can only be due to erroneous awareness of the world forces operating in those times. They may have been barbaric then, they continue to exist even today.

However, after a millennium of quiescence, the resurgence of this great Indic philosophy is now plainly discernible with fervor. Following its ardent adoption in the West during the last three to four decades, Buddhism is resurfacing in the East with greater devotion.

Apparently, the Indic *Mandala* is assuming a spatial and geo-political dimension. The trans-national Buddhism today consists of two concentric circles. The first covers the vast Inner Asian space from Mongolia, Buryatia, Chita, Kalmykia and Manchuria to the Himalayan region with its epicenter in Tibet. The region has enormous hydro and earth resources, share common philosophical and cultural outlook, and in spite of being heirs to a great civilization it has been of marginal and peripheral interest to the world.

The outer circle encompasses the vast stretch of the former Soviet space including hydrocarbon rich Central Asia where Buddhism once flourished, but had to retreat in the face of onslaught of Islam in the early centuries of the previous millennium. The *Shambhala*, therefore, is currently under threat of triple forces of Sinification (fortified with irreligious Marxism), Russification and Islamization. These together with other violent forces, manifesting through terrorism, like the Bamiyan's destruction by the Taliban, threaten the every existence of this sacred world.

It is gratifying that the historical and spiritual importance of Hambo Lama Itigelov and others are being revived in the Siberian region. Hambo Lama Itigelov as a historical figure is well known to the Buddhist world. A great monk of Anninsky Datsan in Buryatia, he was great practitioner of medicine and a master on the Buddha's nature of emptiness. He authored an encyclopedia of pharmacology. Hambo Lama was a great social reformist and an active worker who tried to protect the Indian philosophy from the invasion of the Red Guards.

Revival of Buddhism in Siberia is of great importance to India in terms of restoring the lost linkages. Buddhism could become a new factor in enhancing Indian interests in Siberia, especially exploring new opportunities for investment in mining, energy, agriculture and human development.

Even in China, the Communist's vociferous campaign against Buddhist institutions seems to have become outdated, the doctrine of peace is finding new patronage of the Chinese state. The Chinese, since 2006 held major Buddhist congregations drawing world's attention. The convention of the first World Buddhist Forum, first since the Communist revolution, held in Hangzhou and Zhoushan City, Zhejiang Province in April 2006 is a pointer in this direction.

For the Chinese, Bamiyan conventionally epitomized the ascent of Mahayana order and their node on the famed Silk Route. Buddha's obliteration by the Taliban naturally had a resonant impact on the Chinese reminding them their past ordeal under the Arabs in 751 CE. The event seems to have triggered a wave of upsurge among Chinese for preserving their heritage. Chinese neo-entrepreneurs are zealously resurrecting the Bamiyan replica next to the world's largest 71 meters Leshan Buddha in Sichaun province, even contemplating for a Disneyland for Buddhism creating over three-thousand Buddha replicas in Leshan.

For the Karzai government rebuilding of Bamiyan Buddhas is a "cultural imperative" which may be completed by 2009 end with support from UNESCO and other heritage agencies. The project costing $30m may restore the Silk Route heritage that drew millions of travelers for over 1600 years. Bamiyan city that once had 20 luxury hotels for international tourists could get its live back providing hopes to half a million Hazaras trapped in tyranny and poverty.

Bamiyan tragedy also appeared to have rekindled the post-Soviet Central Asians to restore their hitherto decrepit and dilapidated Buddhist legacy. In the rest of Asia, especially in Southeast, Buddhism is a spiritual quest—a currency of well-being and prosperity.

Interestingly enough, even for Islam notice the benign-ness of Buddhism as opposed to Western ethics. Plethora of write-ups and analysis by Islamic scholars are coming to fore covering a range of historical and ethical association between Buddhist and Islamic principles. They range from Buddha's depiction in the Arab-Islamic literature to worshipping of idols at the Kaaba in the form of Buddha by the inhabitants of Mecca and Medina prior to Prophet. Islamic scholars write that the man from *Kifli* (Arabic rendition of Kapilvastu) finds reference twice in the *Quran*. Similarly, 10th century *Tarikh-i-Tabari* described the Buddhist community as Ahamira (red dressed). There is a certainly renewed attempt for hindsight in demystify Islam as a fundamentalist force. The paranoia and prejudice toward the Muslims, carried over for centuries must stop at one end. The flawed Western interpretation of Asian history, particularly depicting Buddhist-Muslim standoff in South and Central Asia on religious rather than economic or geopolitical motives, confusing military warfare with religious onslaughts *et al* may have helped to perpetuate the prejudice. History is also full of Buddhist-Muslim friendly interactions and cooperation, alliances and exchange of trade, frequent scholarly exchange and spiritual advancement that were not without advantage to the humanity.

Most heartening of all is that even in its birthplace, India, where Buddhism was once routed out, is making a comeback albeit as a Brand symbol of rising India. Economists now feel that Buddha-Industry could transform the lives of millions, providing lucrative career options to a large youth component of his land. India's corporate believes that the country is sitting atop millennia-old tourist mines. This is what a recent FICCI-ICRA study said that Sakyamuni could potentially generate $1 billion revenue for the country. There are scores of Buddhist sites in India directly linked to spiritual destinies of millions in Asia. With ever-increasing adherents in China, Buddhist traffic to India estimated to rise by 400 per cent in the near future. India could also easily tap or divert millions of Asians taking pilgrimage to China annually. Aptly the Government policy is recently showing more finesse, indicating a more potent and tangible component in pursuing a goal. Steps taken to restore Nalanda's legacy could help scores of Asian schools to trace their lineages to eclectic institution. It would be fitting as also a way of investment by the governments of Uttar Pradesh, Bihar, Andhra Pradesh, Maharashtra, Orissa, Chhattisgarh and Madhya Pradesh to encourage Asian countries and societies to build their lineages and institutions while providing incentives in form of allotting them with lands.

However, lot more needs to be done in conceptualizing Brand Buddha. More than its market import, Buddhism needs a cultural tagging—a source of knowledge-based soft-power lever. There are however many challenges ahead and a synergy is required for a nuanced and adept policy pursuit. With China culturally opening up, we are inevitably going to witness a resurgent Buddhism in that country. Not only India needs to view it as a benign phenomenon but also recognize Chinese Buddhism in its institutional form, something India has ignored for too long. There are many Brand names of Indian masters such as Kasyapa Matanga, Dharma Ratna, Kumarajiva, Paramartha, Prabhakaramitra, Vajrabodhi, Bodhidharma, and Gunavarman, and Chinese masters like Faxian, Xuanzang and Yijing, who played profound roles in providing foundation to a civilisation of vast magnitude and influence. Invoking their roles could create a new market phenomenon and space for moderation and rationalisation in Sino-Indian relations.

While on the other hand, a Buddhist China could also entail implications. Adroit Chinese are likely to assume a foremost role over Buddhism, at least on the Asian scene. Not only would they like to control the trend and nature of discourses on Buddhism but also use it as a vehicle of influence and instrument of pragmatism in major parts of Asia. Chinese may also finally view the Dalai Lama and a settlement with him in this paradigm. The challenge before Indian policy makers, therefore, is to retain its cultural leadership and plays a meaningful role in shaping the course of this great phenomenon in the 21st century. Buddhism was India's ancient geopolitical tool that could still be employed to meet the challenges of the new millennium.

13

Siberia as Integral Part of Russia in the Era of Globalisation

Felix N. Yurlov

How to Weaken and Split the Russian Federation: Dreams about a Siberian Republic

The disintegration of the Soviet Union heralded the end of the former world order, based on bipolarity and opposition of the two super powers. At the same time, the dismemberment of the USSR ushered in a new era, in which the "winners" did their best to further strengthen their position. Using the historic chance they tried to ensure their leadership in the 21st century and to perpetuate beyond a generation America's decisive role as Eurasia and world arbitrator. The creation of such a system required further transformation of former Soviet territories in order to suit the US self-interests.

The emergence of America as a sole superpower gave birth to theories aimed to preserve and expand this power in time and space. The fundamental idea behind this attempt was to convince the world that no state could match America in military, economic, technological and cultural power. But the weakness of this idea became quite apparent in a decade or so after the disintegration of the Soviet Union.

To perpetuate the US leadership, or "forced imperialism", or "benign hegemony", as some American authors prefer to call this leadership, short term, medium term, and strategic measures were to be taken.

An important part of this strategy relates to Russia and the newly formed states—Ukraine, Kazakhstan, Azerbaijan and the Asian

Republics, Uzbekistan in particular. After the "orange" revolution in Ukraine, Russia's influence in this state was substantially undermined. The "rose" revolution in Georgia and the failed "tulip" revolution in Kyrgyz Republic added to Russia's geopolitical concerns, as well as its loss of the positions on the Black, Caspian and the Baltic Seas. These concerns may grow immensely in Siberia and the Far East when we take into account the vast resources and sparse population of this region.

The idea of further disintegration of Russia was mooted quite some time ago, just after the demise of the Soviet Union. The general outline was as simple as that: to strengthen the American base on the Eurasian continent, so that Europe could become a springboard for the advancement the international democratic (meaning American) order deep into Asia, including Siberia. One of the ideologues of this theory Zbigniew Brzezinski holds that the disintegration of the biggest state in the world (that is the USSR) led to the formation of a "black hole" in the very centre of Eurasia. Thus America is facing many-folded tasks, one of them being to prevent the resurrection of the "Eurasian empire", which could hamper the implementation of the American geostrategic aim, i.e. creation of a larger Euro-Atlantic system.[1]

It needs to be stressed that though tsarist Russia had indeed been an empire, the Soviet Union could hardly be considered as such, for at least three reasons. First. The former Soviet republics had the right to self-determination, which they made use of at the time of disintegration of the USSR. Second. In spite of the centralisation of power in the Soviet Union, the republics had a substantial amount of authority at their disposal, which helped them to preserve and develop their national cultures and traditions, though on a limited scale. Third. During the year of Soviet Power, there was a noticeable rise of national elites, which made possible the formation and governance of the new nation-states.

As a result of disintegration, the Soviet Union, from the state of great territorial power, was transformed into numerous independent states, and Russia became a state with a limited access to the external world. Russia sharply turned to the West, seeking friendship and cooperation with America and Europe. But Russia became too weak to claim equal partnership with America and other Western countries. And they treated her accordingly.

Soon the Russians started changing their approach to the West. They sensed that the pro-American bias served the interests of the

West at the expense of Russia. The new possibilities, created by the disintegration of the USSR, were used by the West for its political and economic ends. The Russians also began to understand that the West was not the only geostrategic choice or alternative for Russia.

The West in turn, predetermines the only alternative for Russia—that is cooperation with it on certain conditions. One of them is the rejection by Russia of its so-called imperial past, which in reality means complete subjugation of its politics and security to the interests of the West. Thus, the survival of Russia as a state is put on a trial.

These conditions could not be accepted by a country with a thousand-year history, vast territory (including Siberia) and world's biggest natural resources. Russia can survive as such only as a great power. Otherwise it will cease to be Russia and become something else. Some leaders in the West, like John Major, the former British prime-minister, said quite openly and cynically, that Russia's role in the future should be confined to the supply of raw materials to rich countries of the West. For that purpose about 60 million Russian people would suffice. The US Secretary of State Madeleine Albright expressed herself on the subject more or less in the same vein.

Such a perspective obviously could not suit Russia's interests. Instead of becoming a junior partner of the West and America, it took steps to strengthen its economy and to increase its military power. Any outside attempts and pressure to weaken its geopolitical position were considered detrimental to its security.

It is not accidental that the ghost of Harold Mackinder—the geopolitician in the beginning of the 20th century, was revived by Western politicians. He was the father of the concept of Eurasian pivot area, which should include the whole of Siberia and the bigger part of Central Asia. This concept was later transformed into "heartland" of Central and Eastern Europe to serve as a springboard in order to dominate the Eurasian continent. "For America" after the Cold War, Brzezinski adds, "the chief prize is Eurasia".[2]

Later Adolf Hitler also dreamt of "Lebensraum" (living space) for the Germans and tried to fulfill his design at the expense of the Soviet people. What was the end of it is very well known.

Some people in the West cannot reconcile with the thought that after the disintegration of the Soviet Union, Russia still remains in charge of the world's largest piece of real estate, spanning ten time zones and dwarfing powerful America, Europe, and China. Hence their recommendation: Russia should not engage itself in a futile effort to regain its status as a global power. A loosely confederated Russia, composed of a European Russia, a Siberian Republic, and a Far Eastern Republic would be more suitable for them. According to their thinking, each of the confederated entities would be able to tap its local creative potential, now "stifled" by Moscow. In turn, a decentralized Russia "would be less susceptible to imperial mobilization".[3] In this case, "a non-imperial" Russia could then be accepted as the region's major economic partner, although no longer its "imperial ruler".

Behind all these strategies lies the fact that Eurasia is home to most of the world's politically assertive and dynamic states. Eurasia accounts for 75 per cent of the world's population, 60 per cent of its GNP, and 75 per cent of its energy resources. Thus, the immediate task for the US is to ensure that no state or combination of states gains the ability to expel the United States from this supercontinent, or even diminish its decisive role. "A benign American hegemony" must discourage others from posing such a challenge.

According to some American strategists, a Greater China's geopolitical influence is not necessary incompatible with America's strategic interest in a stable, pluralistic Eurasia. What is important to note in this connection is that China's growing interest in Central Asia (and Siberia) constrains Russia's ability to achieve a political reintegration of the region under Moscow's control.[4]

Though the original idea to use China against Russia was quite obvious, it could not be implemented until today. On the contrary, some further developments, including creation of the Shanghai Solidarity Organisation, comprising both China and Russia as its leading members, was a movement in the opposite direction.

As of late, we are witnessing more anti-Russian rhetoric by some American politicians. For example, John McCain, a US senator and a candidate for the Republican presidential nomination, called Russia "revanchist", and suggested to exclude it from the G-8, and include Brazil and India instead. He proposed to institutionalise the new quadrilateral security partnership among the major Asia-Pacific democracies: Australia, India, Japan, and the United States.

At the same time McCain pronounced that dealing with a rising China will be a central challenge for the next American president. But in case China proposes regional forums and economic arrangements, designed to exclude America from Asia, the United States will react. He said, however, that China and the USA are not destined to be adversaries.[5]

Presently, new ideas are being formulated in the West in regard to Russia and the world order. They are based on the assumption that during the last decade Russia changed dramatically. In the 1990s, it was a weak state, which could be dictated what, and how to do, and where to move. Now, a much more powerful Russia sees itself as an independent Eurasian and world power.

Some experts think that in this new strategic environment NATO and the European Union need to articulate a new strategic rationale for "expanding the democratic West and devise a new approach to dealing with Russia". They speak about another opportunity today "to advance Western values and security, and redraw the map of Europe and Eurasia once more".[6] They hold the view that Russia's efforts to oppose the West would be futile. In this context they specifically mention Ukraine and Georgia, as well as Azerbaijan and Armenia. They also do not exclude the scenario, when Russia, using its energy supplies and influence, would emerge as an authoritarian capitalist alternative to the West.[7]

In reality, much will depend on the change in the correlation of forces—economic, political and military—in the world. As of today, the advantage is on the side of the Asian countries, including Russia as a European and Asian power.

Russia and Siberia—Problems of Development and Globalisation

Russia's economic development in the last five years has revived hopes that it will regain its leading positions in the world after the disintegration of the Soviet Union. During this period, Russia's GDP increased more than 50 per cent. The government's financial policy eliminated the need for foreign loans. As a result the country was able to beef up its budgetary and hard currency reserves to about $500 billion against possible financial crises.

This was the result of the economic situation on international markets, specially the rapid growth in energy prices. Russia's economic development was driven by the export oriented resource sector. The growth largely came from the extensive exploitation and development of oil fields. Nonetheless, the contribution from the non-resource sectors to the nation economy essentially increased. This was followed by a decline in oil output by the major Russian companies, including Sibneft.

Lately, Russia demonstrated that its economy is capable of

growing at a high rate even without a rapid expansion of its resource sector. The most troublesome trend was the decrease in the competitiveness of Russian goods compared to imports. While domestic demand grew by more than 50 per cent, imports accounted for over half of this increase.

At the same time there are some serious long-term challenges. One of them is the reduction of the Russian population including that of Siberia. This problem can be solved by birth rate stimulation, better health services and immigration, primarily from the former Soviet Republics, with the aim to stop depopulation. In the meantime, Russia has to reduce emigration from the country. It relates to Russia in general and to Siberia in particular, where we have a great deficit of population.

As far as Russia's foreign policy is concerned, there should be a definite turn to the growth of political and economic relations with the Asian countries, including China and India. The main objective of Russia's Asian policy must be the development of its eastern regions—Siberia and Russia's Far East.

The Russian Far East already participates in integration processes, oriented to China. The Asia-Pacific countries account for 85 per cent of all foreign trade of the Russian Far East, and its economic relations with the neighbouring countries are much more intensive as compared even with the European region of Russia.

At the same time, there are potential dangers associated with the full reorientation of the Asian part of the Russian Federation to regional economic centres, especially China. It may happen as a result of the insufficient economic and social development of Russia's Asian region—Siberia and the Far East. This is why Russia attaches great importance to the new project—*Discovering Siberia Anew*, which is intended to boost the social and economic development in this area. The aim is to increase the share of the Asia-Pacific region in Russia's foreign trade to 35 per cent. This can be achieved by expanding energy cooperation since the majority of Asian and Pacific countries are in need of new energy sources, and Russia can be a potentially reliable partner.

In Siberia and the Far East the emphasis is placed on the diversification of transport routes of Russia's energy resources to Asian consumers, particularly to China, India and Japan. Russia and the Asian countries could cooperate in building Trans-Siberian pipelines and developing infrastructures for tanker oil export and liquefied gas transportation.

The formation of Russia's new policy towards the Asia-Pacific countries is impossible without transforming its own policy thinking, which has been traditionally focused on the Euro-Atlantic space. This is more important as Asia is developing its economy more rapidly than the West. Therefore, it should be a sort of Look East policy. But it does not mean that Russia should curtail its trade and economic ties with Europe and America.

Until the middle of the 20th century, the resources of Siberia could not be fully used because of the First World War and the Civil war in Russia. The real chance to harness the riches of Siberia presented itself during the Second World War and after. It was only in the 1950s that Russia started in earnest to implement what was envisioned two hundred and fifty years ago by our great scientist Lomonosov. He said that the riches of Russia will grow with Siberia.

Siberia is extraordinarily rich in minerals, containing ores of all valuable metals, including uranium. It has some of the world's largest deposits of nickel, gold, lead, molybdenum, diamonds, silver and zinc, as well as extensive unexploited resources of oil and natural gas. Most of these are in the cold and remote eastern part of the region, which makes their extraction difficult and costly. Siberia has the world's largest forests. Timber remains an important source of revenue despite the fact that the logging rate in the East is much more rapid than that of the forest recovery. The See of Okhotsk is one of the richest fisheries in the world, producing over 10 per cent of the world's annual fish catch, though fishing has declined substantially since the collapse of the Soviet Union.

Industry in Siberia developed and increased greatly until the 1990s, but declined immensely after the demise of the USSR. Still Siberia's rating looks very impressive in some groups of goods. It occupies a leading position in such important industries in Russia as timber and paper (more than 30 per cent of the total production), fuel (more than 20 per cent), chemical products (more than 15 per cent). Today, Siberia provides about a quarter of Russia's industrial output. Some indicators of economic efficiency for Siberia considerably exceed the Russian economy average, including labour productivity and wages.

About 70 per cent of oil and 90 per cent of gas come from the West Siberian Basin, which covers an area of 1.3 mln square miles. As Russia increasingly participates in the global economy, the importance of its oil and gas resources for the country is also increasing. Russia exports a significant amount of oil and gas to Europe, Ukraine and Byelorussia. 25 per cent of all gas consumed in Europe comes from Russia. With the construction of new gas and oil pipelines from Russia to Europe the amount of gas and oil export will substantially grow. And, Russia itself is the world's second largest consumer of natural gas, and fourth largest consumer of oil products behind the USA, Japan and China.

In the last decade the consumption of oil and gas in Russia increased significantly. And it will definitely grow more as the whole territory of the country has not yet been covered by gas supply. At least 40 per cent of the population is still not provided with the natural gas, though we had cent per cent electricity supply for the entire population in the Soviet Union.

In the West Siberian Basin production projections for oil indicate that sufficient oil volume exists to maintain the current rate of its extraction for 25 to 40 years. But a continued development will require significant investments and technology advancements. There is also a potential for the development and recovery of big volumes of natural gas. All these have global implications for the world economy.

In addition to the West Siberian Basin there are other major oil and gas reserves in other parts of Siberia, particularly in the area close to Lake Baikal, which, incidentally, has one fifth of the world's fresh water resources. The mighty Siberian rivers Ob, Enisey, Lena and their tributaries also carry huge amounts of fresh water.

As far as oil and gas reserves are concerned, further explorations are carried in other regions. One of them is Schtokman, located at the shelf of the Barents Sea, which may yield huge amounts of oil and gas for many decades.

While discussing the problem of Russia's natural resources we should not ignore some very important concerns. First. These resources will not last forever and they are not renewable. Second. Their production and the following consumption negatively affect the environment. Third. Oil and gas production in the arduous climate of Siberia is very costly. It is three to four times more expensive than the extraction of oil in the Persian Gulf countries. Fourth. There is a shortage of qualified workers and engineers not only in Siberia, but in Russia as a whole. And fifth. Russian workers do not get a proper wage for their grueling work in the harsh conditions of North-West and North-East Siberia.

It is also a matter of deep concern that Russia, as we put it— "sits on an oil and gas needle". It means that Russia's economy depends to a very great extent on the export of crude oil and gas, which amounts to more than 60 per cent of the value of all goods exported from the country. The high price of crude oil (up to $100 a barrel and even more) has no relation to labour productivity and diversification of the production of other goods. The present model of the economic development of Russia does not seem to be a balanced one.

There are less than one million workers and engineers in the oil and gas sector while the whole work force in Russia is more than 75 mln people. It can be said that Russia's economy is following the development model of the oil producing countries of the Persian Gulf, which is very vulnerable, as it depends on the prices of oil. In spite of huge profits the unemployment rate of the local people in the Gulf countries is growing every year.

There is a debate in Russia on how and to what extent to use the natural resources, which are abundant but not unlimited. Sometimes, comparisons with other countries are helpful. In India, for example, there was a discussion on how to save the country's raw material reserves. The case of China was mentioned, which is importing now more than half of its requirements of iron ore after exports depleted its own reserves.

India is a major exporter of iron ore to China. It is projected that within 20 years India may face a situation similar to that of China and will be forced to import iron ore. Therefore, the question of protection of India's own resources and even banning the export of iron ore to save domestic steel industry is very much on the agenda.[8]

Similarly, Russia, in spite of its rich natural resources, in Siberia and other places after some time may face the same problems. The answer to it is to carefully exploit the present and future resources of oil, gas, different ores, minerals and timber.

And instead of selling crude oil we have to process it to get different petroleum liquids and other products which cost much more. Unfortunately, during the last 20 years not a single oil refinery was built in Russia. So, for domestic consumption of oil products we are surviving on the same 40 or so refineries constructed in the Soviet Union.

Nevertheless, things are slowly changing. Steps are taken to develop not only oil and gas resources but other branches of industry in Siberia and elsewhere in Russia. They include the production of durable consumer goods such as automobiles, washing machines, TV sets, refrigerators and the like. Russia is taking initial steps in production of consumer goods from timber instead of exporting raw timber.

A recent report by the scientists of the British, American and German institutes identified global risks which could be triggered by global warming. One of these risks is drying of the Amazon Basin, linked both to logging and global warming. Another one is the damage to Northern pine forests, including those in Siberia, caused, in part, by frequent fires and vulnerability to pests in warmer, drier conditions.[9] And all these may happen earlier than projected in the 2007 report by the UN Climate Panel.

The importance of real economic development—plants, factories, and different enterprises producing goods for popular consumption, should not be underestimated at a time when the economy in some developed countries is slipping into recession. Former Federal Reserve Chairman Alan Greenspan recently said, "Global economic influences today are stronger than almost anything that monetary or fiscal policy can counter them with".[10]

One more point to mention. Objectively speaking in today's Russia we witness the emergence of a new model of economy, characterized by a consolidation of state-led capitalism. Russia, China, some countries of East Asia and Latin America follow this economic policy, which is different from the Anglo-Saxon model, where the state stays out of running business.

According to some recent studies, the developing countries had a 69 per cent share in the incremental growth in the world output in 2006, on a purchase power parity basis. China had a 29 per cent contribution to the incremental world output. The USA and the European Union put together only a 22 per cent share.[11]

One of the reasons for the development of the state capitalism is the growing demand for natural resources to sustain high growth. And the state gets actively involved in allocation of these resources, based on national priorities. All this does not mean that Russia may start closing down its economic boundaries and isolating itself from the rest of the world. I think Russia will continue to share with the rest of the world its culture, knowledge, expertise, and ideas, as well as resources in return of the same from our friends, colleagues and partners. It applies fully to our longstanding and tested friend and strategic partner—India and its people.

Notes and References

1. Zbigniew Brzezinski. *Velikaya shakhmatnaya doska,* Translated by O.Yu. Uralskaya. Moscow: Mezhdunarodniye otnosheniya, 1999. Originally published as *The Grand Chessboard. American Primacy and Geostrategic Imperatives* (Basic Books. A Division of Harper Collins Publishers), p. 108.
2. *Ibid.*, p. 43.
3. Zbigniew Brzezinski, "A Geostrategy for Eurasia", *Foreign Affairs* September/October 1997: 50-64.
4. *Ibid.*, p. 61.
5. John McCain, "An Enduring Peace Built on Freedom. Securing America's Future", *Foreign Affairs* November/December 2007, Campaign 2008.Part lll: 19-35.
6. Ronald D. Asmus, "Europe's Eastern Promise. Rethinking NATO and EU Enlargement", *Foreign Affairs* January/February 2008/*http:www.foreignaffairs.org/20080101*
7. *Ibid.*
8. *The Economic Times*. 05.02.2008.
9. *The Times of India*. 06.02.2008.
10. *The Hindustan Times*. 31.01.2008.
11. *The Economic Times*. 05.02.2008.

14

Imagining a Russia Minus Siberia: Issues and Implications

P.L. Dash

Introduction

In certain academic circles in Moscow, an insinuating thought is being hotly debated, overtly or covertly, but mostly privately, that the Russian Federation faces political instability to the extent of secession. This is not about political instability before the impending presidential elections. It is about Russia getting vivisected by various forces sweeping the country through the post Soviet years. The debaters, mostly academics, political analysts and intellectuals of different hues without any party ideology, argue that in and around St. Petersburg there are rumours spreading about forming a political block comprising of St. Petersburg itself, Karelia and Finland, the Baltic states and the Scandinavian countries. The intention is to form a bigger Balto-Finnsih and Scandinavian, unified complex with common economy and political structure, if not yet state borders; the argument sounds provocatively absurd though. There are, however, rudimentary concepts formations in their inceptive phase demanding such a complex. The future shape of things are yet to come.

In another area, with regard to the Caucasus in the South, there have been growing apprehensions that a strategically important area has already slipped out of the Russian clutch. Much as Russia likes to contain the fissiparous tendencies in that region, it all the more precipitates the situations snowballing into terror right from the heart of Moscow at Nord-Ost theatre that was taken hostage to underground train blasts in Moscow to everyday occurrences in

Chechnya to Beslan where the gruesome tragedy of school children brutally killed by hostage takers two years ago were indeed heart rendering. Precisely, the Caucasus is in ferment, its spiraling effects are felt across Russia. The way Georgians have reelected Mihaiel Saakashvili to power in their January 2008 elections after their November, 2007 street protests has added to further Russian worries because the issues of Abkhazia, Azharia and Ossetia are likely to remain unsettled.

On the other spectrum of former Soviet prefectures, Central Asia and Kazakhstan are by far a separate unstable entity across the underbelly of Russia. Five independent states, who cannot wish away Russia easily, willy-nilly, follow the inevitable for the last fifteen years. Resource rich and dictatorial, with relative political stability and fluctuating economic performance, the Central Asians have been passing through the thrills and frills of their so called post-Soviet democracy. For the Russian Federation, Central Asia assumes a danger zone with the pervasive economic proliferation of China into the region as well as widespread religious proliferation of Islamists from Afghanistan. Thus as long as Central Asia remains sandwiched between dwindling Russian influence and growing Chinese presence and Islamic influence, it remains a danger zone for Russia. Infested with increasing menace from the Islamic fundamentalists and narcotic traffickers, it is all the more an absolute danger zone for all in the periphery, including Russia, China and the Far Eastern periphery.

In the whole swathe of landmass with abundant resources and emaciated demography is Siberia, both east and west of Lake Baikal. The region is vast, largely unpopulated, thoroughly inaccessible and heavily endowed with oil, natural gas, diamond and metal. It is this landmass that has been vital for Russia's growth in recent years. Given that oil prices have soared from just $17 a barrel when Putin came to power eight years ago to $100 a barrel in 2007-2008, Siberia's economic development merits academic discussions and policy debate. However, territorial bickering with the neighbours such as China and Japan had jeopardized the prospects of regional cooperation for development of the region throughout the Soviet years. The two parallel rail links—the Trans-Siberian railway built by the Tsar in early twentieth century and the Baikal Amur railway built by the Soviets through the 1970s—are the only surface connect for the common masses to the region with mainland, European Russia. The airfare from Moscow to any city in the region is prohibitively high and there is countrywide condemnation of Aeroflot fare policy in this regard. The visible mismatch of the region is evident in the enormous natural and mineral endowment vis-à-vis nakedly visible underdevelopment of Siberia and the Far East. Russia has the greatest challenge to overcome this asymmetry in the emerging context of posturing its region to the world and evidently in the context of globalization. Hypothetically, if the Siberian region does not develop fast enough under the Russian dispensation, would it ensue separatist tendency in the area east of Lake Baikal? Will the region fall prey to greater Chinese and Japanese proliferation with a strong intent to create a cooperative platform to tap the resources of the region? Or Will the Siberian region be arena of war over resources? While in the current situation, the first and the last propositions are highly improbable, the middle platform is significantly probable. This paper traces the security implications of many of the ongoing efforts to draw conclusions about the inevitability of Siberia as a resource rich region in the scheme of things to come for regional cooperation minus which there will be unending conflicts and chaos.

Clash of Interests

The Far East and Siberia of the Russian Federation border with five countries—Mongolia, China, North Korea, Japan and the USA. Three of these five countries—China, Japan and the US—are going to play a significant role in shaping future agenda of development in that region simply because contiguous countries, more so if they are economically powerful, play an influential role. The paradox of the Far East is that all these three countries have inherent differences with Russia bequeathed from Tsarist and Soviet eras. Historically, when Alaska was sold to the US in 1860s by Alexander II for a meager sum of $7.5 million, it curtailed Russian naval influence and fishing rights in that region substantially. Russia then and since, has been living with the tantrums of the US that assumed colossal proportions when both were super powers in the Soviet ear. The US has never lost sight of the resources located in Siberia and adjoining areas of the Russian Far east. In the fast changing and globalizing world, the US objectives are still more valid. It does not have any territorial disputes with Russia and wishes to bank on the goodwill to tap Siberia's oil, gas and other resources. In the APEC, the Asia

Pacific forum for economic cooperation, the US-Russian attitude has been synonymous with regard to regional economic cooperation and both countries are well aware of the imperatives of changing times.

The other two countries—Japan and China—are on a different footing with long standing territorial dispute with Russia. The Kurile dispute in Russo-Japanese relations has jeopardized normalcy in economic relations between the two countries. Russian political and military leadership feel that giving away the chain of four disputed islands—Habomai, Shikotan, Itorofu and Kunashiri—to Japan will precipitate two immediate challenges. First, it would open up the Sea of Okhotsk to international navigation, thereby endangering the Russian Far East and posing a strategic and security challenge for Russia to handle. They draw attention to the strategic vulnerability that may cost Russia dear should the island be ceded. And secondly, giving away the Kuriles islands to Japan will generate internal dissensions within Russia with soaring demands for territorial independence elsewhere across the country. But economic cooperation with Japan is inevitable and efforts were made in that direction so as to hold the island disputes in abeyance and proceed ahead with economic cooperation. Tangible results, however, have not followed these efforts and bickering continues to rent bilateral relations.

The other Russian apprehensions center around possible joint US-Japan maneuver in that area to elbow out Russia not only from the Far Eastern and Pacific strategic space, but economically from the Siberia altogether. The efforts the US have been making in the Caspian to bypass Russia and build oil and gas pipelines from Baku in Azerbaijan via Tbilisi in Georgia to Ceyhan and Irzhurum in Turkey has further made Russia suspicious of the US motives. Should it ever allow foreign direct investment in Sakhalin, Khabarovsky Krai and Sakha or consider turning it into a Special Economic Zone with free for all trade facility, the matter should not slip off hands. This apprehension grows stronger day by day and Russia relates gingerly to any development despite all out efforts through Putin years to develop the region through international cooperation. Russia's participation in the APEC is geared in that direction although Russia cannot extricate itself from the regional implications stemming out of the activities of international actors.

China is yet another telling story. China's recent saga of economic boom has several ramifications for the Russian Far East. The vast eastern flank of the Russian Federation east of Lake Baikal is a territory scantly populated. Roughly some seven plus million people, inhibit in the areas in contrast with twenty times more that demographic number living in China. The illegal migration of Chinese to the Russian Far East is a real headache for Russia, and Russia in post-Soviet years, whether under Yeltsin or Putin, has virtually failed to choke the steady flow of Chinese migrants that continues unabated. China's upfront and adroit diplomacy with all its neighbours, mainly with ex-Soviet republics is commendable. It has bought a piece of land from Kyrgyzstan in 1999 near the Bedel pass in Naryn oblast to settle border dispute between the two countries, although it has not been finally settled. It has been actively engaged with Kazakhstan in oil exploration and pipeline politics in ensuring its energy security in a varied way. A direct pipeline has been built between Kazakhstan and China that would supply oil to the Xinjiang province and its adjoining areas. And with the Russians, it has resolved most of the outstanding territorial disputes, save a few islands in the Amur-Ussuri-Argun rivers sector in the Far East.[1]

The rapidity with which Putin has resolved the longstanding Sino-Russian territorial disputes conveys a clear message of bilateral rapprochement. China's growing economic prowess served as a miraculous mismatch with Russia's declining power in general and weakness in the Far eastern sector in particular to precipitate a speedy solution to territorial disputes. Both countries have apparently prioritized economic imperatives to prevail over other unsettling issues and proceeded ahead with relations in tune with the demands of changing time. Further, the globalization priorities have driven the two countries to open up to the outside world and bury the hatchets of the past in their respective backyards. Therefore, most, if not all, pronouncements of the APEC and SCO summits are overtly pro-cooperation and anti-conflict in nature, where both China and Russia are active members.

Thus it is evident that despite a section of Russian intellectuals considering different pockets of their own country infested with the virus of separatism, the world perceives Siberia and the Far East very much as an inalienable part of Russia and takes into consideration its active role as a catalyst of economic growth of that region. On her part Russia too has never shirked back its role from the Far Eastern region. However, the hitch lies in the inadequate attention being paid to that part of the Russian world. The irony of prevailing reality is evidenced in the stark paradox of 75 percent of all natural and mineral wealth concentrated in Siberia and Far East, whereas an equal percentage of all Russian wealth is getting circulated only in its two big cities—capital Moscow and St. Petersburg. And also nearly all industrial enterprises are located west of Lake Baikal, while resources lay east of the lake. Some revamping of the existing scenario is urgently called for in favour of allocation of resources to achieve developmental targets of the underdeveloped Far East and Siberia. When clash of national interest is rapidly paving way to creating a new platform of cooperation, it is undesirable to stick to old conflicts and thereby miss the bus to industrialize the neglected, backward region.

Such a configuration of potential actors in the far Eastern flanks of the Russian Federation creates a peculiar strategic alliance possibilities, where, apparently, Russia and China are getting closer and Japan and the USA work hand in hand to checkmate the growing influence of China as well as to retain Russia weaker with the status quo of its post-Soviet debility. However, China's record economic growth in the last two decades plus Russia's economic bounce back to the limelight dim that prospect of having clear alliance and partners. The Sino-Russian relations through the Putin years have warmed up as never earlier. The Indo-Russian strategic partnership is also a unique phenomenon of mutual alliance. Much as they wish, the US and Japan cannot ignore the weighty role of China and India in the Far Eastern Asian sector of Russia. Nor they can wish away Russia itself easily. Since Japan also wishes to procure energy from Sakhalin, it may spurn any US advances to block its prospects of bettering its relations with Russia. However, the real roadblock is the continuing Russo-Japanese territorial dispute over the Kuriles that stubbornly show no sign of improvement or dying down. Will mutual economic compulsions drive the two countries to a rapprochement and final settlement of border disputes? This is a question that future will throw at us and possibly decide.

Russian Problems

Raging debates within the country that have raised the issue of Russia losing Siberia one day are primarily three: i. inaccessibility of the region, ii. dwindling demography; and iii. inadequate infrastructure. All three aspects are so intrinsically interrelated that one from the other is difficult to differentiate. For centuries Russia has not been able to build a highway between Moscow and Vladivostok, while it has avidly taken away the oil and gas wealth of the region. Professor Stanislav Menshikov, who lives and works in Holland questions the Russian authorities about their true intentions and asks "What sort of developed country you expect of Russia when it does not have a direct Highway linking Moscow with Vladivostok?[2] Road as a means of communication infrastructure is essential for development. And interior Siberia does not have adequate number of highways and link roads to its major cities. In the vast expanse of land stretching across north of the trans-Siberian railway, there are no connecting roads shown in the political maps. In between the space of Trans-Siberian railway and Baikal Amur railway—the two parallel transport lifelines of the Far East—there are few connecting roads. If this has been the lack for centuries, it cannot be overcome overnight. Russia does not seem to have any grand plan of building communication infrastructure in that area too soon because the Russian press is just quiet about development of the region so far.

Far too long has Siberia and the Far East of the Russian Federation been a raw material appendage of Moscow. In post-Soviet years, although Siberia's oil and gas wealth has helped Moscow to garner a huge kitty of more than $256 billion dollars in Consolidation Fund, little of this money is earmarked for Siberia's development beyond the oil and gas sectors. The post-Soviet debate has centered on who should finance the big developmental projects. While the prevailing view predominating the debate points at market taking care of everything, the reality of the matter boils down to a striking tussle between the private and public sector, both throwing the ball at one another to undertake road projects. This rotates the debate around a 'public-private-market merry-go-round' and the state conveniently abdicates its responsibility of infrastructure building in difficult to access areas. Professor Menshikov asserted that "the less the development, the more the nationalism."[3] And conclusively, the longer it takes, the more harmful it will be for Moscow.

The demographic danger is not only visible across the country, but more tangibly discernible in Siberia and in the Far East. The population is scant, cities are few and villages are far too scattered. This author was privy to travel in the twilight of Soviet years from Irkutsk to a village, Ust-Ordinsky by car; and from there to Lake Baikal. It was the onset of autumn at the end of August and the

Taiga was on nature's yellow fire, piercing the mind and thoughts of a traveler from the vantage point of an outsider to observe. In the midst of sylvan Siberia, traveling miles and miles on, one could hardly see a village or town. To locate a filling station was a mind-boggling job, and development was far too behind; still farther was Moscow. I am sure many Russian planners must not have seen those remote, thick, lovely woods, as Robert Frost wrote, "dark and deep". But Russia has her promises to keep. Full of birch and pine trees, intermittently interloped with linden that added a coppery touch to the yellowness, in the entire surroundings, only the meandering Angara was throwing its azure look at us from time to time. Nothing much must have changed since those years. Baikal was marveling at its best in the glistening rays of a slanting sun.

Depopulation is a serious problem for Russia, more so in the far flung areas. In the past few years, it has been reported that some 300 small villages have disappeared altogether from the map of Siberia because over the past 15 years the Russian Far East has lost more than a million people. Inhabitants of these villages have migrated westward to heartland Russia, to more hospitable areas, where opportunities are more and living standard better. Even those who had been sent by the Soviets in a strictly regulated migration system and received pecuniary incentives for going to backward areas to help that area develop, have decided to come back to their respective places of earlier residence. Thus with a tottering demographic figure hovering over 7 million people on a vast territory, Siberia lay sans development, awaiting an opportunity in the future to progress. Whether China with her skilled population and thirst for resources would fill the gap through a Sino-Russian rapprochement for development of the region is yet to be seen. Nothing tangible has been worked out in that direction.

Untapped resources and underlying underdevelopment are due to woeful infrastructure in place. One could say, except in cities, it is the absence of infrastructure that has led to underdevelopment. In recent memory, when Novosibirsk was developed through utter Soviet determination, or port facilities in Vladivostok and Sakhalin were developed for fishing and naval purposes, it was just isolated locale that received attention of the authorities, while a huge expanse from Khanti-Mansi to Chukchi via Sakha and across Khabarovsky Krai lay barren and underdeveloped. Their underdevelopment precipitates the urgency for Russia to pay adequate attention to that area, particularly in the context of a fast globalizing Far East with new actors actively eying the natural resources of the region. The complex interplay of these actors in the regional scenario brings in the question: What if Russia remains minus Siberia? However, that day is not near in foreseeable future, nor it would be feasible for anyone to exclude Russia from Eurasia, particularly from its Far Eastern flank.

Why it is not feasible to exclude Russia from the emerging scheme of things in Siberia and the Far East? Simply because, when the Soviet Union was dismantled, only the political superstructure was demolished and political leadership toppled; and not the economic base. The economic base—a highly rich endowment of Russia, remained intact and virtually unchanged. Foreigners could not gain a foothold on it. Whatever they got they got by manipulating the new superstructure they put in place. The resources were too huge in size to be tapped quickly. Russia was too large a country to penetrate too quickly. This was why with little planning and reorientation, Russia has bounced back from minus four percent annual economic growth rate to a sustained 7 plus percent in recent few years and has been looking forward to future with crimson hopes. Siberia is Russia's backbone and minus Siberia it would be spineless. The leaders know this very well, and therefore would like their country to play a befitting role in that region in the years to come despite any demand for autonomy and independence of that area.

The Kuriles Dispute

What ails Russia's overall picture of bilateral and multilateral conduct in the Far East for over a century is the frosty Russo-Japanese relations over four small chain of islands located close to Japan's Hokkaido island. Historically these islands have alternated possession between Russia and Japan. For Russia these islands provide a protective, security coverage for Sakhalin, the Sea of Okhotsk and Kamchatka peninsula. They also extend Russia's limit of naval access to the Pacific sans which Japan would prevail freely over the Sea of Okhotsk. For Japan it is a question of national pride to regain possession over their northern territories, which they had once owned. This tussle between national pride of Japan and territorial primacy of Russia has led both countries to lock horns with each other, and the matter remains unresolved. As a Japanese scholar, Fuji Kamiya, had written: "the two countries have been consistently out of kilter on the northern territory issue. And as time goes on, the possibility of resolving the issue in Japan's favour is lessened, if indeed it ever existed."[4]

Harking back to the ownership of these islands over the past over hundred years, one sees that the defeat of Tsarist Russia in the Russo-Japanese war of 1905 had taken away these islands from Russian possession. The Portsmouth treaty had vested the possession of these islands with Japan and Japan had retained them until it was defeated in the Second World War in August 1945. Following the declaration of Allied Powers, Stalin had decided to regain firm possession over the Kuriles once and for all, and ever since the dispute continues to becloud the Russo-Japanese relations. The uncompromising position held by both parties in negotiations over the last fifty years has resulted in a virtual stalemate. The outcome of all bilateral negotiations over a period of fifty years have very often weakened the Japanese position to face a hard bargainer like Russia. In the late 1970s as Russia enhanced its troop presence in the Far East, it heightened Japanese security concerns and the territorial issues preoccupied both countries. However, Russia has also often demonstrated flexibility to accommodate some of Japanese aspirations, if not all, which Japan has utilized well to its advantage on time. These were the missed opportunities in mid 1950s, the in late 1960s and then in late 1980s and so on.

The wave of positive changes that began to sweep across East Asia after Gorbachev came to power in March 1985, generated hopes for a settlement. Gorbachev's visit to Japan in 1991 was the first ever any Soviet topmost leader had undertook to Japan. His policy of New Thinking in foreign and domestic policies had virtually replaced old stereotypes in Soviet East Asian policy. And the decade between 1985-1995 witnessed major strategic changes. Russian foreign policy had to grapple with the pangs of transformations within the country and this posed a true global challenge: not one challenge, but simultaneous, as mark Katz described, three challenges such as the Western challenge, the Muslim challenge and the China challenge.[5] One would like to add another challenge and that is the Japan challenge. Two countries—China and Japan have preoccupied Soviet and post-Soviet foreign policy space sizably in recent years. Russia has resolved most of its differences by the end of 1999, particularly the border disputes with China in the Ussuri-Amur sectors. "With the exception of two small areas including Xeixiazi island or Bolshoi Ussuriisky island as it is called on the Russian side, all boundary issues have been basically resolved.[6] Subsequently, during Putin's state visit to China in October, 2004, both countries had signed a supplement to their border agreement that completed the delimitation of boundaries between Russia and China. However, the territorial disputes with Japan have remained unresolved. These disputes, as they continue to engage Russia actively in the Far East, trammel the progress in bilateral relations.

Within Russia, there are three clear pressure groups, favouring or disfavouring the settlement of Kuriles disputes. These pressure groups are: the military, the business tycoons and the political elite. The military argues in favour of Russian strategic advantage in retaining the Kuriles, while the business lobby argues in support of Russia's economic benefit out of greater economic, commercial and technological cooperation with Japan. The political leadership is sandwiched between the two prevailing opinions and the issue perennially evades a solution. Further the hardened attitude of Japan makes betterment of Russia's bilateral relations with Japan hostage to and resolution of the Northern territory dispute. Both countries are so located in an uncompromising predicament that a forecast is difficult to make as to when they would descend down to a compromise. But who know? The way Russia and China settled their border disputes under Putin or even the unexpected way the Soviet Union crumbled to pieces were never foretold by anybody. Russia may throw up a surprise in Russo-Japanese relations too in the years to come.

The Wider Challenge

Although the broad spectrum of problems facing Russia pinpoints at the fundamental questions of Russia's national interests, the real challenges are how to overcome economic underdevelopment of an area vastly endowed with natural resources. Precisely, the potential of Siberia and the Far East awfully mismatch the developmental agenda of Moscow for that region. It is not only the question of administering an inaccessible region and keep on harping on its security and strategic significance, but also pay needful attention to rid off the pathetic underdevelopment. The core developed sectors are oil and gas plus fishing; the rest lay unexplored. What singles out the Far eastern sector in this context are the enormous economic weight the country has to attach to resource rich Siberia and the Far East. Far too long the region has been neglected. With the rise of Asia and the east, time is now most appropriate for the Far East to rise too. When the developmental ethos shifted scene from Europe to Asia, it would not be far off when Russia would concentrate on devising ways for growth of that region. At least the southern flanks across the Mongolian, Chinese borders can be economically developed. In this context, Kamchatka, Sakhalin peninsula and Khabarovsky Krai will be the hub of development. Joint venture potentials are enormous with both Japan and China and Russia could well tap the taper of time to overcome its backwardness and turn its Eastern fringe into an industrial hub. If Japan across the Sea of Okhotsk, can be a prosperous country, why not Russia's Khabarovsky Krai?

Overlooking the region far too long will further raise doubts as much about Russia abdicating its responsibility in that region as about its separation from that area. So far no foreign power has even imagined to distance Russia from the Far Eastern sector. A weak Russia in the years to come may repeat history to share and finally sell away territories as it did under Alexander II with regard to Alaska. Although the possibility looks remote, one could never take for granted the shape of things to come. Dearth of population which one could call virtual depopulation, absence of labour savvy laws to invite migrant workers to the Far East, chary approach to upcoming joint ventures from both Japan and China and other countries, plus lack of focused policy on Siberia and the Far East would further pit a resource rich underdeveloped region against developed Japan and China and very much again their desire to help the region develop. The quicker Russia realizes this contrast its eastern flank has been passing through for years, the better would be its position to look at the overall progress of that area. Focusing only on the military strategic aspects of the Far East without much of economic development may not only mar the prospects of that part of the world to be a part of the globalization process but may also finally turn that region into an arena where all interested countries will scramble for resources; and wars on that basis may not be ruled out.

The unfolding of post-Soviet development in the Far East and the jockeying and lobbying of various actors to regain their influence in the changing scenario are of paramount significance for the future shape of things to come. There is an apparent fear of a rising China. Every country therefore tries to face the China challenge, take measures to counter Chinese moves and make possible alliances bypassing China. However, much as countries do not wish to accommodate the aspirations of China, the Chinese involvement, engagement and meddling has become an inevitable regional factor for consideration. Therefore all major surrounding countries around China—Russia, Japan, the US as well as India and Korea—have their China policy attuned to the changing regional scenario. In this regard, at least two broad groups are at interplay and their emergence is near certain in the regional scheme of things.

The first group at interplay is US-Japan-India to face the growing China challenge in the Far East. In this group everyone has its own interest and all of them put together have the regional agenda of containing China. The second group is Russia-China and India to contain the growing US role not only in the Far East, but also in Central Asia. There are two other subgroups: China and Russia to counter Japan and India and Russia to counter China. The equations in bilateral and multilateral relations within the ambit of regional organizations such as APEC and SCO do not necessarily reflect the mutual competitiveness primarily because there are urgent imperatives for creating a common platform for peace and economic cooperation. All countries are aware of the acute need of striking a balance between conflicting interests and maintaining peace in the region.

Conclusions

To visualize Russia sans a role in Siberia and the Far East is well nigh impossible. To think of Russia minus its sharp focus on the Far Eastern sector is also equally impossible. Those forces who write off Russia's role in the emerging shape of things to come in Siberia and the Far East do not understand the strategic depth Russia enjoys across its territorial expanse stretching across eleven time zones. Russia also understands the nuances of diplomacy to build her relations in tune with her national interests and throughout the Yeltsin and Putin years, Russia has been trying to mend fences with China, to better relations with Japan and also take into account the US presence across its expansive fringes from the Caucasus through

Central Asia to Siberia and beyond to the Far East. Russia has a role that no other country can play in this area.

Settlement of boundary rows and disputes with neighbors has remained a top priority area of negotiation in Russian diplomacy, but Russia is a hard bargainer and its diplomacy bounces back and forth weighing judiciously her national interests. Therefore it is early and unpredictable to think of a Russia minus Siberia or the Far East and vice versa. However, in the discernible horizon, contours of cooperation are visible in the upcoming areas of mutual synergy. And it is this cooperation that matters more than anything else for harmony of the future of Siberia and the Far East.

Notes and References

1. For details, please see Iwashita Akihiro, An Inquiry for New Thinking on the Border Dispute, background of "Historic Success" for the Sino-Russian Negotiations in *Siberia and the Russian Far East in the 21st Century: Partners in the "Community of Asia"* Slavic Research Centre, Hokkaido University, Sapporo, 2005, pp. 95-114.
2. "What Awaits Russia after 20 Years?" The Discussion of Stanislav Menshikov with journalist Yulya Mironova, *Izvestiya*, 28 July, 2007.
3. *Ibid.*
4. Fuji Kamiya, "The Northern Territories, 130 years of Japanese talks with Tsarist Russia and Soviet Union", in Donald S. Zagoria (Ed.), *Soviet Policy in East Asia*, A Council on Foreign relations Book, Yale University Press, New haven, 1882, p. 122.
5. Mark N. Katz, "Russia's Security Challenges", in Iwashita Akihiro, *Eager Eyes Fixed on Eurasia: Russia and its Neighbours in Crisis*, Vol. 1, Salvic Research Centre, Hokkaido University, Sapporo, 2007, pp. 135-147.
6. Ni Xiaoquan, "China's Security Interests in the Russian Far East", in *Siberia and the Russian Far East in the 21st Century*, *op. cit.*, p. 58.

15

Russia's Policy Towards the Asia-Pacific Region in the Post-Cold War Era

Sreemati Ganguli

The Asia-Pacific region, stretching from the Bering Straits in the North Pacific to Cape Horn in South America, is called one of Asia's most complex regions for its economic potentials as well as for its strategic importance. This article attempts to focus on Russia's policies towards two of the most important countries of the region-China and Japan in the post Cold War era and on to what extent, these policies are shaped by the complex inter-relationships among the three major actors in the region—China, Japan and the U.S.

For Russia, the Asia-Pacific region is vital for sustained economic development, particularly for the Russian Far East and Siberia (RFES), and for comprehensive security. The areas where Russia has potentials for serious engagement with the region are trade, supply of energy, arms trade and multilateral security mechanisms.

In 2006, Pacific nations were Russia's second big trading partners after the EU and the bilateral trade have been growing by 20 per cent each year. Over the last three years, the share of 11 countries of the region (China, Japan, North Korea, South Korea, Taiwan, Hong Kong, Singapore, Thailand, Mongolia, Vietnam and India) in Russia's foreign trade increased to 13.4 per cent, as compared to 4.3 per cent with the U.S., Australia and Oceania. Over the next decade, Russia's six major trading partners in the region (China, Japan, North Korea, South Korea, Taiwan and Hong Kong) alone, are expected to account for 20 per cent of Russia's total foreign trade, while the whole region will account for about 30 per cent.[1] The RFES region has an increased importance as a gateway for trade with the Asia-Pacific region-Vladivostok and Khabarovsk have become centres of business contacts, and after the loss of port facilities on the Baltic and Black Seas, the Pacific ports of Vostochniy, Vladivostok, Nakhodka and Vanino have grown in importance for Russian economy. Russian policy-makers, like Dmitri Rogozin, the Head of the Duma Committee on International Affairs and Alexander Losyukov, the Deputy Foreign Minister, stressed on the need for an Asia-Pacific policy to boost economic cooperation with the Russian Far East, as such a policy would boost the economic development of the RFES region as well as would make Russia more economically active in the Asia-Pacific.[2] To Dmitri Trenin, the future of the Russian Far East is going to be Russia's main geopolitical problem of the 21st century. He argued that at the heart of this area's instability is the failure of the traditional mobilization model of development and the delay in achieving development model based on private, mainly foreign capital.[3] This situation demands increased economic interactions between the RFES region and the Asia-Pacific.

The energy resources of Siberia and the energy requirements of two growing economies of China and Japan have catapulted Russia into a major energy power in the Asia-Pacific region. Oil exports from the RFES to the Asia-Pacific is expected to comprise a third of oil shipments abroad in 2020, when Russia expects to supply as much as 310 million tonnes per year to world market, according to a Report by the Russian Natural Resources Ministry. By 2020, Russia plans to explore new fields and produce 80 million tonnes of oil per year in Eastern Siberia. Output from the Sakhalin island shelf off the Pacific Coast is expected to increase to as much as 26 million tonnes per year by 2010, according to the Report.[4] There are a number of proposed pipeline projects between the RFES and APR regions—the China Natural Gas Pipeline, the Japan Natural Gas Pipeline, the mega –ambitious Trans-Asia Pipeline Grid Project from Siberia to North-West Australia, and most important, the East Siberian oil Pipeline. Through a compromise formula on the actual routing of this Pipeline, Russia tried to balance its relations with both China and Japan, as it was finally settled in 2006 that the first phase of the route would start at Taishet and end at Skovorodino and from there, one branch line would go to Daquing in China and another to the Kozmino Bay, to reach the Japanese market. A study by the Asia Pacific Energy Research Centre in 2000 estimated that joint energy projects between the RFES and APR regions could provide a myriad of benefits to both the regions—enhanced energy security, new opportunities for resource development, facilitating foreign capital flows in eastern Siberian region and regional development and cooperation.[5]

While China has registered itself as the biggest client of Russian arms exports (with over $1 billion arms trade annually), Russia has tried to diversify its arms trade partners in the region and Malaysia, Vietnam and Indonesia are increasingly becoming the markets for Russian arms.

Russia faces a number of security challenges in the Asia-Pacific region, signifying the need for Russia to engage itself in constructive multilateral interactions in the region In the Press Meet following the Plenary Meet of the tenth Session of the ASEAN Regional Forum in October 2003, Foreign Minister Igor Ivanov emphasized on two major problems facing Russia in the Asia-Pacific-the struggle against terrorism 'given that from the Asia-Pacific region comes considerable support for the terrorist structures and organizations which operate in the North Caucasus' and the instability in the Korean peninsula.[6] Alexander Ivanov, Head of the Department of ASEAN countries and general Asian issues in the Russian Foreign Ministry, prioritized security threats in the region thus nuclear developments on the Korean peninsula, the U.S. plans for an exclusive Missile Defence System in Asia, the Taiwan problem, challenges of globalization, separatist trends in a number of Asian countries, terrorism and natural disasters.[7] For the Presidential Envoy to the Far Eastern Federal District, Konstantin Pulikovskii,[8] the most important threats are the 'information threat' posed by the lack of mutual information –sharing between the RFES and the APR regions and the continued problems in energy and its transportation. As the solution of these problems require multilateral engagement and involvement, Russia has activated its interactions with all the important multilateral organizations in the region—the ARF, the ASEAN +10 Post – Ministerial Conferences, SCO and APEC. It is also in the process of involving itself in the Council for Security Cooperation in the Asia-Pacific (CSCAP), Northeast Asia Cooperation Dialogue (NEACD), the BOAO Forum for Asia, the Asia Cooperation Dialogue (ACD), the Asia-Europe Meeting Mechanism (ASEM) and the East Asian Community.

However, prospects of Russia's engagement are fraught with uncertainties as there are areas of disagreement between Russia and the other three major actors in the Asia-Pacific region:

Though China is Russia's main partner in trade and chief market for its energy and arms supplies, but there are suggestions for Russia to be cautious of China's growing economic as well as demographic reach in the RFES region. Also, the ultimate routing of the East Siberian Pipeline shows that Russia wants to balance its relations with China, by developing relations with Japan, so as not to let China have an economic advantage as a monopolist consumer of Russian energy in the Asia-Pacific region.

The issue of four Kurile islands/Northern Territories remain the major irritant in Russo-Japan relations. As the Sea of Okhotosk remains a strategic area for Russia, the Kurile islands of Habomai, Shikotan, Etorofu and Kunashiri provide a protection against American Anti-Submarine Warfare. According to Russian military and naval commanders, both these islands and the Russian Far East still are on the list of potential targets by the U.S. Navy. Another area of major concern is the possibility of a blockade of the Le Perouse (Soya) strait by the U.S. Navy, which would disrupt sea-lines of communication between the Russian mainland, Sakhalin island and the Kamchatka Peninsula. So, the return of these islands by Russia to Japan would drastically alter the strategic balance in the North-West Pacific and that would not be in favour of Russia.[8a] And the fact remains after so many Declarations, like the Tokyo Declaration of 1993, the 1997 Hashimoto Declaration, the 1998 Moscow Declaration and the Programme for Cooperative Exploration of the South Kuriles of 2000, to name a few,[8b] the issue is still far from being resolved. Also, Russia's conventional forces deployed in the Russian Far East and Russian naval presence in the Sea of Okhotosk are perceived as threats[9] to Japan's security.

The Russian SSBN Bastion in the Sea of Okhotosk in the North Pacific continues to be the significant strategic area of concern for the U.S. in the North Pacific region and the major justification for its increasing naval activities and cooperation with the Japanese Maritime Self-Defence Forces in the area. On the other hand, the U.S. policies have made Russia more serious of its commitment to protect the Sea of Okhotosk and strategic sea-passages in the area. The technological capabilities of Russian strategic forces and the so-called 'capable to destroy' syndrome (meaning Russia is the only country capable of destroying the U.S.) have made U.S.-Russian strategic relations more complicated in the North Pacific region. The contiguity of both the U.S. and Russia to the region is vitally important for the strategic significance of the region. As the 1992 Presidential Report to the U.S. Congress 'A Strategic Framework for the Asia-Pacific Rim' indicated that 'the residual power projection capability of Russian naval and air forces—stationed close to our Northeast Asian allies—in Siberia and Russian Northeast Asia remains a major concern. In addition Russia retains a formidable nuclear arsenal which must still be factored in our strategic calculus'.[10]

Interplay of Interests

The Asia-Pacific region plays an increasing role in the global economy, it accounts for about 60 per cent of the world's production, 50 per cent of its trade and 48 per cent of total global investments. It is justifiably called 'the region of the 21st century' and the' locomotive of global economy'. This economic importance of the region has made it strategically significant and has induced the four powers into inter-relationships among themselves. In the context of the complex dynamics of interactions among these powers, reciprocal hedging through clever use of diplomacy and military cooperation is evident. We will now look into the inter-relationships among the other three powers, which Russia has to take into consideration while formulating its own policies towards this region.

For the U.S., the Asia-Pacific region is 'a place of great geopolitical consequence' as its trade with the region surpasses that with Europe, with more than $500 billion in trade and more than $150 billion in investment, and as this region consists of some of the most critical sea-lanes. This is evident in the Rand Corporation Report 'The Role of South-East Asia in US Strategy Toward China' (2000), which commented that 'Economic growth in the region, which is important to the economic security of the US, depends on preserving American presence and influence in the region and unrestricted access to sea-lanes'.[11] The U.S. also maintains an impressive military presence in the region—the U.S. Pacific Command (PACOM) interacts with 14 of the 45 countries of the region; it has a troop-strength of 1,00,000 (with 60,000 based in Japan, 37,000 in South Korea and the rest in Guam); and has bilateral military alliances with Australia, Thailand and the Philippines and access or basing rights with Malaysia and Singapore. The security and economic potentials of the energy resources of Alaska region is another vital incentive for the U.S. to involve itself in the Asia-Pacific region. The 2005 assessment by the U.S. Geological Survey estimated that there are undiscovered but technically recoverable mean resources of 4 billion barrels of oil, 37.5 trillion cubic feet of gas and 478 million barrels of natural gas liquids in the Central Alaska North Slope and the adjacent offshore. According to the Arctic Energy Office, the North Slope is estimated to have a total oil-in-place resource, including undiscovered but technically recoverable oil of 100 billion barrels, over 200 tcf. of gas and 5 trillion metric tons of coal.[12]

Notably, Z. Brezezinski's 'The Grand Chessboard' has been instrumental in laying the groundwork for a compelling vision of U.S.' vital global interests in the post-Cold War era. For him Eurasia, extending from Lisbon to Vladivostok, is the 'grand chessboard' on which the struggle for global supremacy continues to be played and hence, it necessitates an integrated U.S.' Eurasian geostrategy. This geostrategy, according to him, purports to forestall five worst possible scenarios and of these, two are related to our topic—first, Russia's alliance with China in the east and second, an eventual consolidation of Sino-Japanese interests.[13]

Mutual strategic balancing between the U.S., the traditional dominant power and China, the rising power, for gaining influence in the region offers a most interesting scenario. For the U.S., two core questions remain regarding China's present status—whether China is a revisionist state or not and its future intentions—whether China will venture to challenge the regional or even the global power order with increase in its economic and military capabilities: by purchasing power parity (ppp) standard, China's share of global GDP has grown from less than 5 per cent in 1980 to approximately 16 per cent in 2006, second only to the U.S. and China's global exports, from $150 billion in 1996 to almost $1 trillion in 2006. Also, China is the fourth largest market for U.S. exports and China is the largest source of U.S. imports. China's military modernisation programme, focussing on developing a leaner force to fight shorter high-intensity wars, is another cause of worry for the U.S.—Beijing has downsized its force from 4.2 million to 2.3 million in 2005, and is in the process of developing a blue-water navy and of upgrading its air force with Russian-built SU-30 and indigeneously developed fourth-generation F-10 aircrafts.

Some of the important policy documents of the U.S. government like Security Cooperation Guidance of the Department of Defence and Quadrennial Defense Review called for 'influencing strategic directions of key powers',[14] referring to China. Ashley Tellis also suggested to 'cultivate ties' with India and key allies in Southeast Asia 'to create structural constraints' to discourage Beijing 'from abusing its growing regional power'.[15]

The U.S. took steps to increase its defence ties and security cooperation with a number of South-East Asian countries like Singapore, Thailand, the Philippines, Indonesia and even Vietnam to balance China's regional influence. But Japan remains the most important ally of the U.S. strategy of strategic balancing or hedging of China. To that end, the U.S. even supported Constitutional reforms to allow expansion of Japan's military potentials. It was evident in the participation of Japan in the U.S.-Thai-Singaporean 'Cobra Gold' military exercise in 2005 and in the U.S.-Japan military –technical cooperation, particularly in the joint technology research on the Navy Theatre –Wide Defence (NTWD) missile defence systems under the TMD (Theatre Missile Defence) Programme of the U.S. The proposal of creating 'greater policy coordination, including studies on bilateral cooperation in dealing with situations that may emerge in the areas surrounding Japan' under the U.S.-Japan Joint Declaration of April 1996 as also the commitment of this bilateral alliance to ensure peace and security in the Taiwan Straits, under their Joint Declaration of February 2005 bear testimony of Japan's role as the so-called 'northern anchor' of the U.S.' Asia-Pacific policy.

China and Japan have areas of disagreement like the territorial disputes over the Senkaku/Diaoyudao islands and the continental shelf in the East China Sea, over the sea-lanes in the South China Sea, the security situation in the Taiwan Straits and TMD issue. But for both, the most important point of difference arises from their respective search for influence in the region-while Japan sees China as a 'threat' to its future leadership role, for China Japan is its main strategic rival. Another concern for China is the growing militarism in Japan's foreign policy: the U.S.-Japan security cooperation; Japan's participation in the TMD programme; the factor of ambiguity in these programmes as to whether the geographical area of application of these include China or even Taiwan; and the Japanese government's attempts to reinterpret the Constitution to allow Japan to engage in collective self-defence with the U.S. All this, according to Chinese scholars 'increased the capacity of the U.S. military to intervene in the Asia-Pacific...[for] without Japan as a forward base, U.S. military forces would have to retreat east to Hawaii and south to Australia'.[16]

However, for China, the U.S. efforts to contain the rise of China remain the most serious threat. This was supported in the 'Study Reports on the International Situation-1997-98' where Yan Xuetong of CICIR warned of potential conflicts between the U.S. and China as a 'desperate' U.S. struggled to maintain its leading position vis-à-vis a rising China.[17] In a move to counterbalance, China has made efforts to expand its circle of allies in the region—like the increase of trade relations, the deepening of relations with ASEAN, the expansion of bilateral military ties, particularly with Indonesia and the Philippines and the cultivation of economic interdependence with Japan (as between 1993-2004, Japan was China's largest foreign trade partner, and is now third after the EU and the U.S.). All these moves are aimed at presenting China in a less threatening light to the regional countries so that any probable confrontational U.S. gesture towards China could garner support from very few of them.

Japan tries to balance its relations with both China and the U.S. through subtly distancing itself from the triangular U.S.-China-Japan vortex, by economically (through trade) and politically (through cooperating in regional multilateral fora) engaging China as also through 'power balancing'[17a] of China, by developing a number of bilateral relationships with neighbouring countries like Myanmar, Vietnam, two Koreas, India and significantly Russia. Japan's 'Eurasian Diplomacy' as well as 'Silk Road Initiatives', pursued since 1997, are aimed at engaging Russia as also the Central Asian and Caucasus states through various trade and energy initiatives.

There is no denying the fact that China and Russia do share major mutual concerns, like the NATO actions in Yugoslavia without the UN mandate, the TMD issue and the issue of U.S. military bases in Central Asia. And their strategic partnership, in a way, connotes their preference for a multipolar world order, as has been reiterated time and again by their Declarations, like the 1996 Shanghai Agreement for a strategic 21st century partnership, the 1997 Joint Declaration on the Multipolar World and Emerging New International Order, the 2001 Treaty of Friendship and Cooperation and the 2005 Declaration on the World Order in the 21st Century. If we take note of these Declarations, alongwith the Statement issued by the SCO (a Russo-Chinese joint initiative) in 2005, calling for the specification of a timetable for the U.S. withdrawal from Central Asia and the joint naval exercises, codenamed 'Peace Mission 2005', in Shandong Peninsula in the Yellow Sea under the aegis of SCO, all this becomes significant in the context of the regional security framework in the Asia-Pacific.

Simultaneously, there is a growing trend of advancing mutual cooperation between the U.S. and Russia. During the immediate period after the disintegration of the USSR, the U.S. seemed to be reluctant to recognize a weakened Russia as a power to reckon with in the region. Like the Chapter 'How We Can Influence the Future' in the 1993 White house Report 'National Security Strategy of the United States' did not mention Russia in the U.S.' future scheme for Russia, as also the Report 'Defense Strategy for the 1990s: The Regional Defense Strategy' by Dick Cheney, the Secretary of Defense in 1993.[18] But there has been a perceptible change in U.S. stance regarding Russia's role in the evolving security order in the Asia-Pacific region. It has been suggested by scholars[18a] to involve Russia in existing multilateral security and economic organizations in the region and to develop a Northeast Asian security organization to manage power-equations among the U.S., Russia, Japan, Korea and India. Notably, two Conferences, held by APCSS in 2003 and 2005 respectively (the last one in collaboration with the Far Eastern National University of Vladivostok) focused on U.S.-Russian perspectives on security in the Asia-Pacific region. Two of its most significant recommendations included U.S.-Russian joint cooperation in transnational, economic and ecological security challenges facing the Russian Far East and joint consultations on issues influencing regional transformation in the area.[19]

Conclusion

The debate over Russia's European or Asian character has been one of the central themes in Russia's foreign policy, though there also has been a trend to strike a balance between these two identities. As V.I. Lenin commented that geographically, economically and historically, Russia is not only a European country, but an Asian one as well. President M. Gorbachev's ways of balancing the USSR's pro-West approach to find a 'Common European Home' with his gestures to the East, like the famous Vladivostok Speech of 1996 and the Krasnoyarsk Speech of 1988 to search an Asian identity for the Soviet Union is significant.

After the disintegration, this search for a balancing 'Euro-Asian' identity for Russia lost momentum during the Atlanticist period under Foreign Minister A. Kozyrev. But a number of events that followed, notably, the expansion of NATO to include the post-Communist East European states, NATO's war against Yugoslavia, the NMD initiative by the U.S., the positioning of the U.S. military bases in Central Asia during the U.S. 'war on terror' campaign in Afghanistan and the Iraq War-compelled Russia to look towards its East, the Asia-Pacific region in particular, to stay relevant in global politics. Some scholars like Richard Sakwa[20] commented that the debate over the orientations of the Russian foreign policy was mainly a debate 'over the attitude towards and meaning of 'West' and 'East'. For him, there developed a 'multilayered' approach over the identity and perception of the East among the scholars and he focused on three of the most significant approaches. According to the first, the East is a 'zone of geopolitical contestation and affirmation', where a Sino-Russian strategic partnership is presented as an attempt to counterbalance the West. The second one concentrates on the geo-economics of the East, as the Pacific Rim has overtaken the Atlantic basin as the centre of global economic activities and recommends more economic engagement of the Asia-Pacific region with the under-developed Russian Far East. The third approach represents the East in a geo-ideological mode, where the East represents 'not only a spiritual alternative to Western materialism but a broader alternative to the West in general'. In this article, the East, particularly the Asia-Pacific region, is presented from both the geopolitical and geo-economic perspectives, but the article does not approach the issue of Russia's involvement in the region in a simplistic, linear mode of so-called East-West binary as there are innate competitions among the states in the region as well and also between them and Russia.

In the post-Cold War era, Russia struggled to adjust itself to its own diminished status, both economically and strategically. The situation had a strange resemblance with the global realities prevailing in the post-Crimean war, post-Paris Treaty world in 1856 when Russia had to agree to the demilitarisation of the Black Sea. Then Alexander Gorchakov, the Foreign Mister of Tsar Alexander II, tried to reorient Russia's foreign policy with the aim of a return to great power status through the use of predictable and non-aggressive diplomacy to build favourable alliances in order to 'reduce and eliminate the distance between the existing status quo and the acceptable order'. Notably, Russian Foreign Minister Igor Ivanov commented, at the MGIMO Gorchakov Lectures in May 2000, that 'we have started not only to interpret, but also to implement his

(Gorchakov's) legacy which is remarkably suited to (our) current tasks'.[21] Russia's preference for a multipolar world order, in place of the existing largely unipolar one, requires Russia to stay relevant in regions that are economically and strategically significant. For Russia, the Asia-Pacific area is such a region.

Notes and References

1. Cited from Timofei Bordachev, 'Asia's Future and Russia's Policy', Russia in Global Affairs, No. 3, July-September 2006, *http://eng.globalaffairs.ru/* printever
2. Press Sluzhba Gosduma, RF, 9 December 2000, cited in Leszek Buszynski,, 'State Consolidation and Foreign Policy in Russia' in E. Friedman-S C Kim (ed), *Regional Cooperation and Its Enemies in Northeast Asia,* Routledge, London, 2006.
3. D. Trenin, 'The Asian Vector in Moscow's Strategy', *Nezavisimaya Gazeta*, 27 October 2003.
4. Cited in *Russia, America and Security in the Asia-Pacific, www.apcss.org*
5. APERC, Institute of Energy Economics Natural Gas Pipeline Development in Northeast Asia, April 2000, cited in Anna V. Shkuropat, *New Dynamics in Northeast Asia: The Russian Factor*, August 2002, *www.strategicstudiesinstitute.army.mil/pdffiles*
6. Transcript of the MEET, June 18 2003, *http://www.mid.ru*
7. Interview to ITAR-TASS, 12 April 2005, *http://www.mid.ru*
8. Izvestiya, 23 July 2002, cited in Rouben Azizian, 'Russia and the Asia-Pacific: Trends, Threats, and Common Threads' in *Russia, America and Security in the Asia-Pacific, www.apcss.org*

8a. VI Ivanov, 'Russia and the United States in Northeast Asia and the Russian East', in T. Akala (ed) *Politics and Economics in the Russian Far East: Changing Ties with Asia*-Pacific Routledge, London, 1997.

8b. See Yuri Tsyganov, *Russian Policy* Toward *Northeast Asia: In Search of A New Approach*, CERC Working Paper Series, University of Melbourne, 2/2003.

9. See N. Yamaguchi, 'The Future of the U.S.-Japan Security Relations' in Mike Mochizuki *et al., Japan and the United States: Troubled Partners In A Changing World*, Institute for Foreign Policy Analysis, Cambridge, 1991.
10. '*A Strategic Framework for the Asia-Pacific Rim*', Report to the Congress 1992, Office of the Assistant Secretary of Defense for International Security Affairs (East Asia and Pacific Region).
11. Cited in *http://www.converge.org.nz/abc/2003*
12. Oil and Gas Assessment of Central North Slope, Alaska, 2005, *http://pubs.usgs.gov/fs/2005*

13. Zbignew Brezezinski, *The Grand Chessboard: American Primacy and Its Geostrategic Imperatives*, Basic Books, New York, 1997.
14. U.S. Department of Defense and U.S. Department of State, 'Foreign Military Training oin Fiscal Years 2004 and 2005' Volume 1', 2005, *http://www.state.gov/t/pm/rls/rpt*
15. Ashley J Tellis,'Indo-US Relations Headed For a Grand Transformation?' YaleGlobal, July2005, *http://yaleglobal.yale.edu*
16. Lu Guangye, 'Going Against The Tide of History, Threatening World Peace', *FBIS-CHI-1999-0617*, 18 June, 1999.
17. See *http://*globalsecurity.*org*/military/library/*report/2000*
17a. See Reinhard Drifte, *Japan's Security Relations with China Since 1989*, RoutledgeCurzon, London, 2003.
18. See Vladimir S. Ivanov, 'Russia and the United States in Northeast Asia and the RUSSIAN Far EAST' in Tsuneo Akaha (ed) *Politics and Economics in the Russian Far East: Changing Ties with Asia-Pacific*, Routledge, London, 1997.
18a. See Evan S. Medeiros, 'Strategic Hedging and the Future of Asia-Pacific Stability', *The Washington Quarterly*, Winter 2005-06.
19. See Executive Summary, 'Russia and Russian Far East: Transnational Security and Regional Coopeartion,' 2003 and Executive Summary, 'United States' and Russian Perspectives on Asia-Pacific Security', 2005, *http://www.apcss.org/core/Conference*
20. Richard Sakwa, 'Putin's Foreign Policy: Transforming 'the East', in Gabriel Gorodetsky (ed) *Russia Between East and West*, Frank Cass: London, 2003.
21. Both these quotations cited from Flemming Spidsboel-Hansen, 'Past and Future Meet: Aleksandr Gorchakov and Russian Foreign Policy', *Europe-Asia Studies*, 54(3), 2002.

16

Asiatic Vector of Soviet Economic Policy*

E.T. Artemov

The most important feature of the Russian state is its huge unevenly populated territory. In addition to this, its other characteristics are different conditions of economic management, multi-ethnicity and multi-confessional nature of its population which has preserved the «historical codes» of various civilizations and cultures. Hence follows the natural economic and technological heterogeneity of space as well as differences in the standard and quality of people's lives that are different in different territories. These heterogeneities pose as a potential threat to the sustainable development of Russian statehood and Russian society. The problem is heightened at critical junctures of history. This initiates a political struggle often due to diametrically opposite views about an optimally acceptable national and territorial policy as well as a regional policy.

That is what exactly happened after the collapse of the Soviet Union. The Soviet policy of assimilation and development of the entire space under its control, the essence of which was to shift production and population to the east, was declared as flawed. The effect of ideological, military-strategic and political-military imperatives of the "totalitarian state", which consciously sacrificed "effective development of the economy and especially the social sphere", was accounted for that.[1] The space was proclaimed as a "scourge" of Russia. "We give to our immense space much more than what we get from them, as if they suck out the juice from the organism of the country, constantly pushing her to the path of extensive development. Had there been an ocean splashing beyond the Urals, then Russia would have long become a full-fledged member of the community of civilized nations. The question is of course, not to renounce one or the other spaces. The question is about the

* Translated by Susmita Bhattacharya, Fellow, MAKAIAS, Kolkata

awareness of their role, positive and negative, in the country's development, of the need to reduce the burden of expenses and increase the economic and social effects through sound regional policy and making right geopolitical decisions.[2] Hence, the need for a new development strategy followed. In a number of works, it has been referred to as the concept of compression of intensively utilised space. In practice, this should mean changing the vector of regional development from the east to the west, and a transition to a strategy of prioritizing 'improvement' of the European part of Russia. It is suggested to be selective about focused development in the east concentrating on areas rich in oil, gas, gold and other resources.

Today similar and even more radical ways to relieve the "spatial burden" of Russia are being discussed globally. A number of analysts see the solution to this problem in some variations of 'internationalisation' of the Far North, Siberia and the Far East. Even the opinions about the need to separate Siberia are being expressed. Naturally, these views are not supported by Russian researchers, publicists and politicians. Nevertheless, the idea of restricting the 'frontier' and 'internationalization' of development of the eastern regions is still dominant. These concepts are being used in preparing policy documents. This is mentionable especially in the case of formalising the draft concept of sustainable development of Arctic zones of the Russian Federation, where the main hydrocarbon deposits are concentrated.[3] It is considered as raw material reserve as well as biosphere resource of worldwide significance. Hence, here there is a policy of focused development, encouraging outflows of "surplus" people and rejection of integrated regional development, etc.

There are certainly definite reasons behind such suggestions. But they hardly can be considered indisputable. Obviously there has to be some comparisons of different approaches and viewpoints. An analysis of previous strategies and practices of development of the eastern regions demands special attention. Only an objective assessment of their strengths and weaknesses will help us to understand the root of contemporary problems, identify the best strategy for the future taking into account the logic of long-term changes of Russian statehood and Russian society.

From this point of view it is appropriate to look into the Soviet policies of development of the eastern regions in the context of a long term historical perspective. First of all, it should be noted that their origins stretch back to the distant past. Two and a half centuries ago the famous Russian scholar M.V. Lomonosov stated, 'The might of Russia will increase through Siberia and the Arctic Ocean'. It was a very bold prognosis but was based on the objective existing realities. Starting from the second half of the 16th century the country actively began to assimilate huge expanses lying to the east of its historical heartland. Within the next hundred years it annexed territories which area-wise exceeded those of central and western Europe. Nonetheless, the main orientation of political and economic expansion of the Russian state for the next three centuries was towards the west and south. Here however, its interests clashed with the interests of neighbouring countries who were her geopolitical rivals. It provoked permanent military and political conflict which necessitated huge resource backup.

In contrast to the west and south the path to the east and north-east was open in political sense. But economic assimilation of the annexed territories once again was not an easy job. First of all it was hindered by the natural, geographical and climatic factors. The enormous space of the Urals, Siberia and the Far East was not congenial for living and carrying out energetic economic activity. Their assimilation demanded time, huge expenses were involved and purposeful efforts were necessary for constructing a network of stable transport communications. Hence a specific assimilation policy for the eastern periphery was drafted. This policy was orientated towards utilization of easily available natural resources. It was the military-strategic imperatives and requirements of the central regions of the country that determined the character of economic involvement. Such an approach may be referred to as semi-colonial, since Asiatic Russia was considered as a resource of development of the 'metropolis'.

The overall policy of assimilation of the eastern regions changed in due course, especially in the 19th and 20th centuries. The changes were carried out within the framework of "capitalist industrialization" and its ideologue was the famous political figure S. Yu. Witte. He enunciated the so-called "Trans-Urals plan" of economic development, envisaging rapid construction of transport infrastructure in the Asiatic part of Russia, establishment of new fuel energy and metallurgical enterprises here, mass resettlement of the "surplus" rural population to this area from the European regions.[4] Such strategy of economic assimilation of the eastern regions was influenced by both internal and external factors. On the one hand, there was a calculated move to achieve rapid economic growth and to remove obstacles in the path of social development (in particular, to solve the problem of agrarian resettlement in European Russia). On the other, to consolidate the military, strategic and economic position in the Far East and Central Asia that were experiencing the growing pressure of the neighbouring states and world powers.

The critical situation in the western frontiers also motivated Russia to increase the productive potential of the Urals and Siberia. This mindset was specially observed during the First World War period. The eastern regions were considered as a natural place for establishing "rear fortified sectors" that could sustain the country's war industry. But there was not enough time for actualizing the ambitious schemes. The shocks of the Revolution stood in the way of such methods. They were reanimated in the 1920's and the 1930's when the Bolshevik regime took the course of forced growth of economic, military and political power of the Soviet state. Despite proclamations about discontinuities from the past, the Soviet regional economic policy indicated sufficient continuity with pre-revolution projects.[5] The eastern regions were considered as a prospective source of natural resources and as a rear region with respect to external frontiers especially the west. Therefore the strategy of assimilation was aimed at building separate production enclaves here, the products of which were oriented towards domestic consumption connected with strengthening military and economic potential. The classic Stalinist variant of Soviet development emphasised this Antarctic, militarist component of regional policy. As a result, up to the 20th century the economic assimilation of Asiatic Russia was carried out in a selective manner with little consideration for the exclusive needs of the regions.

The Soviet economic system created pre-conditions for realizing such a policy. It was bent on implementing the strategy without consideration of the expenses. It was based on the monopoly status of state property and centralized distribution of resources. In their opinion such an approach was workable especially when priority tasks were less in number. As early as in the 1930s the large-scale projects, at that time solely concerning the eastern regions, were based in the Urals and Siberia. Ore and coal resources received prime attention and the new fuel and metallurgical base was built that entailed a complex build up of machines and chemical productions. There was a spurt of railway ventures (Turksib, that started from the Urals and the Kuzbass), aiming to strengthen inter-regional connectivity (European and eastern regions as well as Central Asian republics). Nonetheless, by a rough estimate the share of the Asiatic Russia in industrial production of USSR increased from 6 to 7 per cent to 16 per cent in 1930s.[6] During the same years the construction of a large industrial base started in Central Asia which was the southern belly of USSR's macro zone. On the one hand industrialization in Central Asia was motivated by the need to situate industrial enterprises in close proximity to the resource reserves of raw materials. On the other it was regarded as a means to overcome the 'economic and cultural backwardness' of the regions. The latter concept as a matter of fact, reflected the aspirations to highlight social homogeneity of the country and thereby consolidate the position of the ruling regime.

During the Second World War period the predominance of the eastern vector in the regional economic policy was fully manifested. The temporary loss of the vast territories close to its western frontiers accounted for this Soviet policy. The role of the eastern regions sharply increased. Hundreds of enterprises were shifted here from the European part of the country and the main capital building process started here. Urals, Siberia and Privolzh'e became the nucleus of the war economy of the USSR. The Central Asian republics with their substantially consolidated industrial base were also part of it.[7]

In the post-First World War decade, there was prospective planning of the country's economic development and largely on the basis of pre-War schemes. Expansion of the productive base and defence sectors of the industry was prioritised. The economic assimilation of the eastern regions was precisely geared to such interests. The Angara-Yenisei region's developmental programme was announced as priority task. The areas rich in hydrocarbon resources and with a prime concentration of minerals were chosen as prime construction sites of power-consuming industries. Large-scale ambitious programmes were implemented in the war industry and primary attention was given to 'the sword and shield' nuclear missile building. In this connection three plants were erected in the Urals for working on related materials. Later on primary enterprises for producing nuclear supplies and nuclear ammunitions were built, scientific research and experimental designing centres were established and so on. The decisions to construct them were primarily guided by security issues, availability of strong electro-energy base and rich water resources and the possibility of attracting skilled labour forces. In other words, these enterprises were sort of war-industry enclaves in the regional economic complexes and were significant in terms of additional reserve of resources.

Nevertheless, a definite transformation of the Soviet regional policy took place in the mid-1950s due to both internal and external factors. The Soviet Union turned out to be a world super power. It reached a position comparable to the United States in terms of national income standards, level of industrial production and competing appreciably in the realm of science and technology as the leading sectors. However, it did not mean that there were no problems. The systematic redistribution of resources in favour of basic and defence industry made other sectors lifeless. The agrarian sector, the productivity of consumer goods and the social sphere reached rather low standards. Simultaneously there was the need to re-energise especially because the society was exhausted by a perennial 'emergency situation'. Thus, the consumer-oriented constituent emerged in Soviet economic strategy alongside the drive to sustain the war-industry. It was premised on the twin factors of improving the living standards of the population and simultaneously intensifying the defence component. It may be said that the policy of creating a socialist analogy of "consumer society", popular in the western countries, was formulated.[8]

The change in general strategy entailed a shift in the regional policy. The necessity of a complex approach in the development and distribution of the productive forces for solving the social problems was conceived of. The consolidation of positions of the local bodies, i.e. the party organs in the structure of state administration began which contributed to the making of a new course of action, exemplified by the reform of the Sovnarkhoz or the Council of National Economy. Nonetheless the attitude towards the eastern regions as a strategic rear and support-base of deficient raw materials remained unchanged. It was especially visible during the assimilation of western Siberian oil and gas province. The country acquired powerful resources from these sectors which could be utilized in solving regional and state problems. However this option was utilized irrationally. The growth of oil output and its export without looking at the expenses, became the priority. The foreign exchange that was earned was directed to seal the loopholes in Soviet economy: the purchase of provisions, equipment, consumer goods from outside, increase in the financial base of arms race became redundant measures of foreign policy.[9] Such a policy resulted in socio-economic disproportions and limited the opportunities of the eastern regions to utilize their potential as prospective partners. The failure to fulfil the desired objective of development in comparison to other sectors created further complications.

Similar problems were observed in the southern macro zone of the USSR. It had its own specific features. Earlier the country had two separate segments: the west and the east, detaching backward regions in the east. A different scheme was observed during the last years of the Soviet Union. It envisaged detachment of the European territories and the Urals (now referred to as "old industrial" regions), Siberia and the Far East, Kazakhstan and Central Asia.[10] Such a scheme quite completely reflected the existing diversity in the conditions of management and the content of regional policy. The high rate of population growth and labour resources were the distinctive features of the southern macro region. Therefore there were the attempts to develop primarily the labour-intensive sectors. Simultaneously separate branches of the agrarian sector developed intensively especially cotton culture. Cotton production had immense strategic significance for the economy of the USSR. The border location of the Central Asian republics played an outstanding role in the socio-economic planning. Efforts were made to utilize them as 'springboards' for increasing political and ideological influence of the Soviet Union among Third World countries. Hence attention was given to their achievements in the social sphere, preservation of cultural heritage and the build up of a suitable infrastructure, expansion of transport communication system etc. As far as participation in the international labour market was concerned, there was hardly any change in the eastern regions of the country up to the 1970's or later.[11] The state monopoly in foreign economic relations did not give exclusive opportunity to the regions to realize their competitiveness in world economic relations.

The Soviet regional policy was derived from the system of political and economic relations in the country. But radical changes at the end of the 20th century did not mean negation to former practices. The fact is that the Russian society changes very little with time. The specificity of its culture and national character of the population are recognizable. The mechanisms of social organizations also function in the similar way. The geopolitical and geo-economic position of the country is retained. In such a situation it may be predicted that the former policy of economic assimilation of the eastern regions would continue. Despite the emergence of numerous autonomous units of economic activity, a decisive role is played by the state which gives absolute priority to the national (as considered by the ruling elite) requirements. Its development policy will be accompanied by intensification of the Asiatic orientation in the foreign economic and foreign policy spheres. The latest practical moves by the Russian leaders support the sustainability of such a trend. They do not envisage "internationalisation" of Siberia. But to talk about the idea of the latter's exclusiveness from Russia, it can hardly be taken seriously. If such a scenario is implemented, it will at least already become a different country with different identity. It can be referred as Moskovia, but not Russia.

Notes and References

1. Yurii Pivovarov, "Alternativnaya kontseptsiya makroregional'nogo razvitiya Rossii: szhatie intensivno ispol'zuemogo prostranstva", *Mir Rossii* 2 (1996):63.
2. A. Traivish and V. Shuper, "Teoreticheskaya geografiya, geopolitika i budushcheye", *Svobodnaya mysl'*, 12 (1992), 22.
3. S.E. Akekseev, E.T. Artemov, and V.P. Timoshenko, "Arktika i Rossiya: strategiya budushchego", *Nauka, Obshchestvo, Chelovek, Vestnik Uralskogo Otdeleniya RAN* 3, 2005, pp. 3-6.
4. Dmitrii Gavrilov, "Ural, Rossiiskii Sever, Sibir' i Dal'nii Vostok v "zauralskom plane" S.Yu. Vitte, In *Gornozavodskoi Ural XVII-XX vv., edited by* D.V. Gavrilov Ekaterinburg: URO RAN, 2005, pp. 498-253.
5. A.A. Dolgoluk and A.I. Timoshenko. Proyekty kompleksnogo khozyaistvennogo osvoyeniya Sibiri v XX v. In *Vostochnye regiony Rossii: Strategiy i praktika osvoenii,* Novosibirsk: Nauka-Tsentr, 2006, pp. 252-253.
6. Vladimir Mozhin, (ed.) *Planirovanie razmeshcheniya proizvoditel'nykh sil SSSR. Osushchestvleniy politiki KPSS na etapakh sotsialisticheskogo stroitelstva,* Moscow: Ekonomika, 1985, p. 25.
7. Yakov Chadaev, *Ekonomika SSSR v gody Velikoi Otechestvennoi voiny (1941-1945),* Moscow: Mysl', 1985, pp. 182-184.

8. Evgenii Artemov, "Istoki krizisa sovetskoi sistemy", *Ural'skii Istoricheskii Vestnik* 17 (2007), pp. 105-106.
9. Iegor Gaidar, *Gibel' imperii. Uroki dlya sovremennoi Rossii,* Moscow: ROSSPEN, 2007, pp. 179-183.
10. Nikolai Nekrasov, (ed.) *Osobennosti i problemy razmeshcheniya proizvoditel'nykh sil SSSR v period razvitogo sotsialima,* Moscow: Nauka, 1980, p. 19.
11. *Ibid.*, 260-261.

17

The Asian Part of Russia: New Step of Industrial Development*

V. Yu. Malov

In contemporary Russia the thesis on the necessity of a search for new "national idea" is heard more distinctly, which principally differs from the paradigm of achievement of western mentality and life style. It would become evident to an ever-increasing number of our fellow-citizens that "His Majesty the Market" is not all-powerful, that it works well only "under the supervision" of a society and state, which are concerned not only and not so much with current profit, but to a certain extent also with long-term goals, which do not always (more precisely extremely seldom) enter into market mechanism. The revival of Russia's position as one of the basic subjects of world civilization may be considered as the strategic goal in the first quarter of the 21st century.

Russia has the necessary potential for maintaining economic growth, strategic, economic and other securities. A high safety margin still remains with the country. The basis of this is the integral potential of our natural resources, scientific and technological achievements, production capacities and quality of labour force. The natural resources of Russia continues to be in demand in the world market, which in many respects also predetermines the attitude of a number of states towards Russia, interested to utilize our natural potential. Russia is bound to find a position in shortest period of time in its treatment of the challenges and threat from the globalising world economy, both from its west and in particular, the east, where Russian territories are rich with natural resources and sparsely populated.

The Baikal Economic Forum of 2000 organised in Irkutsk served as the platform for the President of Russian Federation to resolve

* Translated by Susmita Bhattacharya, Fellow, MAKAIAS, Kolkata

the task of working out both the strategy of economic development of Siberia and transport strategy of Russia. The research studies of the Institute of Economy and Industrial Engineering, Siberian Branch of the Russian Academy of Sciences confirmed the importance of development of the Asian part of Russia's economy. Besides, it is not at all necessary that central Russia outstrip the growth rate of GDP here. What is more, the territorial division of labour has already taken such a form that the processing complex, service sector, branches with high share of added cost are concentrated in the European part of the country and the resource related ones are primarily in the Asian part. But it is the latter ones that determine the possibility of steady progress of entire Russia and assists it to get out of its crisis of the 90's of the last century, without depending on external factors and the third countries.

The role of resources of the Asian part of Russia and its economic geographical position continues to be significant. The outward effect, visible and expressed in the GDP indices, is manifested to a great extent in the west of the country whereas its material substantial base is to a considerable degree formed in the east. That is why we think it necessary to distinguish the problem of development precisely in this part of the country, to give attention to the need of active regional policy in the Asian part of Russia, active state participation in a number of large infrastructural projects the commercial effect of which (in contrast to national economic) does not always blend with the market framework.

The state participation may take different forms and the financial component of such participation is far from being most effective. In our opinion it is more important to create conditions for realization of large-scale projects of private companies whose interests coincide with that of the state at a given period and in a given territory. And what is more, the state, its federal bodies and regional authorities, would be assigned the role of a coordinator of interests of separate companies that is determined to achieve national goals.

The resources of Siberia, both mineral and natural raw materials (including its own territory) are highly attractive for states that are deficient in resources, and this demand is bound to increase in due course. This was often heard of more than 100 years ago and at that time there was an idea that it was impossible to reach Siberia and the Far East only by pursuing commercial interests. It was also clear at that time that it would be much easier and economic to defend such a territory not by serfs and the army but by the active, numerous and prosperous population. The contemporary new geopolitical situation of Russia after the disintegration of USSR is compelling us to seriously think about preserving our territories in the south and water routes in the north. The interest of the state should not just be charted out and be proclaimed but real and effective steps should be made towards economic assimilation of the territory and ensure other kinds of state presence including military presence. The latter factor, perhaps for some more time would be one of the most effective one.

The processes of growth among the population of Siberia and the Far East, which continued for four centuries, have turned backward. This unprecedented phenomenon in the history of Russia perhaps would not have evoked much anxiety after the end of re-emigration of Russian population in the Far East had there not been the threat of Chinese immigration. Reviews of the contemporary demographic situation and prospects of maintaining the Far-Eastern Russian possessions have striking resemblance with the predictions and hypotheses which are more than a century old. The leit motif of the majority of the scenarios of the demographic future of the Far East is the imminent fate and inevitability of the loss of the Far Eastern possessions of Russia. In Vladimir Lamin's view "Yellow labour force, yellow predominance"—the lexicon of pre-Soviet Far Eastern administrators which they used to seek immediate help from the state hierarchy. The authorities in the capital, like today, did not hasten to provide aid since it did not know again just like today what to do and did not find the means to protect the outlying regions of the Far East. The historical comparisons are of course not the directions to solve the complicated problems in a feasible time. But they are indisputably instructive for actually seeking maximum practical solution to urgent problems.

The confusion before the so-called challenge of the new times once again is reigning in the society, though this challenge existed for more than a century. In Russia anything new is almost always something that should have been resolved long back in the past but retained and kept for the future.

At present two interrelated problems are clearly distinguishable:

1. defining a place of the Asian part of Russia in the country's economy and its integration with the economy of the neighbouring states.

2. realization of concrete interregional transport and energy projects, involving the issues concerning the formation of new institutional conditions and their realization.

Let me emphasise that all concrete projects primarily concerned with the exploitation of natural resources, one way or the other are localized within limited territories—the problematic regions in terms of resources.

The quantitative evaluation of national economic efficiency in strengthening inter regional connections is based on calculations by inter-sector and inter-regional model. A supporting transport network in the Asian part of Russia is required for this. The changes in the geopolitical position of Russia are compelling a review of the interrelations with our close neighbours, in the first place with China, particularly taking into account the impetuous growth of its economic development and lack of friendly environment. The desirability of a purposeful state policy to draw in the Russian population here is based on a historical analysis of the processes of migration from China to the eastern regions of the country. Precisely this measure can be a "peaceful defensive factor" that can build a "peaceful safety zone". There are not many regions in this planet the resources of which can be mobilized for world production. Serious debates are going on concerning exploitation of the resources of Antarctica and even of the moon. Against this background the Asian part of Russia looks extremely attractive for the transnational companies for assimilating it, particularly considering cheap resources and skilled labour force, absence of ecological restrictions in the given territory which according to the governmental elite is a "heavy burden on Russia's budget." It is impossible to remain unconcerned to the calls like "putting a brake" on the development of Siberia and the Far East, ignoring these territories either "till good times" or for those who are capable of efficient management than Russia. Amongst political circles and 'independent" analysts of the west, the last option is especially welcome. The best answer to these friendly advices would be indigenous exploration and action for creating a new latitudinal space of economic development in the Asian part of the country, simultaneously bringing a space for independent control of Russia in terms of resources and transport. The settlement of the problems related to lands under industrial assimilation, which considerably restricts the aboriginal people of the North to maintain a traditional

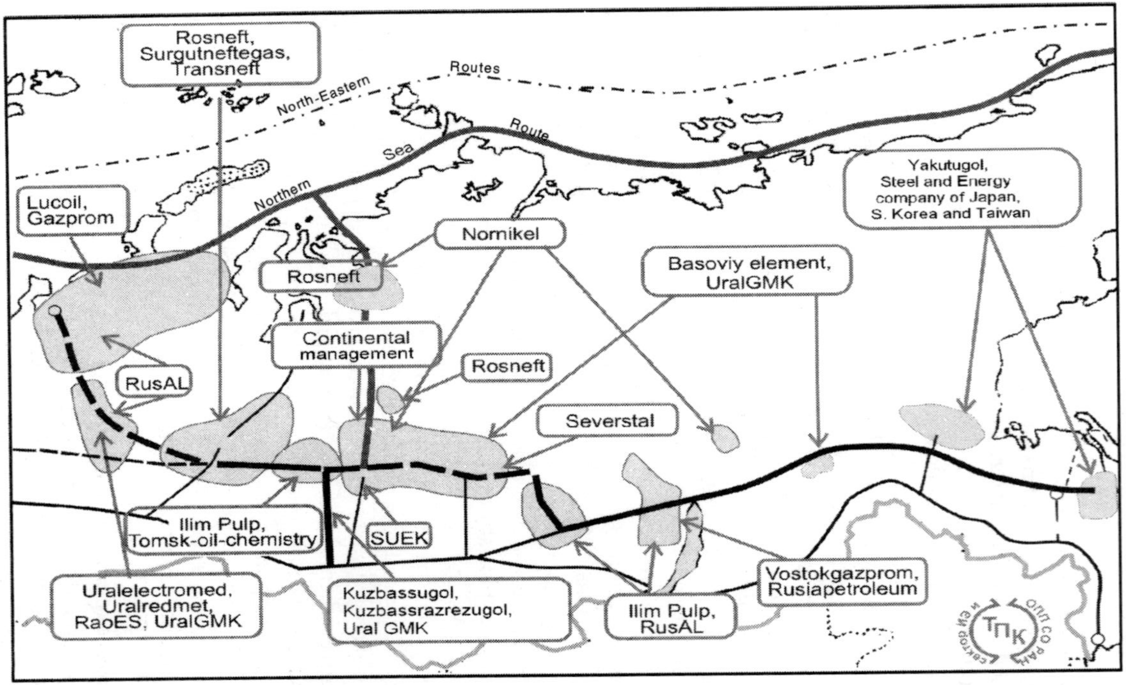

Fig. 17.1: Integrated industrial-transport zones along North Russian Eurasian Railways and large-scale firms' interests

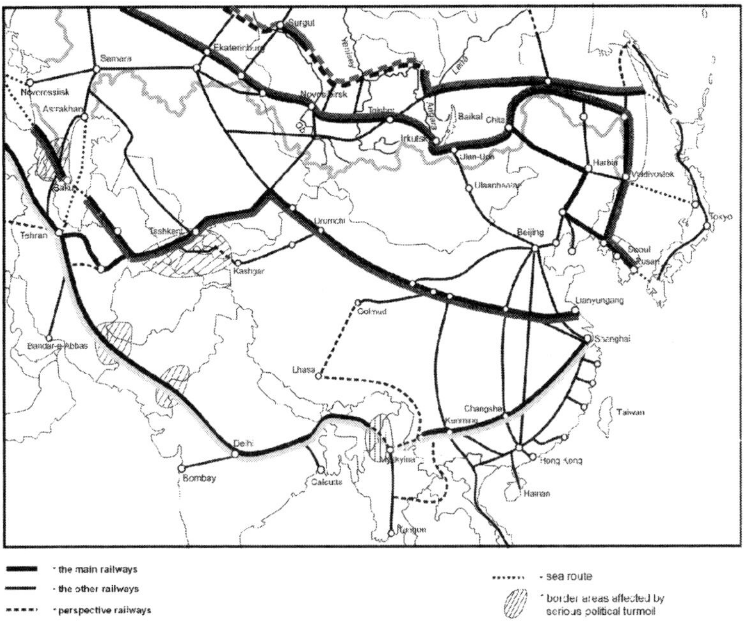

Fig. 17.2: Variants of Eurasian continental transport corridors (Asian part)

way of life, has tremendous significance on selection of paths for further assimilation of the resource-based areas of the Asian part of the country, located especially in the North.

The priority of forestalling development of Siberia and the Far East is extremely important for steady development of the whole of Russia and preservation of the integrity of its economic and political space. "Strangulation" of transport connectivity is the critical economic and political factor here. Strengthening of the eastern vector as an internal and external policy measure by Russia is an effective response of the state to ease out the geopolitical anomalies. The accomplishment of the task through a redoubling of the GDP and the consequent enhancement of the living standards throughout Russia has been assigned an important role. However, it is impossible to accomplish such a task with the presence of growing intra-Russian regional asymmetry and growing gap in the living standards in the European and Asian parts of Russia. The gap can only be reduced by first of all, active regional policy by the state aimed at creating favourable conditions for economic activity in the eastern regions of the country. A supporting transport network is one of the prime conditions here which would be able to meet the requirements of the 21st century such as the new geopolitical situation in the Asia-Pacific region and Russia's new role in it. A modern well-advanced transport infrastructure would be able to transform the special geographical position of Russia to its economic and strategic advantage.

The issues of the second group are examined in the context of realization of large infrastructural inter-regional projects in the spheres of energy and transport, which provide the basis of subsequent economic and demographic development. An approach is suggested for making these projects viable at a national economic level that would have a systematic effect. The energy projects are concentrated mainly on a selective utilization and transportation of hydrocarbon raw materials of the deposits in Eastern Siberia and Yakutsk. The commercial and national economic criteria were compared while selecting the variants. Considering the factor of uncertainty (unyielding to statistical approach) in long-term perspective and the uniqueness of each of the projects, an approach based on random multitudes is suggested. In the projects on energy and transport development of the Far East, much attention has been given to the issue of interaction with the economies of the neighbouring countries like China, North Korea, South Korea and Japan. In the transport strategy of Russia a shift from the national economic level to the regional one is examined in the transport complex of Krasnoyarsk *krai*. The issue of its development as part of the transport sector of the country and as a component of the economic complex of the region has been studied. It shows the paths of its development, serving the interests of the country as a whole and the interests of an individual region and the private companies. It specially highlights the issue of convergent interests in the form of state-private partnership in the construction of infrastructural projects as one of the priorities of transport strategy of Russia. Special attention is required in relation to partnership with private companies having sizeable share of foreign capital in order to actualize such projects in the border territories of Siberia and the Far East.

The availability of natural resources in the Asian part of the country under special conditions of a suitable transport infrastructure is a necessary prerequisite for the development of productive forces of this region and an opportunity to build up enterprises with a long-term perspective (up to 50 years) based on the compatibility factor, the effect and fulfillment of the norms of rational utilization of nature. The volume of output would be helpful in carving out a niche in the future both in the domestic (entailing supplies to the Urals and other European parts of the country) and foreign markets. The integration of oil and gas fields of Eastern Siberia, Sakha republic (Yakutiya) and Arctic shelf is necessary for immediately meeting the intra-Russian consumption in energy and technological raw materials (for the chemical and petro-chemical complex), and making a prominent entry into the energy markets of the countries of Asia Pacific region. The realization of some large projects is necessary to ensure an independent entry into the foreign market. They are:

- development of a network of arterial oil pipelines and capacity-building of the terminals of the Black Sea ports and Baltic pipelines system
- building new outlet of oil to the countries of the northern Europe and extension of the Trans-Siberian oil pipelines up to Nakhodka for entry into the countries of Asia Pacific Region
- constructing advanced pipelines network in the East of Russia with diversified entries to Korean peninsula, China and Japan
- for raising the living standard of the people of the eastern regions of the country would be extremely desirable to build an arterial pipeline to coordinate with mass gas supply in the inhabited areas of "transit" regions (Sakha republic/ Yakutiya and Buryatia, Chita, Amur and Sakhalin *oblast*, Khabarov and Primorskii *krai*).

The prime task should be to concentrate on the construction of the North Siberian Railway as the middle section of the North Russian Eurasia Railways exclusively passes through the Russian territory and connects the ports in the Pacific and Arctic Oceans that are outside the freezing zone. This has been recorded in the final reports of the Baikal Economic Forum (BEF) of 2004. Without this railway it is difficult to combine the tasks of organizing dependable coal supplies of Urals and the European part of the country and the mining deposits of Siberia and organizing the 'Asia-

Europe' container bridge. The completion of the North Sib would facilitate in sustaining the BAM and routing through it a part of the container traffic from the APR countries especially Japan. The economic indices of the BAM could be substantially better if the project to connect railway of Sakhalin Island with BAM is realized (construction of the bridge in Sakhalin with the next crossing in Hokkaido). This is the railway which can be the foundation to form a new latitudinal space of economic development of Russia in its Asian part that would raise the living standard and demographic potential.

It is needed to solve the organizational questions concerning a single and comparable tariff policy separately and "arms" of the trans-Siberia corridor as soon as possible, for "tapping" the container traffic via Chinese (including a TRACEKA variant) routes. The formation of a single administrative structure (considering the growing activity of China for completing this transit) is also a requirement. In addition, it is desirable to have alternative variations of direct sea routes to Western Europe through St. Petersburg or other Baltic Sea-based container terminals in the Russian territory, other than the land routes through the countries of Eastern Europe. The northern sea route is not as competitive for the road corridors as the supplementary route. It should be considerably favoured by the revival of the Siberian rivers as the "connecting links" between the economically integrated southern zone (along Trans Siberia), the new latitudinal one (along the North Siberian Railway) and SMP. (The technical solution of the problems of the entry to the world market would be through the SMP from the remote Siberian territories by the Siberian rivers).

Activation of transit flights through the Russian space may substantially bring high dividends if economically viable conditions are organized for their transit landing, fueling and loading. But at present it not yet possible to combine the efforts of not only various potential consignors but also the authoritative structures in the regions, each of which would like to see its own region as the future legislative center. The latter factor is of topical importance for the territory of Siberia in the light of growing competition for the marketing of goods traffic by air from the neighbouring states. The efficient operation of a supporting transport network requires a congruence of prospects of development and the operation of the regional transport complexes and the corresponding regional centers of goods availability, processing and dispatching. It would create conditions for more effective economic development of the regions, particularly in the eastern part of the country, where the proportion of transport components in relation to the prices of the finished product is very high. Therefore, working out methodical recommendations on the formation of regional transport complexes as fundamental parts of the integral transport system of Russia should be one of the prerogatives of the (scientific) research works. The integration of interests of the state, the regions and private companies (as potential investors) in the sphere of construction of large infrastructural units may be attained by using concessions as a special form of state-private partnership. They can become one off the most ambitious and prospective trends of development of state sector of Russian economy and a basis of the Russian model of a global economy.

The mass scale privatization of all the sectors of industry in the late 1990's led to the elimination of state control over some important sectors which were the basic ingredients of national security. Such a measure should not be allowed in the production infrastructure, particularly in the transport complex. In our view, this is one of the most important socio-political tasks in maintaining integrity of the economic, political and civilizational space of Russia.

A large number of proposals that have been discussed in the given article were upheld by the Baikal Economic Forum of 2006 (in Irkutsk). The premise that the economic complexes of the European and Asian parts of Russia mutually complement each other had contemporary relevance and was therefore considered accurate. By interacting with each other they can make the economic sector highly competitive in the world market, independent of oscillations of the world market or policy of individual states aimed at eliminating the competitors.

18

Transborder Character of Transport Communications*

V.A. Lamin

In 2007, the construction of the first experimental railway line in Russia between St. Petersburg and Tsarskoe Selo entered its 170th year. In the second half of the 19th century this was the only railway running between St. Petersburg and Moscow that stretched upto 700 km.

For a long time the assumption that "railway construction in Russia was absolutely impossible, obviously useless and in any case unprofitable", formulated even before the construction of the Petersburg-Moscow line, was criticized.[1]

An atmosphere of conservatism prevailed in Russia for a long period of time about the role and place of railway in the process of development of transport system using new transport technology. Every new project evoked strong debate that continued up to many years, at times even decades. Thus, the "railway question of Siberia" arising simultaneously with the work on the Moscow-Petersburg railway project was discussed for more than one half of the century. It is unknown how long it would be discussed if there would not have been the threat of Japanese military aggression and danger of losing the removed Far Eastern regions of the Empire. Owing to such a perspective and evidently the delayed Tsar's imperial permission for building Siberian railway, its construction was carried out using high speed technology in one track, with minimum journey and development of station tracks, with sleeper quota reduced by 30 per cent and light weight rail-rolling in the total operational period. The traffic capacity depended on the volume of goods traffic, formed under conditions of Siberian horse-drawn route/road constructed in the 18th century.

---

* Translated by Susmita Bhattacharya, Fellow, MAKAIAS, Kolkata

In spite of these deficiencies and reduced costs as well as time of construction, as a result of which the technical speed of the freight trains was fixed to maximum 16 km per hour, of the passenger "expresses" to not more than 90 km per hour and the weight of the train that was not to exceed 500 tons, the initiators of the project looked into future with optimism. Thus, one of such patrons of railway construction in Siberia G. Kraevskii wrote: "It is hard to imagine what a world-wide revolution caused by the Siberian railway, perhaps equal to the success of Suez Canal to China and Japan, would completely stopped". Relying on the figures of the future carrying capacity, commercial speed and other indexes, G. Kraevskii asserted: "Owing to Siberian railway all the ports of Russia in the Far East, situated on the shortest and round the world route, will play a pre-eminent role in the Pacific Ocean."[2] The business circles in various countries became serious about the future of the Trans-Siberian railway in inter-continental transit. Taking this situation into account even before the completion of the construction of Siberian railway the project of trans-continental railway was laid down to compete with it. In 1895 Takuchi, the editor of one of the Japanese newspapers presented a report to the Association of Economists in Tokyo on the possibility of carrying out the construction of Eastern Trans-Asian Railway before long. According to Takuchi's project the route of this railway was to pass from China through India to Kashgar and then crossing the tunnel of Tian-Shan range, along the territory of Russia (Kokand, Bukhara and Merv) and further through Tehran and Baghdad to Constantinpole and Paris.[3] Takuchi's project, in the specialists' opinion, was fully implementable technologically. But the track from Pacific coast to central Europe by Trans-Siberian railway would be shorter by 3184 versts. This, according to for instance, Kraevskii, was one of the main advantages of Trans-Siberian railway in comparison to the Eastern Trans-Asian railway, proposed by Takuchi.[4]

To counterbalance the Russian trans-continental trade communication links, a project on building a round-the-world railway route was brought forward in the USA. A group of American banks, including Rockfeller's 'National City Bank', came forward with the project to acquire the Chinese Eastern and South-Manchurian railways which were to become the first links of the round the world railway.[5]

The foreign financial and political community sharply reacted to the so-called "Chinese stretch of Trans-Sib", i.e. construction of its eastern section through the Chinese territory, "directly" not only to Vladivostok, but also through the South-Chinese railway to Port Arthur. In connection with this stretch one of the English political correspondents remarked, that as long as the Siberian railway made up to its way up the freezing port of Vladivostok it posed no threat. But its way out to Port Arthur would be fraught with threat to the interests of England and other west European powers in the Asia-Pacific region, as Russian presence in the Pacific Ocean may become predominant.

The country's specialists assessed the eastward connecting links of the Trans-Sib through Chinese territory. The official publications were optimistic about the great future of Russian trade in the south-eastern region of Asia through the Chinese stretch of the Transsib.[6] The other experts suggested that KER built with Russian money will exclusively serve China's welfare and insisted on the need to construct the eastern section of Trans-Sib in Russian territory from Chita to Khabarovsk and further joining the Ussuri track up to Vladivostok. They were concerned that KER would become a distinctive boundary of Russian territorial expansion in Asia. About the initiation of the "Chinese stretch" S. Yu. Witte asserted, "for the Russian people the border post separating them as European race from the people of Asia has been shifted beyond Baikal to the steppe of Mongolia. In due course its place will be at the last point of the Chinese Eastern Railway."[7] Similar arguments about the prospects of Russian presence in Asia had wide publicity in the government circles determining the Russian policy in the East concerning railway. Thus, even before S. Yu. Witte, M. Umanets, a popular writer wrote in 1889 about the need to consider the military as well as cultural-ethnographic priorities of the country. The Russian wooden plough and harrow should follow without fail the Russian banner and exactly the same way as the mountains of Cancasus and sands of Central Asia did not stop the Russian soldier, they should not stop Russian migrant/resettler".[8] The opponents of this foreign policy line called for objectively appraising the future of Asian countries. In their perception the Asian countries were inevitably to be liberated from the 400-year long military, political and economic domination and other dependence on the European race. They thought that the soldiers' colonies under triumphant banners, plough and harrow of the European colonists have no future. In spite of the calculation that CER would become a "colossal Russian pump for pumping out resources, they affirmed that in due course, when China, lying on its back today, would rise on its feet," the Chinese stretch with a cost of 300 million of gold roubles, undoubtedly, would come under China's ownership. And the railway communication with Vladivostok, in view of the refusal to construct Amur line in Russia's own territory would become interrupted or extremely difficult.

The Russo-Japanese war of 1904-1905 dispersed the mirage of Russian colonial policy much earlier than the non-official opponents had assumed. At the conference on communications in Siberia held at Irkutsk in December 1906, it was ascertained that the war disturbed the calculations done on the basis of earlier propositions on the role and significance of the Siberian railway in international trade and transit to the world.[9]

The reassessment about the predominant role of Trans-Sib in a Europe-Asia transit zone continued for almost 100 years. The period passed through two world wars and a lot of things changed and in Asia, perhaps more strongly than anywhere else. Most importantly the prognoses on lack of prospect and end of 400 year old colonial domination came true.

Within three years after the defeat by Japan Russia had to complete the eastern section of Trans-Sib in its own territory. The construction of the Chita-Khabarovsk railway basically was completed during the years of First World War. The advantages of railway running in its own territory was immediately visible in transportation of arms and other military goods, supplied by USA and Canada and also in the dynamics of agrarian assimilation of the Russian Priamure and further as was predicted by critics of the "Chinese stretch". In 1935 CER had to be sold to China at a price of US $12,261,16,135 thousand and 64 cents in today's exchange value. After the Second World War USSR recovered the Far Eastern territories lost by Russia at the beginning of the 20th century and restored the right to CER and lease of Post-Arthur. After the formation of ideologically related Peoples' Republic of China USSR relinquished the lease on Port Arthur and transferred CER to full ownership of China. During the strained situation of "cold war" communist China was regarded as a vector to counterbalance the disproportion in war technology and economic potential between

USSR and the former allies in the Second World War, now fighting against it.

The CER, constructed at the end of the 20th century with an expansionist purpose, was predicted by the opponents as not having fulfilled the hopes and calculations placed on it. But it undoubtedly "stretched" the transport communications of China with Europe, in comparison to trans-oceanic routes. The analogous trans-border function was prescribed to Utan-Bator railway built in the second half of 1940s and the railway "Druzhba" constructed by USSR and PRC, which opens an exit door from the western regions of China to Europe through Kazakhstan.

There is no doubt about the pioneering and up to date role of the sea and oceanic communications in the formation of a system of trans border communications. The network of aviation communications the second constituent of the transborder system, came into existence at the end of the 1930s and very soon took upon itself the great bulk of trans border, trans continental and inter-continental passenger traffic. The origin of the network of transborder communications by land must have taken place not later than the maritime coast trading navigations. But its development was hampered not so much by the maritime, trans oceanic and aviation international communications than by physio-geographical, natural-climatic conditions and barriers.

Practically just in the first one third of the 20th century the technology of transport construction and progress in the field of the means of transportation by land, railway locomotive and automobile reached the level enough for getting over any physio-geographical and natural climatic obstacles. In Europe, the relatively even landscape and natural climatic conditions that were similar to North America facilitated a faster system of transborder communications by land. It is significant that even the state and political obstacles on the way of development of the system of transborder communications by land in Europe and USA, in spite of wars, were "softer" than in the countries of Asia, the structure and scales of economy which were determined by the interests of the European centers of the empire. Under the flag of these interests, the transport systems also were formed in the transoceanic possessions of the western powers. Special attention was devoted to the development of oceanic and transport communications connected to the ports.

In fact only after the decline of 400 year old colonial era and fall of the colonial empires the opportunity of economic development and corresponding transport networking leading to socio-economic progress was opened before the Asian countries. Starting from the 1960s expansion of geographical boundaries of automobile and railway communications takes place in all the Asian countries. In contrast to aviation and maritime and oceanic routes operating locally in the territory, in the final points of their routes, the land communications equalize the regional disproportion of the socio-economic development faster and in larger scale.

Apparently it will not take much time when the national land transport systems of the countries of vast Asia would attain the level of development comparable to the European or north American parameters and later on will be united into transborder ones. But it can be positively asserted that these two phases of transport assimilation of the Asiatic expanses are inevitable. In Europe this process took an entire historical era. In North America, it took roughly 100 years in conditions of primordial transportation if one has to consider from the beginning of development of steamship communications and railway network, and later on reconstructed into even more compact road transport. Considering modern material and technological potentialities, rapid progress of technique and technology of transport construction and means of transport, this process can be covered in Asia significantly faster.

It is possible to think that within 15-20 years Asia and Europe will be an the threshold of the need of practical solution of the problem of stable, wide frame unification of the land transport systems of the two parts of the world into trans continental and Eurasian one. The practical interest in solving this problem seems to be mutual and the same for Europe and Asia. Thus, the latter can successfully develop in self-sufficient regime. But Europe without diverse resources of Asia can hardly do that. This fact is particularly proved by contemporary expert power bearers of Asia.

In the format of such perspective the scholars in Novosibirsk has completed a monographic research "Sukhoputnyi transport Sibiri "Land transport of Siberia", as a result of which prognostic outlines of future transborder, world, transport system has been worked out, the schemes of which are presented in the figures (Figs. 18.1, 18.2, 18.3).[10]

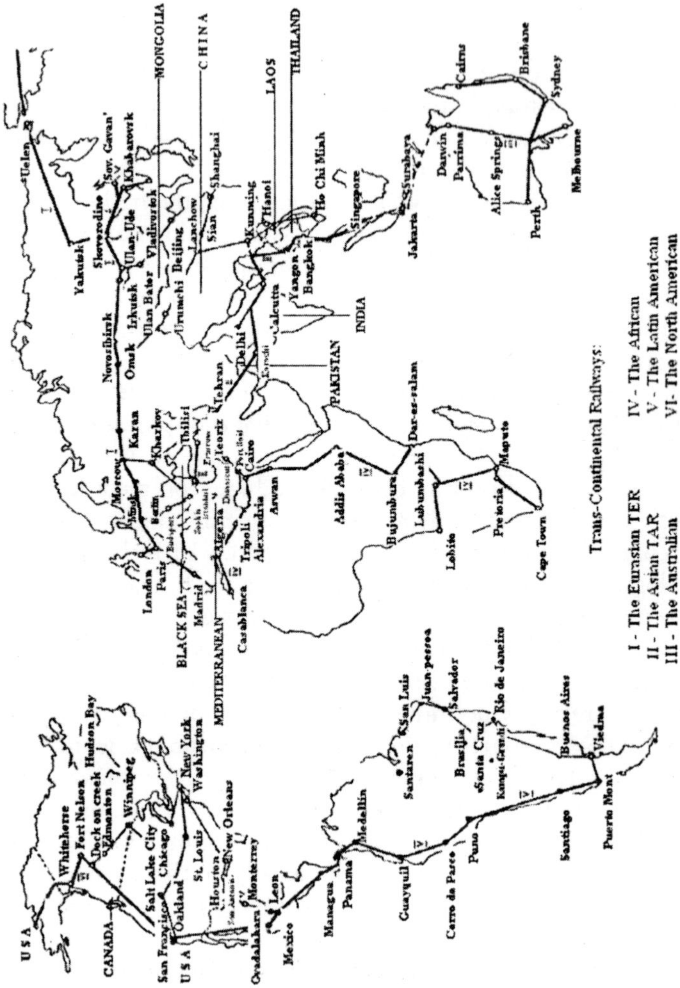

Fig. 18.1: Trans-World/Global Super Rail Road

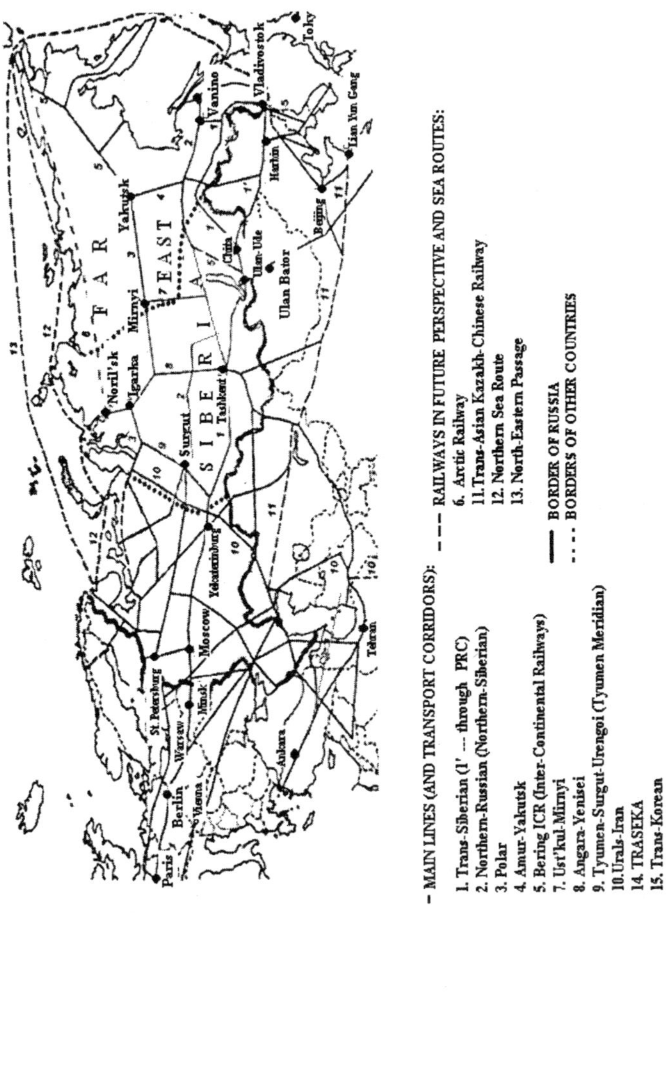

Fig. 18.2: Supporting Railway Network of Asiatic Russia in the 21st Century in the System of Trans-Continental Railroads

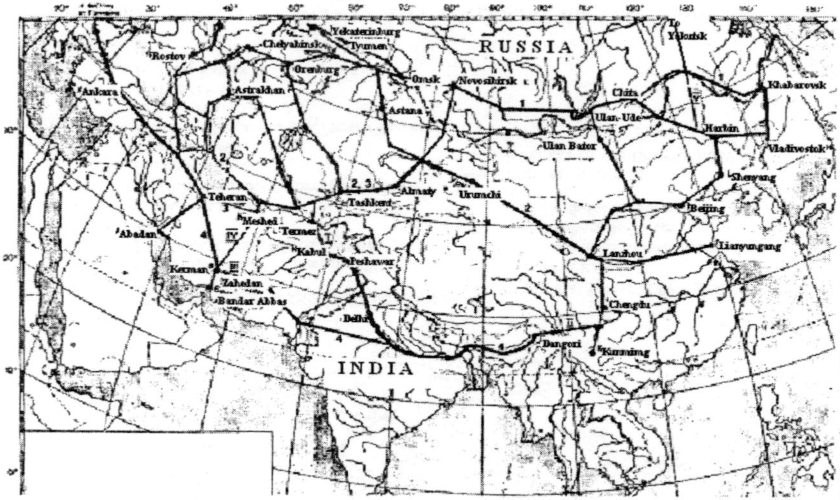

Direct transit routes from India to Russia and to the Trans-Sib:

I - The Western Transit Peshawar-Kabul-Termez
II - The Eastern Transit via PRC Dangori-Chengdu

Possible extension of the supporting transport network:

III - Inaccessible link of Southern Eurasian Corridor of Kerman-Zahedan
IV - Prospective link of Urals-Iranian Railways of Meshed-Kerman-Bandar Abbas
V - Prospective link of future transport corridor from North America via Bering Strait and the Russian Far East to the countries of APR and South Asia.

Eurasian overland corridors:

1. Trans-Siberian;
2. TRASEKA;
3. Central;
4. Southern [TAR].

Source: V.Ya. Tkachenko., V.P. Pertsev, *Sukhoputnyi transport Sibiri. Formirovanie opornoi seti zheleznykh i avtomobil'nykh dorog*, Novosibirsk: IEiOPP[The Institute of Economics and Industrial Engineering] SB RAS, 2003. Figure 1.1 *Planetarnaya zheleznodorozhnaya magistral'*, p. 23; Fig. 1.2. *Opornaya set' zheleznykh dorog Aziatskoi Rossii*, p. 33; Fig1.28/1.3 *Zhelenodorozhnye vykhody iz Indii*, p. 200.

Fig. 18.3: Railway Transit Routes from India in the System of International Transport Corridors and Supporting Railway Network of Asia

List of Abbreviations

1. MKM—Mezhkontinental'naya magistral' [Inter-continental railways]
2. TEAZhM—Transevraziiskaya zheleznodorozhnaya magistral' [Transeurasian railways] железнодорожная магистраль
3. TAZhD—Transaziatskaya zheleznaya doroga [Transasian railways]
4. TRACEKA—Transportnyi koridor Evropa-Rossiya-Aziya-Amerika [Transport corridor of Europe-Russia-Asia-America]

Notes and References

1. P.S. Atreshkov, *O vedenii zheleznykh dorog v Rossii*, St. Petersburg, 1841, p. 10.
2. G. Kraevskii, *Mirovaya—Tranzitnaya Sibirskaya zheleznaya doroga. Soobschenie, sdelannoe v sobranii inzhenerov putei soobscheniya,* 8 Marta 1897 g. Irkutsk: TYP.-LIT. P.I. Makushina, 1898, p. 8.
3. *Japan Daily Mail*, 18 February, 1965.
4. G. Kraevskii, *Mirovaya—Tranzitnaya Sibirskaya zheleznaya doroga. Soobschenie, sdelannoe v sobranii inzhenerov putei soobscheniya*, 8 Marta 1897 g. Irkutsk: TYP.-LIT. P.I. Makushina, 1898, p. 10.
5. A.A. Fursenko, *Neftyanye tresty i mirovaya politika,* Moscow-Leningrad: Nauka, 1965, p. 433.
6. *K desyatiletiyu Komiteta Sibirskoi zheleznoi dorogi (1893-1903). Sibirskaya zheleznaya doroga v ee proshlom i nastoyaschem. Istoricheskii ocherk*. Compiled by S.V. Sabbler, I.V. Sosnovskii. St. Petersburg, 1903, pp. 395-397.
7. Cited in *Istoriya, antropologiya, kul'turologiya,* chast' II; Izbrannye lektsii Omsk: Nauka, 2004, p. 39.
8. *Op cit*, p. 23.
9. *Trudy soveschaniya 1906 g. v Irkutske o putyakh soobscheniya v Sibiri*, T.2., Irkutsk: Izdanie Kantselavii Irkutskogo Generalnogo Gubernatorstgo, 1907. p. 188.
10. V.Ya. Tkachenko., V.P. Pertsev, *Sukhoputnyi transport Sibiri. Formirovanie opornoi seti zheleznykh i avtomobil'nykh dorog*, Novosibirsk: IEIE. The Institute of Economics and Industrial Engineering SB RAS, 2003. Figure 1.1 *Planetarnaya zheleznodorozhnaya magistral'*, p. 23; Fig. 1.2. *Opornaya set' zheleznykh dorog Aziatskoi Rossii*, p. 33; Fig. 1.28 *Zhelenodorozhnye vykhody iz Indii*, p. 200.

19

International Transport Corridors of Eurasia: Socio-Economic and Geopolitical Dimension*

M.N. Baldano

The geopolitical location of Russia between Europe and Asia and its dynamic centres of business activity have a special and key role in maintaining Eurasian relations. The territory of Russian Federation is situated at the intersection of trade routes between the countries of Europe, Central Asia and Asia-Pacific region. The international transport routes across Russia cover the shortest distance cross state borders for minimum number of times and pass through a territory with single legal space thereby ensuring less time for delivery of goods. Besides, Russia has a developed network of railways and waterways with reserves of traffic capacity, and also has a developing network of motorable roads which enables it to avoid the need of large investments in the layout of international corridors.

Till 2020 it is expected that greater attention will be given to the problems of forming a supportive transport network based on the principles of transport corridors. In the conditions of formation of a new model of development of world economy, transport is considered as an instrument for realizing national interests and integrating Russia into the world economy.

In West and Central Europe, where communications are more developed in comparison to that of East Asia, the basic network of transport corridors has already been completed. But, the system of pan European corridors does not fully meet the geo-political and economic interests of Russia. In the present setup they do not provide the transport approaches to a number of regions—which are important participants of foreign economic activities, and also the economic relations of the world centers of business activities, do not enable

* Translated by Susmita Bhattacharya, Fellow, MAKAIAS, Kolkata

actively utilizing the transport communications of Russia for maintaining international transcontinental communications.

Despite considerably lagging behind the majority of European countries in the field of transportation, Russia has been earnest about building intermodal systems. The International Transport Corridor or ITC passing through the territory of Russia has been constructed in conformity with geography and structure of the existing and prospective international transport communications. At present the intensity of trade between the markets of South East Asia and Europe is growing. For assimilating the powerful goods traffic Russia needs further development of the existing ITCs and construction of new ones. The ITC system in Russian territory involves two Eurasian corridors "North-South" and "Trans-Sib", Northern shipping routes/ sea lanes, two pan-European corridors and also the corridors connecting the north-eastern provinces of China through Russian sea ports of Primor'e krai with the ports of Asia-Pacific region.

The trans-Sib corridor is an alternative to the traditional sea route for delivering containers to Europe from South East Asia around India and through the Suez Canal. According to experts, for making the Trans-Siberian corridor viable to contemporary demands, it is necessary to develop transport routes and modernize seaports of the Far East and north-western region, joining this corridor with the international communications. The international transit in latitudinal direction by Trans-Sib would not only facilitate additional financial sources, but will also be conducive to the growth of internal transportation and development of the eastern region of Russia.

The international Eurasian "North-South" transport corridor would connect the northern and central Europe with the states of the Persian Gulf and India. The utilization of these lines for transporting international transit goods through the territory of Russia ensures substantial reduction of their delivery period owing to considerably short stretch of the routes (by 2-3 times) in comparison to those transported through southern sea routes through the Suez Canal. The transportation of transit goods through Trans-Sib might amount to 600-800 thousand containers and through the "North-South" corridor to 80-100 thousand containers.

The northern sea line—the international transport corridor highlights transportation by the shortest route between the Western Europe and ATR countries. The state's role in the activation of the arctic transport system is meant to create favourable conditions for dependable functioning of the Northern Sea line and to build transport infrastructure to maintain this process. This need is dictated by the conditions of development of large-scale projects in the Arctic for assimilating the hydro-carbon deposits and securing their transportation.

According to an estimate by experts, an additional gross national income can be realized due to the transit potential of Russia for Eurasia. The predictions are as follows: taking into account the growth in goods turnover by 2010, GNP can reach more than 6 million dollars and may rise up to 20 million dollars in 2015. The transport services might, thus turned into the largest item of national export after oil and gas and raw materials.

While addressing the Conference on Russo-German logistics of 8th February 2007 the minister for transportation of Russian Federation I.E. Levitin emphasized, "considering the geographic advantages of Russia the logistics in our country is capable and should become a new sector of economy of Russia comparable by scales to such traditional sectors as the export of energy carriers and armaments". He also mentioned that for Russia the logistics of becoming a sector of national economy is a new process and we are still at the beginning of the journey.[1]

The route of the future Eurasian transcontinental railway would pass through the main regions of Russia with high concentration of fuel-energy, mineral and natural resources and timber resources. In the main zone is located Timano-Pechorskii and Western-Siberian/ Zapadno-Sibirskii oil and gas complexes, Lower and Middle Priangare with their richest and diverse natural resources, the unique Udokansk fields of copper and other mineral resources, Brelsk-Ust-Ilimsk, Upper Lena and Yakutsk (Southern) TPC at the formation stage, new centers of oil and gas fields of Sakhalin, including its shelf area.

One of the important parts in the construction of the transport corridor is the realization of the project of construction of branch lines between BAM and Trans-Sib through the territory of Buryatia. The ITC reaches out to the railway network of Mongolia and China, which conforms to the principles of Russia's transport strategy on working out the projects of construction and development of transit corridors supplementing the basic international transport corridors, with the participation of the subjects of Russian Federation. This way, the completion of the transport system and realization of the strong transit potential of the country for securing Eurasiatic communications would become one of the key elements of the development of Russia's economy.

As far as the regions of Siberia and the Far East are concerned which covers more than 70 per cent of Russia's territory and with unique natural resource potential at its disposal, the problem of state support has a special urgency. The reserves of hydrocarbon, coal, non-ferrous and precious metals, timber, water and hydro-power resources are overwhelming—the extractable explored reserves of oil in Siberia make up 77 per cent of Russian reserves, natural gas and coal make up more than 80 per cent of the reserves and timber resources make up 50 per cent of the total Russian reserves. The new transport construction, which requires one-time expenses but ensures high national economic effectiveness may play a key role in boosting the economy of Siberia and the Far East, populating the poorly assimilated territories and raising the living standard of the population. This has been proved, in particular, by the experience from the construction of Trans-Sib, transport assimilation and formation of Western-Siberian Oil & Gas Complex (WSOGC). More than 200 million dollars were spent on transport and establishment of the WSOGC, which enabled the country to secure huge volumes of oil and gas, mining and to receive within a period of 20 years. From 1980 to 2000 a total integral economic effect resulted exceeding the onetime expenses.

The construction Trans-Siberian Railway resulted in mass resettlement of people to Siberia, establishment of higher educational institutes, setting up large centers of mining, coal and metallurgical industry. The existence of Trans-Siberian Railway helped the transfer of many factories to Siberia and maintaining uninterrupted work in its rear during the War period, which to a great extent determined the victory of the Soviet people in this war.

But at the very beginning of its construction, despite praises, the Trans-Sib was severely criticized, especially after it became known that the Siberian Railway would be built along the southern part through Omsk to Krasnoyarsk, Irkutsk, and further to Vladivostok through Chita and territory of China. The representatives of business circles thought that as a result of such adjustments the Pacific gateway to international trade would remain closed for Siberian trade as before. In view of the impending armed conflict with Japan some specialists asserted that the CER could be a factor in stabilizing the international situation in the Far East. It was also mentioned that it was dictated not only by military and strategic considerations, but not to a lesser degree by prospective significance of CER in international transit of goods and passengers, and also the key position of Russia in the Eurasian transport communications.

Meanwhile the war with Japan was lost. Only after this in 1907 the decision was taken to construct the Amur line of Siberian railway, but actual construction took almost ten years to start.

At the planning stage of the Trans-Sib considerable attention was devoted to the question of substantial expansion of the zone of active economic development of Siberia. In the course of these plans large-scale expedition-oriented explorations of natural resources of Siberia were carried out. Enormous expenses were made for the first time by special geological explorations, geophysical, topographical survey, systematic study of hydrologic regime of Siberian rivers. As a result, in the map of Asiatic Russia appeared Ekibastuzsk, Karagandinsk, Sudzhensk, Antropovsk, Kubekovsk, Kuskunsk, Cheremukhovsk, Malinovsk; Hara-Norsk, Suchansk coal fields. The Siberian Railway financed petro-geological exploratory projects.

The Committee on Siberian Railway from the very inception persistently emphasized that the results of the expeditions would be utilised for restructuring the technological and economic foundations and exploring possibilities of developing iron-smelting, foundry works and building industries of construction materials especially cement.

However, the promised financial subsidies were as usual never allotted for the all-round economic development of Siberia, except 30 million roubles for the construction of production structures like (open-caste mines, brick, lime and cement factories), directly connected with construction of the railway during the period from 1893 to 1902. Thus, the plan of all-round economic development seemed elusive.

At the end of the 1920s, the question of making the Trans Sib a super railway project was raised and the initiators of this project suggested the increase of the traffic capacity at the cost of construction of supplementary lines to all directions of the Trans-Siberian Railway. According to specialists, the transformation of the Siberian railway into a ten-track line could be cheaper in comparison to the construction of a new transport line that would pass through uninhabitable and inaccessible regions of the north. Through the North-Sib Railway or Veliki Severnyi Put (VSP) Great Northern Railway, the possibility of connecting the coasts of three oceans namely Pacific, Arctic and Atlantic and the wider possibilities of an exit to oceanic communications without being liable to foreign policy complications were being explored. It was proposed to locate the large industrial premises, especially the metallurgical ones to the concentrated mineral-raw materials zones and fuel energy resources in the zone of future Northern Trans-Sib, as in the event of war these enterprises could provide the strategic industrial rear that would become inaccessible to any potential aggressor.

But the country's tradition was that the railway, which was highly expensive in terms of capital investments and operational costs, should be constructed only after the exhaustion of the potential of other cheaper kinds of transport communications. This tradition was fully visible in the counter arguments against the VSP/GNR.[2] Nonetheless, the settlement of the question on construction of latitudinal railway became the starting point of the new stage of working out the problems of formation of railway network in the southern Siberia and the Far East. There were discrepancies as well. The most vital one was that the future railway had no exit/outlet to the Arctic coast. The choice between Arkhangelsk and Indiga had to do on the basis of the criteria, drawn from the actually available technological and economic potential, which was determined by the capacities of the operating ports and northern maritime communications in Arkhangelsk and Murmansk. The construction of a new port in Indiga in a complex that had a network of railways had to be started at the end of the second five-year plan or in an extreme case during the third plan.

But the Second World War started, and the Murmansk port along with the railway approaching it was in immediate proximity to the arena of war activities. For preventing breakthrough of the enemy towards Murmansk railway and a port-city desperate efforts were made, but there was no guarantee against a catastrophic situation. The maritime communications in the Baltic were already paralysed in the first months of the War. The Arkhangelsk port, second after Murmansk in the list of the top priority objects of port construction in the north, in spite of the capacity built up during the pre-War years, did not have feasible reserves at its disposal to compensate the Murmansk in the event its loss.[3]

In this situation once again the idea of constructing a port in the Indiga bay became topical, but the construction that had started soon was stopped. The extreme war situation too was a major stumbling block as far as the communication hubs of the country's transport system with the outer world was concerned. The traditionally developed primarily western bound railway connections with the outer world were practically sealed during the initial stage of the War. Similarly the Baltic and Black Sea communication also stopped. The Caspian Sea and land routes through Iran and Transcaucasus were not able to block the Black Sea and Baltic routes. The Trans-Siberian railway outlet to the oceanic communication more or less remained open in the outer world.

History shows that the geopolitical interests of the country were extremely weighty compared to the socio-economic considerations.

One sees a strong resemblance between the contemporary geopolitical situation and the historical situation that temporarily arose during the War years. Russia's borders changed in its western and southern directions. The borders of Siberia in the East that overlapped with the limits of Kazakhstan, its Pacific and arctic coasts and the northern territories of European Russia remained untouched by the national and political metamorphoses. In the conditions that evolved it was necessary to find a solution. The governor of Tomsk oblast N.M. Kress stressed in his speech at the Baikal Economic Forum of 2000 that it is necessary to reconstruct the Trans-Sib providing it with modern equipment in order to bring it to the level that would maintain the safety of the movement and safe-keeping of goods in conformity with the international standards. It is necessary to build a supporting railway network of federal motorable roads from Urals to the Far East and to have here not just one, but a number of motorable highways; organize a system of international air/avian transportation among the countries of APR Asia Pacific Region and European sub-continent, expand and modernize the communication network and pipeline transport.[4]

At present there are four international routes which are used by the Trans-Sib. The first two routes can be referred as transit ones, since the goods cross the former Soviet republics, and the other two can be defined as bilateral. The European transit connects the countries of East Asia (Japan, Korea and China) and Finland by rail and sea transport. For illustration, such products as electronic goods for domestic consumption/home appliances are received for temporary storage in the Finnish customs houses and from these places they are mainly exported to Russia including the Russian Far East. Most interestingly the price of these goods are much cheaper than those received in the Far East by sea directly from Japan. This is explained by the high tariffs on customs clearance. It would be appropriate to name this route as Finland transit. Transportation of goods from Japan and Republic of Korea takes 30 to 35 days by sea, while by Trans-Sib only 20 days. In 1998 as trial a model container train "Nakhodka-Vostochnaya-Brest" was run through the Trans-Sib, which crossed this distance of 1011.538 km.

The advantage of Trans-Sib over sea routes is its speed. But sea transportation is cheaper and is advantageous due to the capacities of sea containers. The Afghan transit connects Japan, Korea and Afghanistan by Trans-Sib and the railway system of the Central Asian countries. The main competitor of this route is the Iranian one, which actively started operating from 2000 and cheaper in comparison to Trans-Sib. The Iranian sea route moves up to Bandar-Abbas and then by land to the western part of Afghanistan. The main goods that are transported are pipes and auto spare parts. The Central Asian bilateral route connects Japan, Korea and Kazakhstan, Uzbekistan by sea and rail using Trans-Sib and railways of Central Asia. The main transportable goods by this route are the items of Korean companies imported in Central Asia. The alternative route through China the "Trans-China Railway" connects the Chinese port Linyangang with Kazakhstan by the Chinese railways. This route is widely used for transporting goods from Japan (transportation time is 3 weeks in comparison to 2 months by Trans-Sib and with cheaper tariff). The Russian bi-lateral route connects Japan, Korea with the Russian regions.

As far as the frequency of use by Japan, if the Japanese ports and Vostochnyi port used Trans-Sib thrice a month, at present it is only twice. The Japanese companies use the sea route practically every day. In contrast to Japan the Koreans use the Trans-Sib much intensely. The volume of Korean and Chinese goods transport is increasing chemical products like rubber, plastic, goods consumption goods and also the goods invested in Central Asia), while the volume of Japanese goods are declining. The lack of guarantee in safe-keeping, high cost of tariffs in the absence/for the lack of normal conditions of the transportation (containers) and poor management on the part of the Russians do not suit the Japanese.[5] Besides, the

Japanese companies recently have been distributing their branches in China, Malaysia and other South East Asian countries because of the low labour cost and from where the products are considerably easily transported to Europe by sea.

Nevertheless, now Trans-Sib is a two-track railway in ferro-concrete lines/trellis, equipped with automatic block system and electric centralization, complex of automatic movement control system facilities, optic-fibre line of communication similar to the space-satellite communication system.

The construction of international transport corridor and further modernization projects refer to the Trans-Sib as a classical example. These are favoured because of the potential of development of industrial infrastructure of 14 oblasts, 3 krais, 2 republics and one autonomous oblast of Russia. Trans-Sib passes through 87 cities including a number large industrial centers and transport junction in them like Moscow, Yaroslavl, Perm, Ekaterinburg, Omsk, Novosibirsk, Kranoyarsk, Irkutsk, Ulan-Ude, Chita Khabarovsk, and Vladivostok. 62 per cent of the total mineral reserves of Russia is concentrated in the territory of Siberia contiguous to Trans-Sib and BAM. Siberia secures 50 per cent of Russia's export. The largest timber enterprises are situated along the Trans-Sib. The economic development of Eastern Siberia, and precisely the territories lying close to BAM, is connected with the mining operation of the deposits of the titanium, magnate, vanadium, copper and platinum ore deposits, chineisk, and with the assimilation of copper ore of Udokansk and coal basins of Elginsk.

In the coming years the goods turnover by Trans-Sib is bound to increase considerably because of the goods that are transported from USA to the Far Eastern region through the Russian ports of Nakhodka and Vostochnyi. With the growth of the volume of transit transportation up to one million containers the total annual revenue is estimated to 8 milliard dollars, and a minimum annual profit of 1 million dollars.

Such a massive international project tends to result in the growth and integration of the economic systems of Russia, Europe and the countries of Asia-Pacific Region.

In order to make its mark in the world, Russia must utilize all the potentialities and opportunities available to it. The construction of international transport corridors would give such opportunities to develop industrial infrastructure, to work out most modern technology within the framework of the project to utilize profits from the functioning of the transport corridor and raise the standards of material and spiritual culture of Russia in the 21st century.

Notes and References

1. *Ekonomicheskaya gazeta,* 9 February 2007, No. 2.
2. V.V. Alekseev, M.K. Bandman, V.V. Kuleshov, Ed. *Problemnye regiony resursnogo tipa: Ekonomicheskaya integratsiya evropeiskogo Severo-Vostoka, Urala i Sibiri*, Novosibirsk. SB RAS Publishing House, 2002, p. 81.
3. A.A. Dolgolyuk, V.A. Lamin, V. Yu. Plenkin i A.I. Timoshenko, *Sibir': proekty XX veka (nachinaniya i real'nost'), Novosibirsk, SB* RAS Publishing House, 2002, p. 146.
4. *Vestnik Soveta Federatsii*, no. 1 (2001):53.
5. *ERINA report, no.* 5 (2005):64.

20

Siberia: The Emerging Energy Frontier

Sudha Mahalingam

For the past few years, global oil markets have been undergoing cataclysmic transformation, upsetting the cozy, if tenuous equilibrium between oil producers and consumers. Crude prices have risen by more than fivefold in the last five years and have reached a point where they can and do impact growth prospects of oil-importing developing economies. Surprisingly, there is no single catalytic trigger that can be blamed for this development. An unfortunate combination of factors and circumstances seems to be at play. Peak-oil-pessimism is one of them. Oil industry watchers, geologists and analysts have come together to field the theory that humanity has already found and exploited all recoverable oil deposits on the planet and that no new discoveries of cheap oil will be found anymore. This apocalyptic theory seems to find resonance among multinational oil companies that are now converging on regions where they believe, are the last exploitable oil and gas deposits on the planet. Quite understandably, Siberia figures high on this list. Siberia and the Russian Far East are deemed virtually the last energy frontier that holds out promise of significant and exploitable hydrocarbon reserves.

For the resurgent Russian state emerging out of the Soviet chrysalis, energy is the life-blood of the economy. Hydrocarbons account for a quarter of the country's GDP, more than a third of tax revenues and almost two thirds of export income. This year, Russia has overtaken Saudi Arabia, hitherto the unchallenged begum of the oil world, to become the single biggest oil producer in the world.[1] At around 10 million barrels a day, Russia's crude production accounts for 12 per cent of current global crude output. Russia is also home to the largest gas reserves in the world. With 26.6 per cent of global gas deposits, Russia supplies as much as 28 per cent of global gas consumption. Europe imports half of its gas and a third of its crude from Russia while Asia, the relative new-comer to gas, imports 10 per cent of its consumption from Russia. In fact, it is common knowledge that Russia is emerging as the global energy superpower, a formidable counterbalance to the Middle East.

Not as well-known, however, is Siberia's primacy in Russia's energy superpower status. Siberia accounts for 78 per cent of Russia's oil deposits and 84 per cent of gas deposits. Gazprom, Russia's state-owned gas company which contributes as much as a quarter of the country's tax revenues, coaxes as much as 70 percent of its gas out of Siberian soil and seas. Within Siberia, western Siberia supplies the chunk of the country's crude output. Three fields, Urengoy, Yamburg and Medvezhye contribute most of Gazprom's gas business. At present, virtually all of this goes to western markets. Yet, Siberia holds out tantalizing prospects of becoming a prominent supplier of oil and gas to developing Asia, particularly to China with its apparently insatiable thirst for oil and gas, but also to South Korea, Japan and even India.

This paper attempts to critically examine Siberia's hydrocarbon potential. The second part of the paper discusses the field-wise energy potential of Western and Eastern Siberia as well as the emerging Russian Far East. It also outlines the possible transit routes for this energy to flow to Asia and other markets. Part III examines critically, the investment environment in Russia in general and the problems associated with developing Siberia's energy resources in particular. Part IV, looks at the Indian presence in Sakhalin and the prospects for future involvement in Siberia's energy sector.

II

Western Siberian oil fields were first developed nearly half a century ago and since then, 70 billion barrels of crude has already flowed out of the region to domestic and world markets.[2] Currently, the region produces 7 million barrels daily.[3] Siberian crude is sweeter and lighter than the Urals blend and as such, l commands a premium in global markets.

The following map and table give the distribution of Siberian and Russian Far Eastern hydrocarbon reserves.

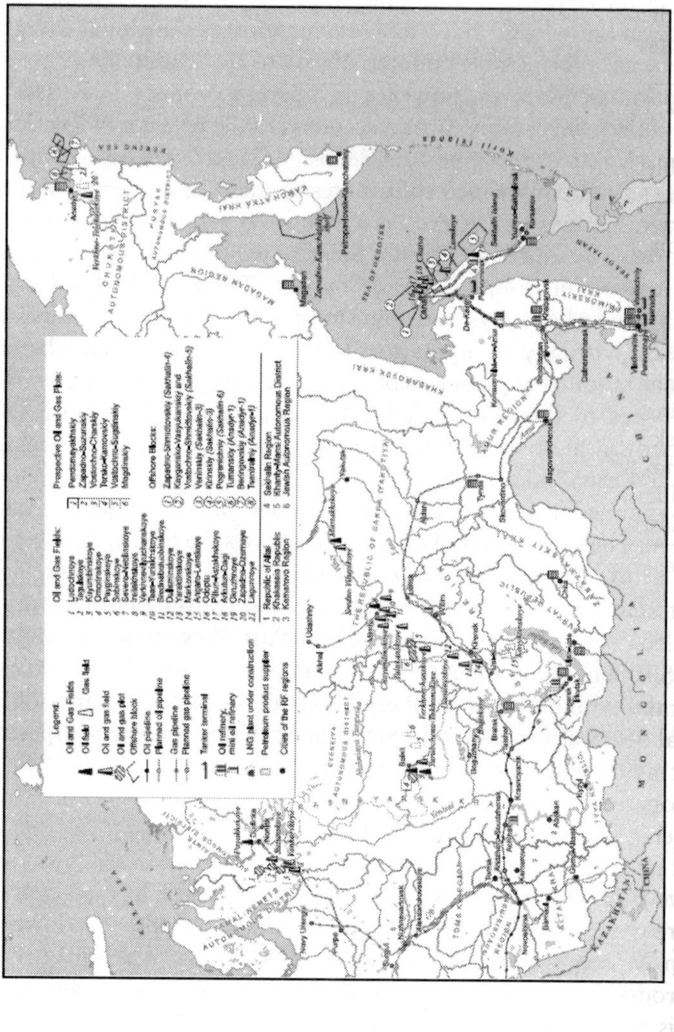

Source: Carnegie Moscow Center

Fig. 20.1: Hydrocarbon Map of Siberia and the Russian Far East

Table 20.1: Distribution of Oil and Gas Reserves by Region (%)

Region	*Oil Reserves*	*Gas Reserves*
West Siberia	53.5	41
East Siberia and the Far East	13.5	19
Continental Shelf	12.4	32
European Part of Russia	20.6	8
	100	100

Source: Oil and Gas Vertical No. 17, 2005 p. 35.

Table 20.2: Forecast of Maximum Production from East Siberia and Far East: Estimates of Gazprom and Russian Academy of Sciences

Region	*Gas Production (bcm) Gazprom*	*Gas Production (bcm) Academy*	*Oil Production (mty) Gazprom*	*Oil Production (mty) Academy*
Sakhalin	72.2	30	23.1	35
Yakutia	53	47.1	8.8	10.8
Irkutsk Region	46.3	53	9.1	13.4
Krasnoyarsk Krai	35.3	19.9	7.1	35.8
Total East Sibera & Far East	206.8	150	48.1	95

Source: Oil and Gas Vertical No. 17, 2005, p. 45.

It is obvious that West Siberia is low-hanging fruit for the Russian petroleum industry. No wonder the Soviet Union focused first on West Siberia, the relatively easier region to access. In 1969, the CPSU Central Committee and the USSR Council of Ministers adopted a special decree on the Development of Oil and Gas Industry in West Siberia.[4] The Yamal Nenetz region and Urengoy fields were developed and pipelines and terminals built to connect the fields to markets. Since then, this region has become an important supplier of oil and gas especially to European markets. However, analysts believe West Siberian fields have matured and that the days of easy gas are gone forever.[5]

In Western Siberia, Yuzhno-Roskoye, the field that commenced gas production last year is considered the region's 'last pearl'[6]. This field is being developed jointly with German technology by BASF EoN Ruhr Gas and Gazprom at a cost of 12 billion US dollars. It has enough gas to supply the entire German consumption for seven years. The deposit, for which Gazprom subsidiary Severneftegazprom holds a license, has 805 billion cubic meters of proven gas reserves, and 5.7 million tons (42 million barrels) of proven oil reserves.[7]

Yamal Peninsula in northern Siberia has not been fully exploited yet. It contains more than 10 trillion cubic meters (tcm) of gas. Royal Dutch Shell which has stakes in gas fields in the region believes it could be as much as 30 tcm, enough to supply the present global consumption for a decade. Most of this is located in Tyumen, Yamal Nenetz and Khany Mansi autonomous regions jutting out into the Kara Sea. However, these fields are a logistical challenge for developers who may have to build artificial islands from which to mount their equipment. It is estimated that this region will require 70 billion US dollars of investment to monetize the minerals. Yamal is considered the world's most difficult region to explore for and produce hydrocarbons. The peninsula is covered with countless rivers and lakes, completely impassable in the summer, and its coastlines are surrounded by shifting masses of pack ice that sometimes tear meter-deep gashes into the ocean floor, making it difficult, if not impossible, to lay pipelines. In fact, it is not clear if there are known engineering solutions for building pipelines from the region.

Shtockman, the world's largest undeveloped gas field is also in northern Siberia, 550 kilometers offshore in the Barents Sea. It is estimated to contain 19 billion barrels of oil and 7 tcm of gas. Many international investors were interested in developing the field and Putin government strung them along for years before it finally decided to let Gazprom go it alone. Total of France is the technology partner for the proposed LNG project and Norsk Hydro and Statoil for crude production. Whether Gazprom has the technology to extract gas from condensate-clogged rocks is a moot question. A pipeline linking the field to Nordstream will need to be built. This will require an investment of 16 billion US dollars. If all these can be achieved, this field will produce 24 bcm daily at peak levels of production.[8]

Vankor is situated in Turukhansk district of Krasnyarsk Krai. It is reported to contain over 250 million tonnes of sweet crude and 76.8 bcm of gas. Vankor underwent several changes in ownership and is now controlled by Rosneft. Drilling began in March 2004 and production is expected to begin this year. Unlike other fields in the region, Vankor's oil could be exported to Europe through the Northern Sea route. However, a substantial part of the productions is likely to travel 5000 kilometers through Transneft and the new ESPO pipeline to Asian and North American markets.

Even as the unexploited fields in western and northern Siberia are being developed, simultaneously, attention is focusing on the vast untapped potential of the east. Geology's generosity to East Siberia tends to be counterbalanced by hostile geography. This in essence, is the region's energy conundrum. Impressive as the petroleum reserves of this region are, a substantial quantity of them are situated in remote geographic locations like the Arctic Circle or in the bowels of the sea, more than six kilometers deep. Permafrost makes drilling and production difficult and ports in the region freeze over for more than half the year, preventing tankers from carrying away Siberian crude to global markets. Gas would remain a stranded asset unless pipelines link the fields to distant markets. Distances as well as terrain are daunting and the technology required to monetize the gas, challenging as well as expensive.

Development of East Siberia was taken up in the mid-seventies by a second decree issued by CPSU. Yet, development proceeded very slowly. Only in the last decade, with energy becoming the driving force of the Russian economy that Vladimir Putin, the then President turned his attention to this region. Also, Putin hit upon the idea of developing the region not only for its hydrocarbons, but also as a security measure. Putin described the situation in the Far East as 'a threat to national security' and stressed the need to invest money in the Far East. The result was a federal government targeted programme called 'Development of the Far East and the trans-Baikal Region upto 2013'[9]

At the same time, Putin conceived a plan to diversify markets as well. The Energy Strategy of Russia up to 2020", approved on August 28, 2003 targets increase in share of oil exports to Asia from 3 to 30 per cent by 2020 and that of gas to 15 per cent and virtually all of this is expected to be supplied by Eastern Siberia and the Russian Far East. These two regions together have 13.5 per cent and 19 per cent of Russia's known oil and gas potential respectively. Further exploration in the region could well increase this figure substantially.

The major gas field in East Siberia is Kovykta, 450 kilometers from Irkutsk. It is estimated to contain 2.3 tcm of gas and condensate reserves of 108 million tonnes. However, the Greater Kovykta regions is estimated to have as much as 10 tcm of gas. The ownership of RUSIA Petroleum which controls Kovykta has changed frequently and drastically even as its mineral estimates got revised upwards. Originally, TNK-BP held 63 per cent stake in the field while China National Petroleum Corporation and Korean Kogas were the other stakeholders as also potential customers for the output of this field. It was estimated that the field could supply as much as 30 bcm of gas to China and Korea through a 4500 km pipeline from Irkutsk to both these markets. However, in 2007, through deft maneuvering, Gazprom managed to grab controlling stake in the field.[10] Commercial production from Kovykta will begin in 2017 and negotiations are on with China for a gas sales contract. However, there seems to be a wide gap between Gazprom's asking price and China's willingness and affordability to pay this price. As of now, it appears that Kovykta gas will supply domestic markets in Russia.

In Yakutia in the extreme northeast lie the Talakan and Chayandinskoye condensate fields which are being developed jointly by ALROSA, the diamond major. This field is reported to contain 124 million tonnes of oil and 47 trillion cubic meters of gas.

Sakhalin I &II are the first fields to be developed in the Far East. Sakhalin has the advantage of being closer to Asian markets which can be reached by tankers, obviating the need for construction of lengthy pipelines. Sakhalin II was discovered in 1986 and enjoys the distinction of being the first PSA project in Russian history. In 2000, Shell bought the controlling stake in Sakhalin II from Marathon and the field became the first project to be developed without Russian involvement. Shell is constructing the world's largest LNG plant with a capacity of 9.6 tonnes per year to ship the field's gas to markets in the Pacific rim.

However, in 2007, through means more foul than fair, Gazprom managed to evict Shell as the majority shareholder although the latter remains operator of the field. Oil production is underway, but gas will have to await the setting up of LNG terminals.

Sakhalin I has 150 million tonnes of oil (1.1 billion barrels) and 500 bcm of gas. It is operated by Exxon Mobil and India's ONGC Videsh has a 20 per cent stake in this field. The promoters plan supply gas to China through pipelines.

In 2007, Russia's arctic expedition named Arktika 2007 set forth to lay claim to the Barents Sea's unknown hydrocarbon deposits. Mir 1 & 2, two submersibles planted the Russian flag in this desolate fringe of the planet in an effort to extend the continental shelf beyond 320 kilometers defined under International Maritime Law. It is believed that the polar regions may contain upto 100 billion barrels of oil and condensates.

Transportation Infrastructure

Development of Siberian and Far Eastern petroleum resources will critically depend upon evacuation infrastructure. Currently, an energy highway of unparalleled dimensions stretches for 5,000 km (3,108 miles) from western Siberia to European Russia and thence to Western Europe. It consists of a dozen steel pipes, each up to one and a half meters (5 feet) in diameter and capable of handling an operating pressure of 70 to 90 bar. It takes about a week for a gas molecule to make the journey from Yamburg to Hamburg.[11] The Baltic Pipeline System connects Urengoy and Uslinsk to Moscow and to Primorsk terminal from where crude is shipped to European and other destinations. There is a proposal to extend this network to Timon Pechora region whose oil is currently being ferried by rail to Murmansk. Murmansk port is also being upgraded to make it an all-weather port.

The other major pipeline system that is being constructed is the East Siberia Pacific Ocean Pipeline (ESPO) which, in the first phase costing 11 billion US dollars, runs 2757 kilometers (1713 miles) from Taishet to Skovordino to carry 1.6 million barrels of oil daily. In the second phase, it will be further extended by 2100 kilometers (1300 miles) to the Pacific Coast from where it could be shipped to Asian destinations and to North America. However, doubts are being raised as to whether exploitable oil in East Siberia would be sufficient to justify a pipeline of this dimension and length. The first phase should be completed this year.

Shtokman gas is proposed to be sent to the Nordstream pipeline 2000 miles away, bypassing Finland and the Baltic States. Construction is slated to being this year. Kovykta, as mentioned earlier, will supply China through pipelines while Sakhalin energy will be bound for Asian markets. There is also a proposal to build a gas pipeline from Sakhalin to northern Japan.

III

Curiously, despite the abundance of hydrocarbons in its own soil and waters, Siberian Far East is notorious for its energy crises. The annual fuel deficit in the Far Eastern region is 7 million tons of oil equivalent, which is covered by supplies from other regions of Russia. The region has also been witnessing major demographic changes with its local population moving westward into Moscow and other cities to be replaced by immigrants from China, South Korea and other Asian countries. Lack of skilled labour will also prove to be a major obstacle to the development of Siberia and the Russian Far East.

Siberian oil and gas production comes at a steep cost due to problems posed by geology, geography and lack of infrastructure. Russian Academician Alexei Kontorovich from the Siberian branch of the Russian Academy of Sciences estimates that developing east Siberian oil will require US $ 87 billion.[12]

Lack of Strategic Vision

However, lack of financial resources is perhaps less of a problem than the lack of a strategic vision on the part of the Russian state. Any serious effort to bring East Siberian and Russian Far Eastern energy to global markets will have to address many critical issues. Foremost among them is the need for technology which may not be available with the National Oil Companies. In today's world, expecting technology transfer and partnership without offering a stake in the project through equity participation, may prove to be elusive. Offshore fields in Western Siberia have been only 1200 meters deep whereas those in the East go down to depths of 6 to 8 kilometers. The climate is far more challenging and the ecology, fragile. It is, therefore, imperative, to involve global majors with experience of drilling and production in similar terrain and climate.

Yet, the only policy of the Russian Federation now seems to be to somehow extend the reach of National Oil Companies to the detriment of foreign companies. Foreign investors are systematically being driven out of controlling positions or marginalized to give way to Gazprom, Rosneft and Transeft, Russia's National Oil Companies with entrenched interests and influence. In field after field, the Russian government and policy makers have found ways and means to evict foreign investors through methods fair or foul to consolidate state control over resources. Sakhalin II provides a typical instance of this tendency. The Sakhalin PSAs were 'grandfathered'[13] when the subsoil law was amended. Yet, Putin effectively wielded the environment card to dislodge Shell from its controlling perch. Russia' environment agency Rosprirornadzor alleged environmental violations in Sakhalin II and levied a fine of 30 billion US dollars. Simultaneously, pressure was exerted on Shell to sell its stake to Gazprom. The threat of fines evaporated as soon as Shell agreed to part with majority stake in the project to Gazprom in return for an obscure field elsewhere. Similar environmental allegations, although on a minor scale, were leveled against Exxonmobil operating Sakhalin 1. For the moment, the American multinational continues to hold on to its position as majority shareholder and operator.

TNK-BP has been evicted from Kovykta on even flimsier grounds of not adhering to agreement to supply the local region although local demand is reported to be much lower than the envisaged supply quantities. Gazprom managed to get a stranglehold on the company for much less than market value. Foreign investors had been lured with the prospect of a share in Shtokman, but finally, Putin signaled Gazprom to go it alone.

Recent amendments proposed to sub-soil law endorse controlling stakes to state firms in 'strategic' fields with more than 70 million tonnes of oil or 50 bcm of gas or those located in the Continental Shelf. There are 32 such field in Siberia (18 in Yamal-Nenets Autonomous District, 5 in Yakutia and 9 – on the Barents, Okhotsk and Kara seas shelf) are about 5.2 tcm. The largest are Kruzensternskoye (1.7 tcm of gas) and Chayandinskoye fields (1.2 tcm of gas). Besides, Severo-Tambeyskoye (929 bcm), Utrenneye (747 bcm), Malyginskoye (745 bcm) and Tassiyskoye fields (441 bcm) have enormous oil and gas reserves. If carried through, foreign investors may have to be content with minority stakes in small and isolated fields.

For their part, foreign investors have also often alienated the Russian government by reporting escalated development costs, far in excess of their original estimates. Higher development costs imply less revenues for the host government, in the form of delayed and lower government take, less taxes and royalties. Company after foreign company has resorted to claiming higher development costs, part of which may be justified because of the scarcity of oil rigs and equipment in the global exploration market. For instance, TNK-BP is reported to have maintained that gas-lifting costs will be 28 to 35 US dollars per 1,000 cubic meters in the East of Russia, though in West Siberia Gazprom reports 3 to 4 US dollars for a similar quantity and independent gas producers 2 US dollars per 1,000 cubic meters. Similarly, operators of both Sakhalin I &II reported escalation in costs, the former from 12.8 billion US dollars to 17 billion US dollars and the latter from 12 billion US dollars to 20 billion US dollars. This will increase the production cost per unit of gas and oil substantially, leaving less for government take and royalties under the PSA. This has no doubt, raised suspicions among Russian policy makers on the reliability of cost estimates quoted by them. It is viewed as a ploy to deprive the Russian state of its share of profits from the mineral wealth from its own territories.

Yet, Russian oil companies alone can neither muster the capital required nor do they have the cutting-edge technologies required to monetize the mineral resources in Russian Far East and Eastern Siberia. According to the Ministry of Energy and Industry, to achieve the necessary volume of gas reserves (6.7 trillion cubic meters) to ensure commercially viable gas production in the East of Russia by 2030, geological and exploration drilling of some 3.45 million meters will be necessary, which means an investment of several billion US dollars.

Domestic funds will hardly be enough to develop this province, Russia's windfall profits from rising energy prices notwithstanding. The Stabilization Fund amounting to 99.7 billion US Dollars as of February 1, 2007 will hardly last five years if it were to be deployed to bridge the gap between required and actual investments, according to Vladimir Milov, a leading Russian energy expert.[14]

The Russian government is considering changes in the tax code for minerals. These changes envisage a reduction of the tax rate for depleted fields, for the production of hard-to-recover reserves and for the development of new oil fields in territories that are not well explored, including in East Siberia and the Far East. Beginning in 2007, companies can receive tax holidays for new fields (up to 10 years for production and up to 15 years for exploration). Companies working in East Siberia are already exempt from mineral production tax, and there have been discussions about possible preferential treatment for companies developing new fields on the shelf, mainly in the Arctic seas and the Far East. Presumably, Gazprom and Rosneft, who divided the continental shelf among themselves, will benefit most from this fiscal innovation.

In a striking departure from the earlier trend, a new breed of investors are coming into Russia, the Asian consumers of Russian energy – Japan's Sodeco, Mitsui and Mitsubishi, India's ONGC Videsh, China's Sinopec, CNPC etc. While some of them might possess the capital for development of the region's infrastructure, they are unlikely to have access to technologies that would be required for successful deep water drilling in depths hitherto uncharted.

Unless Russia puts in place a strategic vision for the development of Siberia's untapped hydrocarbon potential, and follows it up with appropriate policies that encourage and incentivize potential investors and technology partners, it is likely that much of the regions oil and gas will continue to remain underground. Worse, it could lead to haphazard and irresponsible mining in the region, with its attendant consequences for the environment and ecology of the region. The policies must also offer a generous share of the benefits of such development to the local population. The present tendency to marginalize local populations through large-scale immigration of foreign workforce may prove to be counter-productive in the long-run.

IV
Role of Siberia in India's Energy Security

India's presence in Russia's Far East is now nearly a decade-old. Sakhalin 1 which has total recoverable reserves of 307 million tonnes of oil and condensate and 485 bcm of gas was the second project to be given to investors under a production sharing agreement. The initial shareholders were Exxon, Rosneft, Sakhalinmorneftgas and SODECO of Japan. In 2001, ONGC Videsh (OVL) joined the project under an agreement with Rosneft. OVL was to pay 1 billion US dollars in exchange for a 20 per cent stake and in addition, carried Rosneft's interest of another 1 billion US dollars. The sale was also tied to sale of Russian weapons to India. OVL has already committed a total of 2.07 US dollars for the project. As costs escalate, this may go up further.

Sakhalin 1 was India's largest overseas investment and as such, generated much excitement in both countries. It was hailed as a significant step in enhancing India's energy security through supply diversification. In 2007, the field produced 50,000 barrels of oil out of which, a small consignment from OVL's share reached India's Mangalore Refinery. It is unlikely that Sakhalin 1 will become a significant source of crude supplies to India. Crude tankers from

Sakhalin will have to negotiate the cluttered Malacca Straits which China and Japan are trying to avoid. In all likelihood, Sakhalin oil and gas would be shipped to proximate markets in Japan, China and South Korea although for OVL, the investment is a profitable one, especially in a situation of soaring crude prices. Swap deals with Asian buyers of Middle Eastern crude is possible and likely.

Unlike Sakhalin II, natural gas from Sakhalin 1 will be sent by pipelines to markets. China is the logical market for gas from this field. However, there are two obstacles to the promoters of the project realizing market prices for gas. First, Gazprom is now officially the sole agency through which gas can be exported out of Russia. Vladimir Putin designated Gazprom as the sole export vehicle for Asian markets in 2000 and subsequently, extended it to all world markets. Thus, Exxon, the operator of Sakhalin 1 will have to sell its gas output to Gazprom. Whether Gazprom will pay international prices to Exxon for gas exported to China and other countries or will merely offer domestic gas prices which are only a third of prevailing global prices, remains to be seen. If Gazprom does not pay international prices, Exxon may not be keen on gas production and thus monetization of Sakhalin 1 gas could be delayed. Even if Gazprom offers a price less than prevailing international prices, OVL's investment in Sakhalin 1 will yield less profits than it ought to.

The second factor which could dampen gas exports from Sakhalin 1 is China's reluctance to pay prevailing market prices for gas. Unfortunately for gas consumers, global gas prices have got linked to crude prices. With crude prices hovering around 135 US dollars a barrel, gas could well go out of reach of Asian markets. OVL may then have to be content with revenues from crude sales.

In May 2008, India also secured a commitment for a 23 per cent stake to OVL in Sakhalin III. Estimates are that OVL will pay an initial 300 million US dollars for acquiring its stake from Rosneft which holds 70 per cent stake in the field. The field is reported to have in-place reserves of 800 million tonnes.

Although Sakhalin fields may not contribute directly to India's energy security by offering a supply diversification option, it would however, add to the global oil supply stabilizing prices to some extent. By opening up a new source of supply to Japan, South Korea and China, Sakhalin would also free up some quantities of Persian Gulf oil which would then be available to other proximate importers including India.

Conclusions

Despite the remoteness of its location, Siberia's vast mineral wealth is a beacon for the global petroleum industry hungry for new sources of supply. Without Siberian and Far Eastern resources, experts believe Russia is likely to run out of oil in a decade. Therefore, for the Russian state too, Siberia holds out the promise of extending its new-found status as a petrostate for a few more decades. Yet, for Siberia itself and the Russian Far East, their immense hydrocarbon deposits are at best, a double-edged weapon. Exploiting them could bring jobs and prosperity to the region hitherto consigned to economic oblivion by the rest of Russia, but it could also upset the pristine ecology of this environmentally fragile region. Siberia's distinctive culture and rich ethnic diversity are at risk of being submerged by the onslaught of new lifestyles and prosperity brought by oil industry professionals converging on the region from all over the world. Already the demography of the region is strained by the influx of too many 'gastarbaiters' – legal and illegal – and a floating population of oil industry workers – ethnic Chinese, Koreans, Vietnamese and even Indians. The cupidity of global petroleum industry and the urgency of the Russian state to keep the energy taps flowing drive the juggernaut that comes hurtling down the Siberian landscape. Native Siberians have the daunting task of dodging this unstoppable juggernaut from destroying their unique identity and culture.

Notes and References

1. Russia world's largest producer ahead of Saudi Arabia in 2007 at *http://www.gasandoil.com/goc/frame_ntr_news.htm* accessed in June 2008.
2. Poussenkova, Nina: All quiet on the eastern front in Russian Analytical Digest 33/08.
3. *Ibid.*
4. Poussenkova, Nina: The wild wild west—East Siberia and the Far East, A New Petroleum Frontier? Carnegie Moscow Center, Carnegie Endowment for International Peace No. : 4, 2007.
5. Wuest Christian: How long will Siberia's gas last? Inhttp://www.spiegel.de/international/world/0,1518,524140,00.html dated December 18, 2007 accessed in May 2008.
6. *Ibid.*
7. (Ria Novosti, Gazprom to commence production at Yuzhno-Russkoye field on Dec 18, 6th Dec 2007 *http://en.rian.ru/russia/20071206/*

91242419.html) accessed on May 21, 2008.

8. 'Happy New Oil and Gas Year! 2008 will change both Russia and the whole world' No. 1, January 2008 at *http://www.oilandgaseurasia.com/articles/p/64/article/516/* accessed in January 2008.
9. Poussenkova, Nina, *op. cit.*, 3.
10. Russia's Gazprom purchases Siberian gas fields from BP—Washington Post, June 23, 2007.
11. *Op. cit.*, 6.
12. Poussenkova, Nina, *op. cit.*, 3.
13. The term means that existing PSAs would be protected from any amendments to subsoil law. In that sense, they were meant to be sacrosanct.
14. Riley A. "The coming of the Rusian gas deficit' OGEL January 2007.

21

Harnessing Siberia's Power of Natural Resources

Jatinder Khanna

'Land of Nothing' Signifies Everything Lucrative for Russia

"Siberia" comes from the Mongolian root "sibir", which means 'sleeping land'. In the early 1700's, Siberia became a place of exile. It continued to be the last stop for criminals and political prisoners throughout much of the 20th century. Siberia came to epitomize all that was worst about Russia under the communist rule. Now, Siberia is the newly emerging economic and strategic region and is seen as the hub of economic development in the Russia of the 21st century.

Fig. 21.1: The region of Siberia spans 13,488,500 sq km. and is even larger than Canada, which is the second largest country in the world after Russia[1]

Of the 89 entities of the Russian Federation, 29, belong to three major economic areas—West Siberia, East Siberia, and the Far East. The population of these regions collectively referred to as 'Siberia' is about 32 million, or more than 21 percent of the total population of the Federation, and these regions produce 30 percent of Russia's GDP. Siberia is a potent tool for Russia, its claim to become a 'resource superpower'. Could it also prove to be the place which holds the key to the world's natural resource scarcity problem?

Energy Resources

Energy and fuel production served as the backbone of the Soviet economy and its importance has increased during the years of Russia's transition to a market economy. In 1997, for example, the industry provided 68 percent of all federal budget revenues. In Russia today, oil and gas account for about 45 percent of tax revenues, 25 percent of the GDP, and 10 percent of employment.[2]

Russia is the world's second largest oil producer. Russia had an output of 9.7 million barrels per day in 2006 (the most recent year for which figures are available) as compared to Saudi Arabia's output of 11.1 million barrels per day.[3]

Figures cited by the Frankfurter *Allgemeine Zeitung* on May 22, 2002 show that 12 per cent world's known oil reserves are in Russia. Three-quarters of Russia's hard-currency receipts come from the sale of petroleum products abroad.[4]

According to the Address by Industry and Energy Minister Viktor Khristenko at the Fifth Russian Oil & Gas Week in the 2005 G8 Summit, based on Russia's current estimates, oil production may reach 530 million tons and oil export 310 million tons by 2015.

As the source of most of Russia's oil and natural gas, Siberia plays a major role in the country's modern but struggling free-market economy. Siberia holds important energy resources, including 80 percent of Russia's proven natural gas reserves (or 30 percent of the global share), 75 percent of its oil (4 percent of global reserves), and 90 percent (19 percent) of its coal.[5]

The West Siberian oil and gas province was declared the main oil base of the country in this period. Oil production will continue to grow there until 2010-2015.

The Kuznetsk Basin in southwestern Siberia, generally referred to by Russians as the Kuzbas, contains about 600 billion metric tons of low-sulfur coking coal (coal used in steel production); the brown coal deposits of the Kansk-Achinsk Basin in south central Siberia are nearly twice that size.[6]

East Siberia alone accounts for 14 per cent of Russia's oil resources, or approximately 10 billion tons of recoverable reserves. The Russian shelf is rich in gas, especially in the Arctic, which has about 30 per cent of national gas reserves. About 20 per cent, or more than 40 trillion cu m of gas, are concentrated in East Siberia, Yakutia, and the island of Sakhalin.

The remoteness of many of Siberia's oil and gas deposits makes access and transport expensive. As a consequence, Russia's most lucrative potential resources are largely untapped. Russia has proven oil reserves of 60 billion barrels, most of which are located in Western Siberia, between the Ural Mountains and the Central Siberian Plateau. There, only four or five oil and gas fields have been discovered, and a 1996 Petroconsultants study (the latest available) estimated that around 35 million barrels of oil and 5 Trillion Cubic feet (tcf) of natural gas exist in the region. Official energy statistics from the US Government confirm that Russia's ability to harness its energy resources remains far realized especially in Eastern Siberia. Similar is the case with Far Eastern oil fields where the Russian government has estimated it could earn more than $100 billion in profit. Their development, however, will require $55 billion of investment over the next two decades, especially in Eastern Siberia and the offshore fields around Sakhalin Island.[7]

According to the International Energy Agency—On the whole, Russia will need as much as $500 billion as investment by 2020 to maintain and develop its entire energy industry infrastructure.

Precious metals

Russia accounts for over 40 per cent of global annual mine production of palladium and approximately 15 per cent of platinum production.[8] Siberia is very crucial region for Russia with regards to platinum group of metals. The Norilsk-Talnakh region which lies on the isolated Taimyr Peninsula, where Siberia meets the Kara Sea contains more than a third of the world's nickel reserves and two-fifths of the platinum-group metals.[9] Siberia plays host to Norilsk Nickel—a leading precious metal miner of the world. The company is the world's largest producer of nickel (a vital input in the production of stainless steel) and palladium (used for aircraft production, electrical contacts, dentistry, surgical equipment, jewelry and sign production). It also has significant amounts of cobalt and copper.

Fig. 21.2: Map of Russia showing important reserves of PGM

Russia is world's fifth largest cobalt producer and Norilsk Nickel accounts for a major part, with total mine production rounding off to 5000 tonnes in 2005. The metal is widely used in aircraft production and occurs as a by—product of nickel mining.

Russia is the world's fifth largest gold producer. Polyus Gold, a spin off from Norilsk Nickel, is Russia's biggest gold miner. Its output in 2005 was 1.076 million ounces in 2005.

Russia in the Midst of Energy Geopolitics

The development of Siberian energy resources can either result as threat or appear as a promise to the world. And Russia is thinking hard—a fact demonstrated by the Group of 8 summit meeting which it hosted in summer of 2006 in St. Petersburg. The topic on its mind was 'Global Energy Security'—a term which also demonstrates unease that Russia experiences over the immeasurable reserves of under utilized energy resources it holds in its belly called Siberia.

The economic crisis in Russia and its subsequent transition to a market economy in the 1990s has increased the significance of its external economic relations for both the energy sector and its economy in general. In the beginning of 2006, President of Russia, Vladimir Putin visited Yakutia region of Siberia to emphasize the need to step up the efforts to create a unified system for gas production and transportation in East Siberia and the Far East.[10]

For Russia, situations are hardly rosy. Most countries in the world prefer to buy oil and gas from the Gulf countries. To clearly demarcate the divide, Russia recently rejected an invitation to join OPEC, preferring to sell its oil and gas at market price.

After the Ukraine gas-supply cut-off, Russia is perceived as a 'bully' supplier. US Vice-President Dick Cheney reprimanded Russia for increased state control in the sector. EU has accused of pushing its state-owned and natural gas 'Godzilla', Gazprom, in the global energy arena to help it gain leverage. Gazprom aims to consolidate its operations as it sets its sights on companies across the world in a bid to gain cost efficiency.

Much to the chagrin of Britain, the Russian giant expressed an interest this year in buying Centrica, their country's largest natural gas distributor. With the rise of newly industrializing heavyweights like India and China, one presumes that Russia would have to do little to attract customers. The two economic engines are guzzling conventional energy resources like coal and oil. China is the world's second largest oil consumer, after the United States. According to official estimates of China, by 2020, the country's energy consumption is expected to top 3 billion tons of standard coal, with its GDP quadrupled and energy use doubled.[11] Siberia's resources are undoubtedly capable of providing the obvious satiation to this energy hunger given the untapped potential of its extensive resources.

Developmental Policies have Left Siberia in Cold

Years of state-planning resulted in unified and centralized development for electric power, gas, and oil supply systems and the railway network. Post-soviet policies have mainly targeted resource extraction and regional intensification. Oil and natural gas fields were a priority in the 1960s and 1970s first in the West, then in the Far-East and finally in the North.[12] As a consequence of Moscow's planners' ideological stance to 'reduce inequalities' within the country the country ended up with an over-utilized western Siberia and wilderness in the Eastern and Far –Eastern Siberian regions. By 1980s, incomplete projects and extremely low returns on high investment threatened Siberian development.[13]

Apart from Siberia's inhospitable climate, poor transportation links and an underdeveloped physical and social infrastructure, the region also faces problems like high labour turnover and low capital efficiency.

According to IMF Economist Alexei Mozhin, there was a shift of priorities in Siberian development strategy from an effort to endow Siberia with an integrated economy. Earlier, Influx of workers was promoted in regions where they were needed to operate resource industries. This perpetuated a dichotomy, in which 75-80 percent of the population and economic activity continued to be concentrated in the 'European' part of Russia, while about 80 per cent of gas and coal reserves, 75 per cent of water resources and a large part of non-ferrous metals were found in Siberia.

"Build, Build—Whatever Be the Cost"—'Ecocide' in Siberia

The scrambles for strategic resources often jeopardize non-strategic resources (the environment). State planners realized the enormous wealth of Siberia but undermined their own capabilities when it came to managing its resources. Regime after regime, environmental concerns and cost-analysis with a sustainability view point were subordinated to the upholding of the red flag. During Stalin's reign, overtly ambitious projects were the norm. The eventual failure of 500-mile Belomar Canal, stretching from Leningrad proves the point that defective planning took a hefty toll on the adjoining eco-system.

By 1950s the state had established mines in Northern Siberia for Coal, copper, tin, zinc, gold and platinum. Scientists in the Siberian Science City, 'Akademgorodok', planned a paper mill which would utilize Lake Baikal as an excellent industrial setting. Since the start of the project, the level of lake started to rise and destroyed the delicate ecosystem. The chemicals in the lake skyrocketed past acceptable limits up to ninety-eight times the norm.[14] Economist Abel Aganbegian reported that air and water pollution from the mill irreparably damaged the industries of Baikal flora, fauna, fishing and major resources of the region.

Mighty construction projects continued to be envisaged without any consideration of their aftermath. In *Ecocide in the USSR*, Feschbach and Friendly use the Siberian town of Zima to illustrate the ill-effects of state planned industrial projects. During the 1970s, the Chemical Industry ministry established a project to utilize the large chlorine deposit to manufacture polyvinyl chloride and pure alcohol. The factories spewed toxins in the air and in 1989—air in Zima contained the highest level of benzopyrene in the USSR—twenty-two times higher than the tolerable level.[15]

It is true that vast areas remain practically unaffected by human activity, yet in industrial regions air, water and soil are heavily polluted with toxicity. Obsolete Technologies, lack of facilities for rendering and purification of industrial waste are the reasons for large economic centers of Siberia—Angarsk, Bratsk, Kemerovo, Krasnoyarsk, Novokuznetsk, Norilsk—to get on the list of the most ecologically unhappy cities in Russia.

Norilsk, a Soviet penal colony turned multi-billion dollar metal mine, is just miles from the Arctic Circle. Norilsk features in the list of most polluted places in world according to the Blacksmith Institute, where the snow is black, the air tastes of sulfur and the life expectancy for factory workers is 10 years below the Russian average.[16] A 1999 study found elevated copper and nickel concentrations in soils in as much as a 60 km radius of the city. No wonder, there is a common saying there—'If a Norilsk man gets sick in Moscow, the way to cure him is to move him closer to the car's exhaust'.

Energy Powerhouse + Sustainability = New, Improved, Siberia

Presidential Aide Vladislav Surkov's recent speech to United Russia activists showed the government is prepared to sacrifice everything to become an energy superpower.[17] If Russia aims to become a 'superpower', then it has to rethink its long-standing policy of 'development at any cost'. The enormous social and economic costs that it has faced in the past should act as a motivator to discontinue the paranoid control over conventional energy resources.

Siberia has not only huge reserves of fossil fuels but also enormous renewable energy resources and options to develop geothermal, solar, wind, ocean and biomass energy. The share of renewable energy resources (excluding hydro) in electricity generation world wide is about 10 per cent, but Russia's share is less than 1 per cent.[18]

Low prices of conventional energy resources (coal, petroleum, gas etc.) further depress the development of new sustainable technology in renewable energies. No stringent legal framework exists in the regard. The lack of official data available on renewable energy investments in Russia show the neglect that this issue faces within Moscow's policy making circles.

Suggested Shift in Focus

- *Protect the ecology of an economic treasure trove*
  The issue of protecting the virgin lands of Siberia, while extracting resources requires heightened political consciousness. Soviet legacy of exploiting coal, oil and nuclear resources stunts the opportunity for developing alternate forms of energy.
- *Decrease Expenses of Fuel Delivery to Siberia*
  The Russian state bears a substantial cost to deliver energy to Siberian region. The energy cost in remote regions is exorbitant (20-50 times higher than energy costs covered by the central grid). If alternate forms of energy are developed at source in Siberia, then the Russian government can significantly reduce its burden.
- *Exploit the Renewable Resource Potential of Siberia*
  Although, plans are commissioned for developing 'clean energy resources' like geo thermal plants in Kamchatka, several wind farms and micro hydro power stations, Siberia is no where near developing its huge potentials.
  The Alternate Energy Institute warns that '*Water will likely become one of the most fought-over resources in the coming decades*'. In this regard, Siberia-which holds six out of twelve longest rivers in the world and Lake Baikal, (which holds quarter of world's fresh water)-has little to scurry about. (There is no other region in Russia, comparable with Siberia in potential and efficiency of utilization of hydraulic power resources).[19]
- *Reduce Energy Dependence on Conventional Sources and Outdated Methods of Extraction*
  Presently Russia may find alternative forms of energy either expensive in comparison to fossil fuels or unsuitable for large-scale energy production. Even the adoption of technologies which rely on coal, combined with technologies like carbon capture, carbon storage, and zero-emission technology could provide its citizens with environmentally acceptable energy.

Conclusion

Two crucial points seem to be missing from Russia's Siberian developmental agenda: Sustainable development and international competitiveness. Instead there is only one overriding idea of becoming 'the energy super power', which holds out the promise of a footstep in the global geopolitical landscape.

References for Further Readings

1. Weissbach, M. Executive Intelligence Review. 2006. What Did 'Energy Dialogue' At Bush-Putin Summit Mean? Accessed at *http://www.new-federalist.com/other/2002/2922us-russ_engy.html* on 18 January 2007
2. Kaelin, A. The question of development: Siberia's natural resources. Accessed at *http://www.princeton.edu/~gradconf/index_files/piirsgradconfwebsite_files/papers/A_Kaelin.pdf* on 22 January 2007
3. Weisman, S. Russia plays energy card vs. Western investment. 2006. Accessed at *http://www.iht.com/articles/2006/06/11/news/moscow.php* on 12 January 2007

Notes and References

1. Map And Caption from encyclopedia, MS Encarta 2000.
2. Vladimir Ivanov, "Prospects for Russia's Energy Diplomacy in Northeast Asia," *Global Economic Review* (Seoul, Korea), Summer 1999.
3. Energy Information Administration, *Top World Oil Producers 2005, http://www.eia.doe.gov/emeu/cabs/topworldtables1_2.html* on March 15 2007.
4. MS Encarta 2000 accessed at *http://www.nsu.ru/aiesec/english/fortrainees/siberia.php* on 29 December 2006.
5. Saneev, B. Russia's energy policies and Northeast Asia. 1995. accessed at *http://www.nira.go.jp/publ/review/2001winter/saneev.txt* on 1 January 2007.
6. http://www.nsu.ru/aiesec/english/fortrainees/siberia.php
7. Chan, J. Japan outbids China for Siberian pipeline. 2005. accessed at *http://www.wsws.org/articles/2005/feb2005/pipe-f14_prn.shtml* on 20 December 2006.
8. Platinum today 204 accessed at http://www.platinum.matthey.com/production/russia.html
9. Gordon, M. Siberia Tests Russia's Ability To Profit From Privatization. 1997. accessed on 27 February 2008 at *http://query.nytimes.com/gst/fullpage.html?res=9E07E2D7173CF93AA35751C1A961958260&sec=& spon=&pagewanted=all*

10. Tomberg, I. Future Oil and Gas Development in Siberia and the Russian Far East. 24 January 2006. RIA novosti.
11. China to boost use of renewable energy by law. China's embassy in *India. http://www.chinaembassy.org.in/eng/zgbd/t190356.htm*
12. Hill and Gaddy, pp. 80-1.
13. Hill and Gaddy, pp. 93.
14. Josephson, p. 183.
15. Feschbach and Friendly, p. 99.
16. http://www.blacksmithinstitute.org/ten.php
17. Gibson, M. How sustainable is Russia's future as an energy superpower? 2006 Accessed at *http://www.carnegieendowment.org/events/index.cfm?fa=eventDetail&id=860* on 6 January 2007.
18. Karghiev, V. Energy and sustainable Development in Russian Federation. 2005-2006. Accessed at *http://www.helio-international.org/reports/pdfs/Russia-EN.pdf* on 20 January 2007.
19. 'Some Economic Geography' accessed at *http://www.fplib.org/partners/siberia/eco_bus/f1_1.html* on 21 January 2007.

22

Siberia: Scenarios of Colonisation and the Demographic Landscape*

N.N. Ablazhei, E.G. Vodichev

At the time of Russian assimilation, the territories of Siberia and today's Russian Far East were inhabited by Mongoloid-European people. It is believed that at the initial stage of the process of populating Siberia with the Russians annexation to the Russian state was the priority. At a later stage, the purpose was to colonise Siberia. Both these processes of populating, settling and assimilating its vast territories lying to the east of the Urals were inextricably linked. The demographic development of the region reflected the peculiarity and specificity of colonisation of the eastern periphery of the Russian state.

In most general terms and in accordance with accepted patterns, the colonisation of Siberia was accomplished in three basic stages: trade, agrarian and industrial assimilation. This pattern as a whole works and explains the general course of historical process.[1] It should be mentioned that sometimes the historical canvas of the colonisation of Siberia is interpreted according to logic, within the framework of which these stages are considered to have replaced one another, implying a consistent enhancement in the level of development of the productive forces of the region. But the historical process was not one-dimensional. In reality the assimilation of the region was quite a complex picture, in which various trends of development were synthesised. Hence, there can be discussion only about the dominant trends of development at one or the other points of history, which somehow provides an analysis of the given situation but avoids over-simplification of the historical process of assimilation of the region.

---

* Translated by Susmita Bhattacharya, Fellow, MAKAIAS, Kolkata

While talking about the beginning of colonisation of Siberia one usually refers to the period of Siberia's annexation to Russia at the end of the 16th century. However, the process of filling up this region with 'human resources' from lands which had been traditionally part of Russian state began much earlier. It is well known, for instance, that the North Trans-Urals traditionally drew the attention of inhabitants from the north-western territories, particularly, the Novgorod estates. Hence another line of analysis follows the demographic character of Siberia after it was assimilated. It is obvious that there were two parallel trends of colonisation processes—the 'people's colonisation', which in many ways took place side by side with state's policy and secondly the colonisation under regulatory role of the state. But then again, in this case strict division is impossible. On the one hand, even in the absence of any precisely formulated and territorially oriented demographic policy, the state tried though ways and methods tried to influence the process of populating one or other regions. On the other—in practice political action was not always guided by the state's requirements. With regard to Siberia, it meant that the colonisation of this region (in the context of that component, which is related to people's colonisation) started earlier than it was recognised by the state as expedient, and did not develop at all the way as dictated by state policy. Even the campaign of Ermak became a peculiar synthesis of the processes of natural economic and demographic development of the region and the regulatory role of the state, attempting to bring these processes under control, to ensure the colonising processes of resources' and institutional support, and also to legitimise their actions.[2]

At the initial stage, the colonisation of Siberia was closely connected with the processes of this region's annexation to Russia and its legitimisation as a part of the Russian state. It was carried out by economic, legal and military methods. A special role in this process was played by the so-called service class, the Cossacks. Usually the beginning of the stage of assimilation through trade was connected with the campaign of the Cossack detachment led by ataman Ermak, hired by the traders and industrialists of Stroganov. Evidently, it was fur—the main Siberian resource at that time—that became the fundamental cause behind the penetration of the para-military detachments of the colonisers beyond the Ural range. In the 17th century the pelts,.mainly procurable in Siberia comprised not less than 20 per cent of revenue of the Russian state. This colonisation was concentrated mainly in the taiga and tundra regions. The indicator of success of colonisation processes was the growing expansion of 'yasachnaya' or fur tribute system levied on the indigenous population of the region. The main migratory flow during the end of the 16th and the first half of the 18th centuries was from the northern Russian lands.

The demographic potential of trade assimilation of the region cannot lend itself to verifiable estimates. According to the data available in the literature, by the mid-17th century one may say there were roughly 160-170 thousand aboriginal people and a similar number of migrant colonisers. But the question is how far can one rely on this data. However, it is obvious that from the beginning of the colonisation process the automatic growth always remained a primary factor behind the growth of Siberia's population.[3]

By the mid-18th century the role of the pelt business as a source of wealth of the state treasury substantially decreased. The trade assimilation of Siberia played its role in populating the region and was a powerful stimulus for the inflow of migrants and the growth of trade capital. In accordance with the available data, despite the prohibitions by the government of the country on the peasants' migration to the east, the total number of the population of Siberia in one and a half century increased almost by six times. In 1719 it was already 470 thousand, in 1744—590 thousand, and in 1762—760 thousand.[4]

However, the period of trade-business colonisation gradually came to an end. In the 18th century Siberia's potential in other resources was recognized—large reserves of metal ore as well as gold and silver were discovered. Gradually a sense that Siberia is a territory with boundless infinite lands dawned in. And although the agrarian potential of the eastern territories for a long period was called into question, a part of the land could absolutely be engaged in agricultural activities even though for the purpose of internal consumption. Earlier the foodstuffs production (first of all—bread) was supplied to Siberia from the European part of the country, though it was expensive and laborious.

All this raised the question concerning the agrarian resettlement to the region and rapid formation of the social strata of the Siberian peasantry. In the period of serfdom Russia of 18th century when the peasants were strictly living in bondage to the landlords' estate, such an issue could look somewhat premature. But the growing deficit of lands profitable for agricultural operation in the centre of the country prompted authorities to look from St Petersburg towards the interior Russian colonies in the east. In any case, the demographic potential of the agricultural colonisation in an agrarian country as Russia was several times greater than the potential of colonisation through trade-business. Simultaneously, the laws of development of the continental empire gradually demanded an expansion in the direction from the centre to the peripheries. As a result, since the 17th century the agricultural assimilation of the southern belt of Siberia took place, there was a step by step expansion towards the east. The assimilation of the zone of forest-steppes and steppe started, and the people concentrated along the rivers and highways.

The discovery of metal ores, and also gold deposits by the mid-18th century became a powerful stimulus for the development of industrial colonisation of the region. This process had started earlier than agrarian colonisation, but later on merged with the process of agrarian colonisation of Siberia. At the outset of the century, there emerged Kolyvano-Voskresenskii and Nerchinskii silver-melting factories in the Altai and Trans-Baikal. Somewhat later the development of the goldfields started in Eastern Siberia. Though the industrial assimilation of the region was put aside till the beginning of the 20th century, the new demand of manual labour resulted in the revival of production-oriented industries in Siberia. The question about the availability of manual labour was decided in accordance with the established state traditions.

From this time Siberia onwards, Siberia became the polygon for demographic experiments as convicts and the persons sent to exile and condemned to penal servitude by extra-judicial order started arriving en mass. The forced (or penal) colonisation starts in the region. Along with this the state controlled the process of unrestricted colonisation of Siberia, apprehending an outflow of the taxed people beyond the Urals. Penal colonisation was concentrated in the cabinet estates (belonging to the imperial courtyard) of Altai, Trans-Baikal, the belt along the Moscow highway and the border.

As a consequence of the parallel on-going processes of agrarian and the industrial colonisation that had started in Siberia, the population of the region exceeded one million by the end of the

18th century.[5] This trend continued in the 19th century. In the first half of the 19th century Siberia started getting populated with the serfs sent to the region by the decision of the landlords along with state peasants, exiles, and also the self-willed re-settlers, though the number of the latter was relatively less, since the main flow of the migrants was directed to the south. During the years 1820-1840s the state allowed to re-settle in Siberia from the Russian provinces that faced dearth of lands, but penal colonisation was predominant as before, maintaining the mass inflow of migrants to the region who imparted a specific demographic profile to Siberia and a single image in the eyes of the country's inhabitants. By the end of the first three decades of the 19th century the population mark was above 2 million inhabitants.

The "great reforms" of the 1860's had great significance for the changes in the approach to further assimilation of Siberia and correspondingly its demographic development. After the reforms of 1861, which resulted in the abolition of serfdom, the state took new steps for expanding civilian colonisation, which became far more significant compared to penal colonisation, though Siberia remained as the traditional region of penal servitude, exile and deportation of the people. The wide-scale assimilation of the territories of Altai started. The geopolitical interests the government allowed re-settlement in the Far East. Nevertheless, through the entire second half of the 19th century the migration policy of Russia was restrictive in nature. However a new situation arose: a critical mass of population was formed in the region, which influenced the intra-regional demographic balance. As a result the restrictions on the re-settlement of the peasants in Siberia no longer had a restraining effect on the colonisation of the region. The assimilation of Siberia in the 19th century in many respects was carried out by intra-regional (intra-Siberian) migrants.

The peculiarities of the processes of urbanisation in the region prove the domination of the agrarian trend of assimilation of Siberia that prevailed till the end of the 19th century. The first cities in the territory of Siberia were built in the second half of the 16th century. They were the outposts of colonisation primarily carrying out the military, administrative and trading functions. The Siberian cities were extremely thinly populated and practically had no permanent population. During 16th-19th centuries active colonisation in fact had no impact on urbanisation. Only in the mid-19th century the major centres of habitation emerged in Siberia, which not just by name but in essence can be regarded as cities. In Irkutsk, the largest city of Siberia, 17 thousand people lived, in Tobol'sk—15 thousand and in Omsk—almost 13 thousand. Till the end of the century the level of urbanisation of Siberia remained extremely low, lagging behind central Russia. Siberia, as before, was primarily an agrarian region of the Russian Empire, where more than 90 per cent of the population lived in villages.

The construction of the Siberian railway that started in 1893 had enormous impact on the process of populating Siberia. It coincided with the intensification of the agrarian issue in the country that resulted in sharp expansion of migration to the region. From the end of the 19th century Siberia became the main region of the country that was colonized. In 1896 re-settlement issue was taken up by a Resettlement Act. A large portion of the expenditures was on resettlement and relocation of the migrants. In 1885-1886, 165000 migrants moved to the region, during 1896-1900 another 9,00,000 people joined. Thus, the number of migrants to Siberia became comparable with the number of aboriginal people living in the region within a span of five years.

The laws of 1904 and 1906 introduced free migration to Siberia, ensured benefits to the migrants. As a result during the years of Stolypin's reforms (1907-1913) the migratory movement to Siberia reached the highest level. During 1906-1914 about 2.3 million people got settled in the region. The total number of population of Siberia in the year 1897 comprised 5799.8,[6] in 1906—6800.0, in 1914—10263.4, and in 1916—11049.7 thousand people[7], i.e. roughly during 60 years the number of population of Siberia and the Far East increased more than three times, including by two times during last two decades. Such a pace of migratory growth became unique in Russian history.

Transport development resulted in vital changes in the development of urbanisation processes in the region, which turned into an ever-growing serious factor of economic, demographic and cultural development of Siberia. During the first one and a half decade of the 20th century the number of urban population doubled and it increased mainly because of the migrants, who rushed towards the fast developing Siberian cities. Throughout the first quarter of the 20th century the migratory processes in Siberia proceeded more intensively than in other regions of Russia.

The social cataclysms in Russia during the first quarter of the 20th century had effect on the demographic processes in the Siberian region. The first phase of the Civil War caused substantial loss of human lives in the region. According to available data, by the time of its commencement (in 1918) 8324.4 thousand people lived in Siberia (excluding the Far East). The cities that rapidly developed at the end of 19th and beginning of the 20th centuries especially suffered. The Civil War resulted in de-urbanisation. As a result of the breakdown of the socio-economic system the urban population of Siberia was reduced by more than 100 thousand people[8] between 1918 and 1920.

However, by the end of the war (1922) the number of population in Siberia increased roughly by one million comprising 9265.2 thousand people.[9] By the mid-1920's the number of population of the region considerably increased. The All-Union census of 1926 stated 11 million people in Siberia (including Yakutiya) and another 18 million 810 thousand people in the Far East.[10] The fast growth of the population was once again caused by migrations to the region, this time no longer organised and planned, but forced. Practically, the question may be about the mass exodus from the European part of the country to the east, because of a complex of unfavourable socio-economic reasons. A sizeable growth of forced migrants especially took place in 1921-1922, during the famine in the central Russia. By the available estimate no less than 500 thousand refugees settled in Siberia. At the same time and for similar reasons the number of population increased in the Siberian cities, which exceeded roughly by 20 per cent compared to the end of the Civil war.

Already in the second half of the 1920's the planned resettlements in Siberia started once again. The first of them was the resettlement of the small landowning peasants from the central part of Russia, in the course of which almost one million people arrived in the region. Subsequently, during the 1930's and 1940's the resettlement was both voluntary and forced in nature.

Industrialisation, the symbol of Soviet modernisation programme, which started in the 1920's and 1930's, had a determining influence on the demographic process. One of the principles of the economic policy of industrialisation was the policy to expedite the development of industrial centres in the eastern part of the country. It determined some interrelated processes such as the overall growth of population in the region, mainly owing to the migrations, intensification of intra-regional migrations and in principle the beginning of a new stage in the development of urbanisation in Siberia.

In between the censuses of 1926 and 1939 the population of Siberia increased by one third, and of the Far East less than one fourth, comprising 141 million 120 thousand people in Siberia. In the Far East the number of population by 1939 reached 236, m 65 thousand.[11]

Urban population increased at an unusually rapid pace. Within 12 years that elapsed between the censuses of 1926-1939, urban population trebled in Siberia. The growth rates of the urban population in the region were much higher than the country as a whole. Urban settlements in Siberia increased by more than four times and mounted to 200. Large cities, centres of industry, culture and administration emerged in Siberia with more than 2,50,000 inhabitants. Almost 20 per cent of the population of the region was concentrated in large cities as Novosibirsk, Omsk and Irkutsk. At the end of the 1930's the process of urbanisation developed very fast in Kuzbass, exceeding the average index in the country (a seven times growth).[12]

The "human" inflation of the Siberian cities was diverse: according to available data almost one fourth of the new town settlers arrived in Siberia from beyond the bounds of the region, and three fourths from the Siberian villages, reflecting a sharply increasing social mobility of the people. As a result by the end of the 1930's the proportion of the urban population of the region exceeded 30 per cent.

At the same time, from 1930's a trend started showing outflow of the Siberians to other regions of USSR such as Central Asia and Kazakhstan, to the south of European part of Russia, Ukraine and Belorussia. The scales of outflow of population to the western and southern directions sometimes surpassed the volume of inflow. During the 1930's and 1940's the forced migrations to Siberia took place due to political factors. They were the forced resettlement of the members of the so-called kulak families, and somewhat later—ethnic deportations. According to available data, just during 1930-1931 more than 360 thousand people from the families of "kulaks" were deported to Siberia. The total number of people arrived in the region in the course of forced resettlement amounted to not less than 4 million people. The forced migrations considerably influenced the economic development of the region, particularly in the northern and north-eastern region of Siberia. Under their influence the demographic portrait of the region as a whole also substantially changed. The recurrent migrations of those, who were repressed and deported, date from as early as the beginning of 1950's.

The Second World War had a great impact on the demographic situation in the region. On the one hand, it caused large-scale demographic losses. About three million people (i.e. roughly 20% of the population) were mobilised in the ranks of armed forces. During the War years the birth rate declined, mortality increased, though it considerably diminished by the end of the War. At the same time, Siberia turned into the main region for distribution of the people evacuated from the western and central regions of USSR. In 1943 the evacuees in Siberia numbered about one million people.[13] But they were just temporary "demographic injections", since the reverse process already started from 1943 and by the end of the year approximately one half of the evacuees left the region. The evacuation did not become a factor conducive to the demographic development of the territory. The balance between the incoming and outgoing population of the region was negative. Altogether during the War period Siberia lost around 1.5 million people. Simultaneously, the War contributed in the consequent growth of urbanisation of Siberia, as the number of urban population increased by almost 1 million. The population of those cities that had become large centres of defence industry, such as Novosibirsk, Omsk, Krasnoyarsk and others, sharply increased.

In the post-War years, after the completion of restoration processes, the policy of expediting the development of the eastern regions of the USSR once again became urgent. Siberia, particularly its southern part, became one of those territories, which initiated the campaign for assimilating virgin and fallow lands, leading to a substantial growth of rural population in the new grain-producing regions. The series of giant hydropower projects and the construction of industrial enterprises had graver consequences for the demographic landscape of the region. For example, about 50 thousand people used to arrive annually only in the territory of Bratsk-Ust'-Ilimsk territorial-production complex (TPC). According to the data cited in research publications, the number of population of Nizhnee Priangar'e during 1955-1960 increased by seven times and mounted to a half million people. The sharp increase of the demographic weight of separate regions of Siberia in connection with the prospective economic projects continued in the following years. In the provinces laden with oil and gas in northern Tyumen, the population of this region increased by more than one million.

It is of course not that all of them arrived from beyond the region. According to the available estimates, for the construction of cascade of hydropower stations, not more than one fourth of the total people engaged in this sphere of activities arrived to Eastern Siberia from the European part of the country. The rest of them were inhabitants of the Siberian region proper, including the people belonging to rural areas. The acceleration of urbanisation resulted in the resettlement of no less than 1.5 million people from villages to the city during 1950-1959. For the territories with oil and gas the proportion of migrants from beyond the Siberian region was much higher. During the War years the level of urbanisation of Siberia increased not due to the rapid growth of urban population, but because of the decline in the number of rural population. In the 1950's the situation radically changed. By the end of 1950's more than 9 million people lived in the cities of the region and the proportion of the urban dwellers estimated to more than 50 per cent.[14]

The total number of Siberia's population increased to more than 180 million by 1959 and that of the Far East to about 43 million. During the next twenty years the population through Siberia increased to 20 million and through the Far East to 51 million.[15] By 1989 Siberia's population mounted to 241 million and that of the Far East to 68 million.[16]

During 1960-1980's the level of urbanisation constantly increased in connection with the rapid industrial assimilation of the region. According to census data of 1989, 18.2 million people lived in the urban settlements of Siberia. The proportion of the urban population of the region crossed 70 per cent. In a number of regions of Siberia it was even higher. In Bratsk-Ust'-Ilim TPC already by 1980 it rose to 80 per cent and in Khanty-Mansi Okrug (one of the main regions of oil and gas mining) it surpassed 85 per cent.

Simultaneously, it should be mentioned that within this long period the population of Siberia not only increased but also decreased. For example, during 1961-1973 more than one million people left Siberia and went to the regions with more favourable climate, to the European part of Russia, North Caucasus and Ukraine. The total number of those who left the region during 1970's-

1980's was not less than 6 million people.[17] The trend of the migratory flows—from village to city and from the Siberian cities to other regions of the country—had negative impact on the demographic composition of the population, development of productive forces and the social processes in Siberia. It was like an alarm bell, which compelled people to start thinking about the effectiveness and balancing nature of the strategy of regional development in the context of the development of the country as a whole. Unfortunately, the bell was not heard properly and it did not result in changing the socio-economic and demographic policy in the east of the country.

In between the censuses of 1989 and 2002 radical changes took place in the map of the world. Severe socio-economic and political crises gripped USSR, leading to the disintegration of the country in 1991. A new subject of the international law—the Russian Federation became the successor of USSR in its eastern territories. In the conditions of crisis for the first time in four centuries, not taking into account the extreme events of the War period, there was a decline in the population of Siberia (4.8%) and the Far East (1%). In accordance with the census of 2002, above 20 million people lived in the Siberian Federal *okrug* (SFO) and more than 66 million in the Far Eastern Federal *okrug* (DFO).[18] A region that had an active population in the recent past thus was turned into a region with a steady population outflow.

The crisis also affected the process of urbanisation. In the beginning of 1990's Siberia entered into a stage of de-urbanisation, which could only be overcome after ten years. The All-Russian census of 2002 showed that the number of Siberia's urban population mounted to 19.1 million people (73%). The majority (?) of Siberia's cities are small. At the same time in the territory from the Urals to the Pacific Ocean there are four cities of Russia with more than one million population—i.e. Novosibirsk (1397 thousand inhabitants) being the third amongst all, Ekaterinburg, Omsk and Chelyabinsk.[19] The Asiatic territory of Russia was less densely populated and considerably more uneven than the European one. On the whole, in four centuries the number of population of the eastern regions of Russia increased by 178 times. The number of Siberia's indigenous population during the same period increased almost by 7 times.

Thus, the demographic portrait of the region reflects that the intensive economic development of Siberia took place only during the past hundred years. The preceding three centuries were a period, when the matter of populating and assimilating the region was settled. By the end of the 20th century, precisely close to the 1980's and 1990's, Siberia was reckoned among the leading economic regions of the country. But the development was uneven and high level of development was concentrated in western Siberia. Nearly 10 per cent of Russia's population lived in this sub-region, but produced 12 per cent of the total gross product, including 73 per cent of Russia's oil and 90 per cent of its gas. It was exactly the mining and raw materials sectors of production—first of all oil and gas, that in fact determined the high share of the region in the gross product, by far exceeding the proportion of the population. Correspondingly, both the demographic and economic "weight" of the territories of Asiatic Russia, situated more eastward from Yenisei, was much less. For example, the proportion of the population of the Far East in the total demographic mass approximately equalled to 3 per cent of the comparable scales of economy.

The Russian Federation inherited the legacy of earlier expenditures and the bad effects of socio-economic assimilation including the evident underestimation of social factors of development, in particular inadequate investments in the infrastructure and transformation of Siberia into an alluring region. The latter one followed mainly from the circumstance, that Siberia has always been assimilated as an internal colony of the Russian empire, and later on of the Soviet Union. The relation between European and Asiatic Russia in the historical past was always manifested in the form of "imperial centre—colony" dichotomy. Practical realisation of such a strategy resulted in the emergence of many systemic problems both in the country as a whole and in its eastern regions. The eastern Russian territories evoked interest basically from the viewpoint of their resource potential, assimilation of which was done selectively, depending on the military and strategic imperative or the economic expediency of development of the country as a whole, and more often its European part. For centuries with regard to Siberia a de facto semi-colonial approach was maintained, which was oriented toward exploiting the region primarily as a base for economic development of the "centre".

Under the Soviet rule the eastern regions were assigned even more significant role than before in working on the tasks of modernisation. The Asiatic orientation of territorial expansion in the development of productive forces was evident. As early as the mid-1950's it became apparent that the Soviet modernisation programme, in which the eastern regions of the country was not assigned any independent role, was unable to pave the way for a post-industrial society in the country. At this period the political leaders showed their intention to make certain corrections to the previous modernisation scheme which was of extreme nature. In principle, they raised the question about changing the priorities in the development of the entire socio-economic sphere of the society, including shifting the tone of regional and national factors of development. Within the framework of the renewed paradigm the considerations of the state's expediency completely disregarding the interests of the regions could not remain the sole possible dominant.

In practice no serious changes took place and the opportunity to replace the semi-colonial vector of development of the eastern part of Russia by a policy of stable and all-round growth was missed. In spite of the fact that the resources of the eastern regions were extensively included in the economic strategy of the USSR, the programme on replacement of productive forces to the east was put under the "region for the country" concept.

There are no sufficient grounds for stating that during the post-Soviet period the centre's attitude towards the eastern territories of the country has radically changed. However, such a situation, logical enough in the context of the "imperial" scenario of development of the country till 1991, is entering into open conflict with the economic and political values laid down at present. In addition, in the 1990's the state of affairs in the eastern regions of Russia have considerably aggravated in consequence of the accomplishment of structural reforms, which started after the disintegration of the USSR. The accelerated outflow of the population from the east to the west is the integrated index of this. On the one hand, intensification of economic problems would entail the threat of political and social instability in many regions of the east of Russia, and would become a platform for discussions on the advantages of regionalism. On the other, these processes are the bases for discourses on the "lack of prospects" of Russia as a Eurasian country, which are becoming popular in the circles of a certain section of "intellectual elite".

It seems that the next few decades may become a moment of truth. Either the former strategy of semi-colonial development of the "eastern outlying regions" of Russia, which geographically occupies the major part of the country, will continue, and it will result in further socio-economic, demographic, and later on, perhaps, even political and geopolitical complications, or a new strategy will be worked out successfully that would help finding a compromise between the formulas "region for the country" and "region for the region" and securing a new scenario of Russia's entry into the global world as a Eurasian state.

In this the transition from industrial to post-industrial paradigm of modernisation should become the main thing. The rigid centripetal platform, characteristic for the period of rapid industrial growth, in the new circuit of historical development can hardly be effective. The future prospects of not only the Siberian region, but also of the country as a whole, depend on how far the solution of the task of combining the vectors of state and regional development within the framework of the new state strategy succeeds, on whether the making of state policy on the basis of a model of modernisation which takes into account the present-day realities in the global arena, the previous historical experiences and lessons, works out.

Notes and References

1. V.V. Alekseev, E.V. Alekseeva, K.I. Zubkov, I.V. Poberezhnikov, *Aziatskaya Rossiya v geopoliticheskoi i tsivilizatsionnoi dinamike XVI-XX veka,* Moscow: Nauka Publishing House, 2004.
2. D. Ya. Rezun, M.V. Shilovskii, *Sibir', konets XVI-nachalo XX vekov. Frontir v kontekste etnosotsial'nykh i etnokul'turnykh protsessov,* Novosibirsk: Sova Publishing House, 2005, pp. 73-75.
3. Dolgikh B.O., *Rodovoi plemonnoi sostav narodov Sibiri v XVII veke*, Moscow: Nauka Publishing House, 1960, pp. 616-617.
4. A.P. Okladnikov, Chief Editor, "Istoriya Sibiri s drevneishikh vremen do nasikh" dnei, In *Sibir' v sostave feodal'noi Rossi* (5 vols.), Vol. 2, Leningrad: Nauka Publishing House, 1968, p. 184.
5. *Ibid.*
6. *Pervaya vseobschaya perepis' naseleniya Rossiiskoi imperii 1897g. Obschii svod po imperii resul'tatov razrabotki dannykh Pervoi vseobschei perepisi naseleniya, proizvedennoi 28 yanvarya 1897 g., (2 vols),* St. Petersburg: Izdatel'stvo Statisticheskii komitet Soveta ministrov Rossiiskoi imperii. V. 1, p. 476.
7. L.M. Goryurhkin, *Agrarnye otnosheniya v Sibiri perioda imperializma (1900-1917),* Novosibirsk: Nauka Publishing House, 1976, p. 135; V.I. Pronin, "Gorodskoe i sel'skoe naselenie Sibiri b kontse XIX—nachale XX veka", in *Gorod i derevnya Sibiri v dosovetskii period,* edited by

N.A. Minenko, Novosibirsk: NSU (Novosibirsk State University) Press, 1984. Table 1.

8. V.V. Kuleshov, Chief ed. *Sibir' na poroge novogo tysyacheletiya*, Novosibirsk: IEIE SB RAS Publishing House, 1998, p. 24.
9. Volkov E.Z., *Dinamika narodonaseleniya SSSR za 80 let*, Moscow-Leningrad: State Publishing House, 1930, pp. 98-99.
10. Guschin N. Ya., Isupov V.A. Ed. *Naselenie Zapadnoi Sibiri v XX veke*, Novosibirsk: SB RAS Publishing House, 1997, p. 23.
11. Vsesoyuznaya perepis' naseleniya 1939 goda: osnovnye itogi, Moscow: Nauka Publishing House, 1992, pp. 23-24.
12. V.V. Kuleshov ed. *Sibir' na poroge novogo tysyacheletiya*, Novosibirsk: IEIE SB RAS Publishing House, 1998, p. 24-25.
13. Alekseev V.V. ed. *Rabochii klass Sibiri v period uprocheniya i razvitiya sotsializma,* Novosibirsk: Nauka Publishing House, 1984, p. 83.
14. V.V. Kuleshov ed. *Sibir' na poroge novogo tysyacheletiya*, Novosibirsk: IEIE SB RAS Publishing House, 1998, p. 26.
15. *Itogi Vsesoyuznoi perepesi 1970 goda,* 7 Vol., Moscow: Statistika Publishing House, 1972-1973, Vol. 1, *Chislennost' naseleniya SSSR*, Moscow, 1972, pp. 12-14.
16. *Itogi Vsesoyuznoi perepesi naseleniya 1989 goda, 10 Vols., Moscow: Informatsionno-izdatel'skii Tsentr "Gosudarstvennyi komitet SSSR po statistiki", 1989-1990, Vol. 1, Chislennost' naseleniya SSSR, soyuznykh i avtonomnykh respublik, kraev i oblastei, Moscow, 1989, pp. 32-34.*
17. Kuleshov V.V. ed. *Sibir' na poroge novogo tysyacheletiya*, Novosibirsk: IEIE SB RAS Publishing House, 1998, p. 59.
18. *Itogi Vsesoyuznoi perepesi naseleniya 2002 g, 14 Vols., Moscow: Informatsionno-izdatel'skii tsentr* "Statistika Rossii", 2004-2005, V. 1, *Chislennost' i razmeschenie,* Moscow: 2004, pp. 367-371.
19. *Sibir'. Atlas Aziatskoi Rossii,* Novosibirsk-Moscow: Feoriya/Feoria Publishing House, 2007, p. 156.

23

Chinese Migrants and *Migrantophobia* in Contemporary Russia: Stereotypes and Mechanisms of Their Formation*

Viktor. I. Dyatlov

At the turn of the 21st century, the inhabitants of Russia as a whole, and its eastern regions in particular, faced a new challenge. A massive penetration of Chinese migrants, intensification of their economic activities and the gradual formation of permanent Chinese communities started as a result of market reforms, a qualitatively new level of openness to the outside world and establishment of good neighbourly relations with China.

Strictly speaking, the problem is not really a new one. Before the revolution in Russia there existed a large Chinese diaspora playing an enormous role in the economic life east of the country. This was not considered favourable interest in the Russian society, and was a subject of sharp debate and contradictory policy decisions by the authorities.

During Soviet rule the diaspora was eliminated and the problem of mutual relations with the Chinese ceased to be of any interest to the vast majority of the people in our country, which for several generations simply has no contacts with the representatives of this ancient civilization. An exception was the 50s, when within a short-span and short-term policy that highlighted "Russian and Chinese are brothers forever", quite a large number of Soviet people visited China, were able to get acquainted with its life albeit superficially. But a spell of interstate hostility interrupted this process.[1]

Therefore, contemporary Russian society feels and interprets the emergence of Chinese element as a problem that is entirely new and unfamiliar. Every new and unfamiliar thing is itself put on guard.

---

* Translated by Susmita Bhattacharya, Fellow, MAKAIAS, Kolkata

However, there are several factors that create a complex atmosphere of alertness, fear, misgivings, ill will and even hostility centring the Chinese. One may argue that the syndrome of "yellow peril", very widespread at the turn of the 19th-20th centuries, is being revived now.[2]

The fear of China developed in the Soviet period when inter-state relations grew hostile, but at present (and this is a new phenomenon) this fear has spread among the Chinese people.

On the other hand, with the passage of time the natural process of mutual recognition and adaptation, establishment of purely human relations, economic integration, etc. is going on. The acuteness of the problem is somewhat getting removed, though not entirely. The conflicting bilateral relations, the fears and misgivings arising from this and the hostility (syndrome of "yellow peril") are unlikely to disappear in the foreseeable future. The attitude towards the Chinese, and also to the migrants in general, is becoming a constant and quite an important part of public sentiments. This topic is increasingly being used in politics as an instrument of political mobilization and struggle for power.

The phenomenon of Sinophobia, the syndrome of "yellow peril" is a complicated, multi-layered and quite contradictory. The day-to-day mass consciousness of the ideologues, politicians and scholars are contributing to its formation. The basis for its appearance and functioning are real problems, contradictions, conflicts, and the irrational fears, phobias and prejudices.

Certain stereotypes have emerged which have become a regulator of interethnic relations, and an anti-immigrant sentiment—a powerful factor of political mobilization and struggle for power.

This is particularly important because of the unprecedented important role of labour migration in the economic, ethno-cultural, social, political, and perhaps in geopolitical spheres of life. Now it has already become indispensable element in ensuring the vital activities of the host society and on the other hand, an enormous public allergen. Russia is transforming into a country of immigrants—and there can be a radical turn in its character.

So far, the Russian society has not been able to grasp the magnitude of the problem, assess its importance in terms of associated "profit and loss". Especially after several decades of "Iron Curtain" a very complex attitude developed towards the foreigners and "foreign". In addition, this process resulted in radical breakdown of the entire way of life of the country, disintegration of previous relationships and unhealthy formation of new frustrations.

Nevertheless, in the past two decades there were tremendous changes in this sphere. It did not simply mean movement of millions of people. The fact of such a movement was that it had already affected the psyche of the people. An intensive process of comprehension and assessment of the phenomenon is going on in the public consciousness in order to fill out the "blank space" in a radically transformed "picture of the world". This is also necessary in order to develop attitude, strategies and models of behaviour.

The process of comprehension and development of attitudes manifests itself at various levels:

— in everyday consciousness
— in ideological and political spheres
— in scientific studies.

The most important fact is that there is no insurmountable gap between these levels and that an active process of reciprocal action is taking place. Communication and interaction are also occurring. The most striking example is the gigantic number of geopolitical "studies", where the tasks are purely scientific, the *heuristic* ones are marginalized by the ideological evaluation.

These processes are extremely important because the trajectory of the development of Russia—the nature and pace of its economic development, the level of conflict, social and political stability and the nature of the political regime—largely depends on how the role and place of the migrants are comprehended in the society. A way of comprehending the problem and developing attitude towards it is *Migrantophobia*.

Migrantophobia is an inevitable component of the adaptive response of the host society. It swiftly and powerfully joined the already existing xenophobic mentality and gave it a new quality and sweep. Sometimes it also takes the form of previously existing ethnic, racial or cultural phobias. However, it is not only the representatives of the ethnic or cultural groups other than the host society can be perceived as "aliens" or "strangers". Galina Vitkovskaya argues about the existence of *Migrantophobia* in its "pure form" as a reaction of rejection, evaluation of the forced

Russian settlers/internally displaced persons and refugees as "strangers" by the same Russian host society.[3]

Migrantophobia in modern Russia is a huge and multifaceted issue. The study of its scale, temporal dynamics, and dependence on the overall socio-economic situation in the country is a prerogative of quantitative sociology and several influential sociological centres in Russia are quite actively engaged with this problem.

This paper in fact, focuses on how the phenomenon is interpreted and assessed in the sphere of myths and stereotypes. And what is more, the myths and stereotypes related to the Chinese migrants are causing most of all misgivings and fears at the moment. The basic principle here is an operational and purely pragmatic approach to the use of these categories and to understand them as a-prìórì assumptions that are beyond scientific knowledge and judgment. The first stereotype is the formation of an attitude, not so much heuristic but as a means of streamlining social information. Therefore, on appraisal, myths and stereotypes do not need to criticise sources, evaluate and verify them through internal logic and individual postulates. This is equivalent to the human way of knowing the world (along with the scientific one). And in that sense this is also a social reality.

It is the myths and stereotypes rather than positive scientific knowledge that exert prime influence on the attitude of the society and the authorities towards the process of migration and the migrants. These complicated phenomena, which incorporated earlier social experiences and various (including mutually incompatible) ideologies as well as out-of-context scientific knowledge and pseudo-scientific construction. All this lies at the basis of everyday consciousness, day-to-day xenophobic instincts and remnants of 'official internationalism', 'the alien complex' etc.

The paper is concerned with the basic premise mentioned in the text which hardly has any illustrative material and argumentation or reasoning of fundamental principles attached to it. The task of the author is not "to dispel/expose" the myths, to prove their internal inconsistency or deliberate on a-prìórì assumptions. It is much more important to elucidate their basic concepts and the logic of such conceptualization. In principle, though, such a task can be taken only with respect to those mythologies, which act in the form of scientific knowledge, and present themselves as such—and often perceived that way. The thesis "science considers...", "science tells us..." is the favourite form of modern mythmaking.

An analysis of a large number of the most diverse texts provides the ground to distinguish the "cornerstones" of the constructions which are examined as "expansion", "exploitation" and "criminal".

Let's start with "Expansion".

The notion that is widespread is about Chinese migration as a deliberate instrument of expansion and as a focused, planned and organized process implemented by the state. The migrants, according to this line of thinking are not determined as individuals, private persons with their motivations and freedom of will and choice, but an inseparable organic part and the "tentacle" of the state. According to the goals they are expected to achieve they are divided into territorial, demographic and economic expansive segments.

In this context, it is worthwhile to cite the well-known metaphor of "ants",[4] implying mass character, incalculability, orderliness and subordination to the common will of the Chinese people. This metaphor has another dimension: ants—may be reasonable creature, but not human beings. They are not guided by human logic and morality, and therefore attitude towards them is not dependent on this logic. The extreme expression of such approach is the debate on the problem of the Chinese migrants and the Chinese in general in the category of "biomass".

"They have a plan"

A notion that is widely circulated is that there is "a plan" by the Chinese authorities regarding migratory expansion to Russia. It includes a peremptory system of organization, planning and control. It is implemented through coercion and incentives (up to financial rewards to the domicile migrants settled permanently in Russia).

This claim/thesis is widely represented in the mass media, in the statements of the bureaucrats-officials and politicians, and in the works by the scholars as well. This is the view of experts on Chinese migration to Russia, who in 1994 published a book on this subject. According to the experts L.L. Rybakovskii, O.D. Zakharova, V.V. Mindogulov, "China having huge territorial claims to Russia, by all means encourages the entry of its citizens to the latter's territory and founding the base for legal existence. At the same time the economic activities of the Chinese citizens brings huge profits as well... The main purpose of the Chinese penetration into Russia regardless of the forms and channels is to integrate into economic activities, acquire real estate and land, that is, to create economic and legal prerequisites for legitimate acquisition/ seizure of territory... Despite the fact that the Chinese immigration to the Far East Russia is now largely illegal in nature, the existing system of infiltration ensures the legalization of illegal/ undocumented migrants".[5] All this happens, however, in the complete absence of any documentary evidence. [6]

"*Small groups with one hundred thousand people in each*"[7]

This phrase is from the old Soviet anecdotes from the time of Soviet-Chinese military confrontation and lies at the basis of demographic expansion. The Chinese migrants cannot be small in number because there cannot be small number of Chinese at all. Therefore, with very small population of Russia in general and in the east of the country in particular, the Chinese will simply swallow up the local population and will become a majority. Frankly speaking, they are already swallowing up. And even at the farthest corner from the Chinese border live the bearers of such ideas, and one observes how densely populated are the Siberian and Far Eastern cities by the Chinese. In some sense, the Chinese replaced the bears there that used to roam around the streets of most of these cities before.

All these years the most debated question on migration has been: "How many Chinese do we really have in Russia?" There is no accurate statistics available here and not any is foreseen either. The reasons are obvious: illegal component, inefficiency of the state structures to deal with the migrants, and apathy on the part of many people in acquiring correct information.

The figures are incoherent: from 5-6 million to 300 thousand people per year. Besides, the figures that appeared in the early 1990s have remained unchanged and the incoherence is reflected in the newspapers and officials' speeches as well as in the scientific publications. The estimates by serious scholars, and confirmations by the border authorities that the numbers of entry-exit differ just by a few percentages (and that means the illegal component is not so high as is often thought) are simply ignored.

The multimillion estimates of the number of migrants constitute the basis of mass ideology. Those have been confirmed by authoritative accounts of experts. They are exclusive because they are derived through scientific analysis, critical sources and statistics-oriented scientific analysis.

"From a Chinese can born only a Chinese" (P. Proskurin)[8]

Intermarriages appear to be a deadly threat. "Expansion of the Chinese through marriage "is an instrument of demographic expansion. Especially alarming is the strategy of "marriage naturalization/naturalization through marriage", in which numerous illegal migrants (as well as their children and relatives) acquire legal status through marriage, including the fictitious ones. L.L. Rybakovskii and the co-authors have written on these aspects in somewhat inarticulate, but definite terms: "Historical experience proves that the specificity of the population of the Far East and no less specific policy of the contiguous states, including Japan, at different stages of development of the Far East offer a real chance for positive outcome of these long-term, well calculated actions through natural assimilation of the people."[9]

The available estimates suggest a negligible number of such marriages, but it does not matter for the authors who have framed their ideas on that basis. The important thing is that no one has proved that "blood" is the basis of culture, that the Chinese do not adapt and do not assimilate, and that those in whom Chinese blood is flowing on condition "carry a powerful gene of Chinese-ness". References to the pre-revolutionary experience here is not very correct, because the vast majority of Chinese migrants at that time were seasonal and did not set up families nor settled down. That means they got integrated in a very restricted manner.

"Kosovo line"

The myth about compact Chinese settlements in the Far East, about their existence in a lot of places and the predominance of Chinese habitation started taking shape in the beginning of 1990s. Such ideas became stronger in places that were farther from the Far East. The majority of serious people deal with such settlements as a questionable matter. The names are not mentioned. A chilling picture was drawn of how these Chinese enclaves at first would demand autonomy and later on "reunification" with China.

Here are two randomly selected examples to illustrate this point. In 1996, K.E. Sorokin established as an unquestionable and obvious fact a "growing uncontrollable 'creeping' migration of the Chinese to Russia (in our country they number up to 2 million), formation of 'china towns' beyond the jurisdiction of Russian law, especially in the Far East, a mass illegal purchase of real estate to the east of the Urals by the Chinese entrepreneurs, with the help of inaction of the local and central authorities".[10]

In 2005, A. Khramchikhin no less firmly believed that the east of Russia (at the best the space to the east of Baikal, perhaps to the east of the Yenisei, at the worst—to the east of the Urals) in a couple of decades will turn into a giant "Kosovo"... It will be populated by the Chinese, and in both economic-financial as well as in administrative-political terms will become a part of China. And what is more, it will be formally reckoned as Russians (till the time the President no ore appears at Kremlin and gives up de jure claim to what had been lost as de facto), a few citizens of Russia will live in separate ghettos ... In China, they are keenly observing that Russia herself is giving up its east, though surviving at its expense. In China, they are fully aware that their own country will not survive, without taking away the neighbouring territories. The nation wants to live and is solving the question of survival through the only possible way.[11]

Exploitation

Here, the Chinese issue is put into the general set of perceptions that migrants inevitably and automatically lay their claim on the resources of the host society. This implies that the volume of resources is primarily unalterable, therefore, the arrival of new people would automatically take them away from the old settlers. Within this framework some of the most common clichés precisely related to the Chinese migrants should be mentioned:

- — They take away jobs from the Russians,
- — They send off/pilfer our timber, metals and other natural resources,
- — They take out capitals from Russia.

Criminal

The notion about the primordial and all-out criminal nature of the Chinese migrants, like any other migrants in general, is also not left out from the common set of migration related myths. The only specific feature here is that the ominous "Triads" personify it.[12]

Mechanisms and Ways of Mythmaking

One of the widespread ways I would call as "pyramid"—by an analogy of the sad moments of MMM and "Hoper". It relies on reciprocal cross "experts' appraisals" by the journalists, officials and scholars. For example, some information appear in newspapers with reference to anonymous experts from related government structures (and often just like that—without any reference). It is then reproduced (with supporting or even modest-sceptical intonation), by the representatives of the academic—scientific community. After getting "scientific sanction" ("the scientists—scholars write...") the thesis becomes an instrumental phrase of the bureaucratic analysts and officials. Authorised by them, it is already in use as a strong and reliable source in scientific research or academic studies. The mass media circulate the authoritative views of the scholars and practitioners. And thus—through a circle. And each new circle of reciprocal references makes the assertion even more strong and indisputable: "everyone knows, and scientific study corroborates that...". Precisely this way in the publicists', experts' and even scientific circulation the figure of multimillion Chinese migrants in Russia, "information" about the "Chinese enclaves" in the Far East or the number of mixed marriages with the Chinese, was confirmed.

Here is a small illustration of how this "technique" works. The frightening "prognosis-ascertainment" of "marriage expansion" by L.L. Rybakovskii, O.D. Zakharova and V.V. Mindogulov almost instantly was realised into an anonymous expert appraisal that "in the Irkutsk and Chita oblast's about half the men getting married were Chinese". This estimate, somewhat sceptically but without any comment, was quoted by the most prominent specialist on China's economy V. Portyakov.[13]

Now, with reference to his authority the appraisal is reproduced in the press. As an unquestionable fact all of this is being used in politics—and during the last but one elections to the State Duma of Russia, I. Rogozin the leader of "Rodina (Homeland)" constantly told a tale about how some old woman of the Far East happily married for about thirty times to Chinese men and thus became a "tool of their demographic expansion". The Governor of Khabarovsk krai, V. Ishaev is resolutely against mixed marriages, because he is "worried that compact Chinese settlements are emerging in the region, which are increasingly trying to influence the economic and political situation", and a huge number of Chinese want to get married to the Russians for obtaining residential permit.[14] Meanwhile, the number of such marriages in the cities of the Far East and Siberia is insignificant and are estimated literally to ten.[15] And no effort is made to find the accurate statistics.

There is a widespread practice of references to anonymous authoritative sources, and introduction of assessments in scientific—academic circulation without describing the methods of acquiring them ("according to our calculations...", "there are estimates/ assessments...").

It is especially characteristic for the mass media to form verbal and intonational context: loud and catchy headlines, even for absolutely normal and neutral texts, to use alarming ("expansion", "intrusion", "occupation", "Celestial messengers" etc.) or humiliating-mocking vocabulary.

Undisturbed existence of even one person in two totally incompatible worlds of understanding of the problem is very widespread phenomenon. It is very common when an official responsible for the situation with the migrants evaluates it as absolutely normal in the zone of his responsibility ("we have everything under control"), but the overall situation in this area of the country is disastrous. There are two images—one based on one's own observation and common sense and the second formed by the media, statements by the politicians, bureaucrats, simply the men of authority following the already described design/scheme of financial pyramid. The second one is more trusted.

This observation is correlated/corresponds to the results of some sociological surveys. In one of the VTsIOM polls (2002), 57.7 per cent of the Russian respondents answered yes to the question: "Do you think Russia's security at present is threatened by the people of non-Russian nationalities living in Russia?" At the same time, to the question "Do you feel at present any animosity from the people of other nationalities?", 59.7 per cent of them responded "never" and 28.8 per cent—"rarely". According to E.A. Paina, this proves, firstly, that many ethnic phobias are abstract in nature; secondly, preserving the remnants of traditional consciousness characteristic of the empires, when the state is identified with the rulers and some are enemies for him, and for the subjects—some other.[16] There can also be a simpler interpretation—non-discrepant/non-contradictory combination of two mutually exclusive images, described just above, in a single consciousness.

Myths as an Instrument

Myths and stereotypes were formed so quickly and so firmly took their roots in public consciousness for a simple and important reason that they were needed. This is an indispensable way to determine the place of new people and new groups in the hierarchy of relations and status. The model of relationships is formed and functions through them. This is a tool of ideological mobilization and struggle for power. This a tool to serve the bureaucratic-official, regional or corporate interests. Since they are needed, therefore, they are inevitable. But with the change of attitudes of the host society towards the migrants in general and the Chinese migrants in particular, the structure of stereotypes and the intensity of the presence of fears of hostility in them will also change.

Notes and References

1. V.I. Dyatlov and E.V. Dyatlova, "Kitaets v dorevolyutsionnoi i sovremennoi Rossii: reinkarnatsiya obraza?", In: *Vostochnye regiony Rossii: strategii i praktiki osvoeniya*, Novosibirsk: Nauka-Tsentr, 2006. pp. 94-114.
2. V.I. Dyatlov, "Zheltaya opasnost`": transformatsiya odnoi ksenofobii, In: *Rossia i Vostok: problemy vzaimodeistviya. Materialy VI Mezhdunarodnoi konferentsii, Volgograd, 28-30 noyabrya, 2002*, Volgograd: Izdatelstvo Volgogradskogo Gosudarstvennogo Universiteta, 2003, pp. 116-123.
3. G. Vitkovskaya. Vinuzhdennaya migratsiya i migrantofobiya v Rossii. In: Neterpimost' v Rossii: starye i novye fobii. Moscow: Moskovskii Tsentr Karnegie, 1999, pp. 151-191.
4. A.I. Gertzen, for example wrote about the "the Chinese ant-hills" (A.I. Gertzen. Byloye i dumy, In: A.I. Gertzen Sochineniya: (in 9 volumes), Moscow: GIKL, vol. 6., pp. 67-68.
5. L.L. Rybakovskii, O.D. Zakharova, V.V. Mindogulov. Nelegal'naya migratsiya v prigranitchnikh rayonakh Dal'nego Vostoka: istoriya, sovremennost', posledstviya. Moscow, 1994, pp. 35-36.
6. A.V. Lukin, Medved' nablyudaet za drakonom. Obraz Kitaya v Rossii v XVII-XXI vekakh. Moscow: AST: Vostok-Zapad, 2007, pp. 295-296.
7. A. Polynsky, "Sibir's raskosymi glazami", *Tribuna,* 3 Sept. 2005.
8. A popular writer of the Soviet era.
9. L.L. Rybakovskii, O.D. Zakharova, V.V. Mindogulov, *op. cit.,* p. 23.

10. K.E. Sorokin, *Geopolitika sovremennosti i geostrategiya Rossii*, Moscow: ROSSPEN, 1996, p. 107.
11. A. Khramtchikhin, "Zheltoe gospodstvo. Zakhvat Kitayem Sibiri—ne "strashilka". Poskol`ku drugogo vykhoda u nego prosto net", *Politticheskii zhurnal,* No. 27, 2005, pp. 61-67.
12. *Migratsiya i bezopasnost' v Rossii.* Moscow: Interdialekt, 2000. pp. 267-328.
13. V. Portyakov, "Kitaytsy idut? Migratsionnaya situatsiya na Dal'nem Vostoke", *Mezhdunarodnaya zhizn'.* No. 2 (1996), p. 82.
14. V.I. Ishayev, "Kitaiskie zhenikhi okazyvayutsya fiktivnymi muzh'yami", *Rossiiskaya gazeta,* 3 Oct., 1999; "Kitaitsy na Rusi", *Izvestiy,* 26 Jan, 2000.
15. For the situation in Irkutsk see for example: E. Dyatlova, "Brachnye svyazi migrantskikh men'shinstv Irkutska v 1989-1998 godakh (Kitaitsy, vykhodtsy s Severnogo Kavkaza i Zakavkaz'ya i Tsentral'noi Azii), *Vestnik Evrazii,* No. 1 (2001), pp. 30-46.
16. E.A. Pain, *Mezhdu imperiei i natsiei. Modernistskii proekt i ego traditsionalistskaya al'ternativ v natsionalnoi politike Rossii*, Moscow: Fond Liberal'naya Missiya, 2004, pp. 36-37.

24

The Transborder Regions of Siberia and East Asia: The Problems of Regional Paradiplomacy*

Boris V. Bazarov

The contemporary socio-economic and political processes in the world community are taking shape as a result of the interaction between globalisation and regionalisation. The bipolar world has ultimately collapsed, and a new unipolar world is in a formative state. Its further development, in principle, may discard retention or creation of any one state as a super power. It is possible that the new reconstruction of the world would presuppose national-state, racial-ethnic, socio-economic, socio-cultural, religious, political and other forms of pluralism.

Intensification of the regions' involvement in foreign economic activities and international relations has become one of the most striking manifestations of regionalism. Consolidation of these trends is a common natural development and more often defined as regional paradiplomacy.

Regional paradiplomacy signifies a complicated structural interdependence among regions. It is usually differentiated between trans-regional (working out establishment of contacts between the regions of Russia and foreign countries), trans-national (a "network" cooperation between the territorial subjects of the state and trans-national institutions like non-government organisations or TNC) and internationalised (connections between the sub-national units and foreign government institutions).

The forms of all these relations have started emerging in the Asiatic space, but it is obvious that a significant set of issues would require intensified study, both from the viewpoint of practice of the interacting governments, and international as well as existing laws

* Translated by Susmita Bhattacharya, Fellow, MAKAIAS, Kolkata

of those countries. The fact is that federal systems, and also the structures similar to them in their basic features (the European Union) have proved that they are the most efficient guarantors of peace, if they act in the spirit of "considering mutual interests", since such consideration is an integral part of the legal obligations, which ensure the integration of the system.

On the contrary, poorly connected confederations of states, lacking such a principle in their constitutional framework or else some other similar legal system stipulating their integration, could hardly serve this purpose for a sufficiently long period.[1] This comparison is justifiable even with respect to the structures that still remain just as quasi-federal, but which in their approach to the settlement of conflicts never proceeded from a purely confederative model. In this context, it is a correct assertion that after the Second World War, the European Union seems to be the most effective peacekeeping instrument. It would never be able to achieve such a capacity and success, had it been founded on a purely confederation principle. It is difficult to determine such a principle. It is too vague and tenuous to serve the purposes of peacemaking and peacekeeping.[2]

The advantage of federal or even quasi-federal systems thus lies in their flexibility on the one hand, and the binding force of their legislative decisions on the other. But what is more effective is adjustment to the relevant problem of potential synergy.

However, the practice of interaction between the countries and nations in the conditions of the Asia-Pacific region and East Asia will require a clarification of not only the conceptualisation of "regional paradiplomacy", but also changes of some settled character to regulate these relations in a globalising world. Currently, this term means the visits made by regional leaders to the neighbouring states, sometimes more extensive practice of interaction of the officially accredited civil society organizations.

In the vast space of East Asia an unprecedented social tectonic motion has taken place, which brought billions of people into the new global turnover. And what is more, huge masses of people have been demonstrating a new unprecedented quality of the population. The information, scientific and technological progress accompanying this shift has evident features of the change in the configurations of the world's forces. In the face of the recent past, less significant processes have led to the severe-most wars, reaching up to the world wars, the regional conflicts "for re-division of the already divided world", forcible redistribution of markets for products and spheres of influence. But the age that began put into priorities such forms of interaction of the world systems, nations and societies that enable to become more flexible in common universal dialogue.

In recent times, regional paradiplomacy in Russia is reflected in the following types of relationships:[3]

- —Region→ foreign states;
- —Region→foreign governments (this type of relations is carried out directly through consulates and embassies of foreign countries);
- —Region→ federal authorities→foreign governments ("Rosvooruzhenie" collaborates with the administrations of a number of oblast's that produce weapons, to find the best options for its exports);
- —Region→ Region (interregional cooperation programme), as well as cooperation between various organizations in the two regions within the framework of regional programmes;
- —Region→international organizations;
- —City→ federal centre→ international organizations (so, "Roszarubezhtsentr" represents the interests of some Russian cities within the European Programme of "Twin towns");
- —Region→ private international organizations (Nizhnegorod region administration while issuing Eurobond resorted to the assistance of foreign banks and auditing campaigns);
- —Region→ international non-governmental organizations (Greenpeace, Doctors without Borders, etc.);
- —Region→ interregional associations→ federal centre→ international organizations ("Roszarubezhtsentr has signed a contract with the "Siberian Agreement" to provide mediation services in selecting international partners);
- —Implementation of programmes in the regions of international organizations;
- —Region→ transregional organizations→European organizations (regions participating in the Forum of the Baltic Sea or the Barents Euro-Arctic Council may act as agents of EU programmes);
- —Region→ ethnic diaspora→ international organizations (this method is being actively used by Chechnyaand Tatarstan);

— Regional enterprises→ international organizations (the leaders of the largest enterprises of Russia, located throughout the country, are invited to attend the World Economic Forum in Davos);
— The participation of regional structures (enterprises, universities, non-profit enterprises) in the activities of international organizations. The federal and regional structures may be intermediate links in these cases;
— Region→ federal authorities→ foreign financial institutions (Nizhnegorod delegation during the negotiations on restructuring debt to the London Club creditors kept contact with the Ministry of Finance of Russian Federation);
— City→ city (twin relations in the sphere of culture, science, education, sports);
— City→international organizations;
— City→ city→ international organizations (Union of the Baltic cities, for example, works closely with the Council of Baltic Sea, the European Council of Local and Regional Authorities of other organizations);
— Region→ Federal Government→ private companies→ international banking institutions (Government of Tatarstan, with the assistance of the Government of the Russian Federation for restructuring "KamAZ" debt to the European Bank for Reconstruction and Development appealed to an international audit firms, since it was necessary to assess the financial situation at the plant by international standards);
— regional organizations of Russian region, (banks, universities, non-profit organizations, etc.) → regional organizations in the region of another country (banks, universities, non-profit organizations, etc.). The contracts are concluded between the structures themselves without the mediation of regional, central authorities and international organizations.

This phenomenon is quite new. Moreover, irredentist trends have been restricted due to collaboration between the regions of Siberia and the Far East. The development in Russian-Chinese relations indicates a positive shift from 'de-synchrony' to 'sustainable equalization'. All defined trends speak in favour of East Asian direction of the Russian economy that has started gaining momentum. The point is not the weakening of Western paradigm of

Moscow's policy, rather in making inventories of the potentiality of Siberia and the Far East in raw materials with regrouping the growing capital in the East-Asian vector. The political mood of Sinophobia has waned in Russia and the country is heading for rapid revival of contacts in the field of economy, culture and education. But by 2010-2015 the partnership with China would not turn into absolutely "good" or absolutely "bad", because the basic combination of positive opportunities and risks will be maintained and modified.

China made a mark in the world circuit in a gradual and well-calculated way. At the same time, the Chinese experience, like all Chinese reforms are historically of incomplete nature, despite the fact that they have made tremendous positive results. The very historic experiment requires the test of time. It may happen that private companies and individuals, who bear the burden of economic responsibility, have their own interests, not always agreeing with the interests of the state. For them the issue of national sovereignty have considerably less importance in comparison with the opportunity to uphold their rights and their individual international interests.

During Putin's visit to the PRC from 21 to 23 March 2006, the agreements were signed promising considerable growth in trade turnover (up to 60-80 billion dollars by the years 2010-2015), mutual investments and expansion of bilateral cooperation. But the visit once again demonstrated the economic "inconsistencies" of the Russian-Chinese cooperation. Russia's export largely remained (and remains) in military-technical sector and raw materials acquisition. China's machinery export to Russia continues to grow, with simultaneous reduction in Russia's export of the same item.

Russo-Chinese bilateral trade is expected to rise from 30 billion dollars in 2005 up to 60 or even 80 billion dollars by the years 2010-2015. That is certainly not comparable with U.S. trade figures with China, which amounts to more than 300 billion dollars a year.[4]

As stated by Vladimir Putin, Russia intends to change the structure of trade by increasing the share of high-tech projects. In Beijing, Putin declared that "Gazprom" and CNPC (Chinese National Petroleum Corporation) of China would build two gaspipelines: from Western Siberia ("Altai" project) and Eastern Siberia (Kovyktinskii project) with a volume of 60-80 billion cubic meters of gas. This statement practically indicated that Russia in addition to Europe is considering other countries and regions also—notably, China—as prospective consumers of its Siberian gas and oil.

These negotiations reflected the desire of the Chinese side to actually enter into the investment field of Russia. Hu Jintao, in particular, mentioned that 14 billion dollars of Chinese capital investment would be made in the Russian economy. Though quite a long period was set for this—until the years 2010-2015 but, nevertheless, the trend of growth of Asian investment in the economy of Russian Federation, particularly of Chinese, is very important, especially for Siberia and the Far East.[5]

On the military component of Russian-Chinese trade, the increase of its volume through further growth of military orders is still possible. But, it seems that Chinese financial resources for the development of the Russian military-industrial complex has been depleted. As already mentioned, China actually saved the Russian military-industrial complex in 1990's because 90 per cent of it survived on the basis of Chinese and Indian supply orders. However, this period has already passed.

In addition to TEC and MIC, other areas that could be developed in a mutually beneficial basis are also becoming attractive for large-scale Chinese business. They include a range of areas related to telecommunications, chemical engineering, and light industry, transport, car making. China has shown particular interest in the Trans-Sib, which could significantly speed up the transit of its goods to Europe through Russia. There is also scope for separate projects related to nuclear power, as well as further development of space programmes.

During the visit, Hu recalled that China spends 350 billion dollars per year to acquire high-tech equipment from around the world and that if Russian machinery products would be competitive, China will buy it in large quantities. But the problem for Russia is that Russian and Chinese economies, with the similar growth trends are already different qualitatively and structurally.[6]

Insufficient level of integration of Russia into the global economy does not allow it to carry on an equal fight in world markets. This means that commodity products and military industry determine the trade priorities with China. In relations with China, to all appearance in the near perspective we will have to be satisfied with the role of a "junior partner". Despite the positive trends that are seen in Russia over the past one-year and a half, China with their scales of economic growth is notably ahead of Russia. Nevertheless, for Russia this partnership would provide several advantages:

— first of all the alliance with China would lead to build a new "pole" in the global arena;
— huge markets and consequently increase in exports of Russian products;
— new technology;
— improvement of efficiency of domestic production;
— substantial investment funds—investment in real sector and new scientific developments;
— opportunity to attract capital to the Far East and Siberia;
— integration of industry of the Far East and Siberia into a single economic space of APR (Asia-Pacific Region);
— development of transport infrastructure.

Russia has an absolutely real opportunity to be at the crossroads of major trade and economic traffic between the CIS countries and Pacific States, and also between Europe and Asia. The growing need for efficient transcontinental transport between Europe and Asia, as well as political factors associated with the emergence of newly independent Central Asian states, have stimulated the process of developing new concepts of constructing Euro-Asian transport corridors. The routes of these corridors and goods traffic passing through them could potentially have a major impact on the economic interests of Russia.

Simultaneously, the benefits for China out of this alliance or partnership with Russia can hardly be exaggerated:

— Military cooperation, which can be viewed in terms of increasing military influence in the world, as well as in terms of supplies of modern weapons.
— Access to unlimited mineral resources, including gas, oil, timber, non-ferrous metals, etc.
— Access to advanced scientific development and technologies.
— A promising market for industrial products. Border and interregional trade are of particular interest. Trade in the volumes of 7-8 billion dollars is just the beginning of serious and long-term trade relations.
— A Transit Corridor through the territory of Russia, connecting China with Europe and CIS countries.

One may turn to such example in order to bolster the argument for the potential benefits of China. According to specialists, the annual volume of gas consumption in China will increase at least 4 times just by 2010. This means that already by now the official Beijing is facing quite an urgent issue concerning the possibilities of significant increase of imports of "blue fuel". Today Russia is considered as the main supplier of gas to China. However, for this it is necessary for the Russian side to realize with the help of Chinese companies need one of the two mega projects of gas export to China. Though these projects are encountering a number of serious problems related mainly to the timing of payback, their terms and conditions are still being discussed. Russia has a real chance to take a dominant position among the gas exporters to China. In case of such a scenario, Russia would gain substantial economic and geopolitical benefits.

Such prospects and expanding mutual relations have stimulated regional cooperation between the Siberian regions and the provinces of China, especially those in the border. The Siberian regions are the main centres of those natural resources and are the most prosperous economic exchange zones and the vast majority of transit positions should be made precisely along the line of the border trade areas. In addition, the transportation and logistics component of these processes should be improved, which is impossible without normal regional component of the two sides. A bulk of additional factors comes up that would enhance the regional interactions at different levels, which are the inevitable consequence of grow intensity of relations. The centre is not in a position to build an effective rear without the support of the regions owing to the extended stretch of the communications and remoteness of the main actors of the socio-economic process. The sad experience of the past, based on the monopoly of foreign trade persists. That is why, in fact, a thoughtful transition to a regional component of the general policy of the State and intensification of foreign economic activity is required.

A somewhat different situation is taking shape in the axis of interaction in Inner Asia, in the peculiar socio-economic conditions of the Mongolian people. Here the regional paradiplomacy and dialogue between the great states are taking somewhat different course.

In the post-Soviet period, Mongolia was forced to manoeuvre and seek an optimal balance between its economic potentialities, passing from one crisis to another, and the external factors having a complex trajectory of development. However, if the questions of political cooperation between Mongolia and Russia are highly dynamic, as noted in foreign literature,[7] the economic situation, though stable is not very advantageous. According to the data of the National Statistical Office of Mongolia, during 10 months in 2007 the income of the state budget amounted to 1407.5 billion *tugriks*, and the expenditure—1221.3 billion *tugriks*.[8] In the last ten years a trend of excess incomes over the expenditures was observed and the overall budget surplus amounted to 186.2 billion *tugriks*. A similar situation also prevails in respect of the current balance of the state budget, which marked a surplus of 378.6 billion *tugriks*. The increase in budget revenues was 26.9 per cent (mainly from general tax revenues). The budget surplus is enabling the leaders of the country to implement various programmes aimed at improving the welfare of the people.

The GDP at the end of the year will be about US$4 billion (according to a preliminary assessment by EBRD).

The gross industrial production during the ten months of this year in comparison to the prices of 2000 was 738.2 billion *tugriks*, and increased by 131 per cent or 85.4 billion *tugriks*, compared with the same period past year and is sustainable. By different sectors of industry it was: mining—335.1 billion *tugriks* (2.8% growth), electric power, thermal power and water supply—98.2 billion *tugriks* (2.8% growth), food—104.1 billion *tugriks* (a growth of 25.8%), metallurgy—84.7 billion *tugriks* (a two-fold increase).[9]

The freight by all modes of transport amounted to 18.5 million tons, including 11.6 million tons by rail (a decrease of 6.0%), by land transport 6.9 million tons (a decrease of 10.1%).

Mining and sale of gold amounted to 13.9 tons (a decrease of 6.9%).

The state of agriculture is stable. Its foundation is livestock. Till October 2007 there has been a 1.8 million increase of stock compared to last year and the loss of cattle has also declined by a number of 166.9 thousand heads.

On November 1, the harvest of grain was 114.7 thousand tons, 10.3 hundredweight per hectare (down by 4.5%), potatoes—114.3 thousand tons, vegetables—76.4 tons (increase by 7.3%), hay—892.8 thousand tons.[10]

According to the Mongol Bank data, at the end of September this year monetary emission (M2) amounted to 2264.1 billion *tugriks,* which is 46.4 per cent or 717.8 billion *tugriks* more than the same period in 2006. The amount of money in circulation amounted to 323.1 billion *tugriks,* and an increase by 36.0 per cent or 85.5 billion *tugriks,* compared with the previous year. During the period under review the deposits of the citizens and organizations in national currency increased by 72.2 per cent (443.9 billion *tugriks*) and amounted to 1058.7 billion *tugriks.* The foreign exchange reserve decreased by 11.9 per cent (49.1 billion *tugriks*) and amounted to 363.0 billion *tugriks.* The exchange rate of the national currency against the US dollar amounted to 1177,5 (weakened by 1.1%).[11]

On October 23 sessions were held at the Stock Exchange, as a result 8.6 million shares were sold and the amount of the calculated transactions amounted to 20.7 billion *tugriks,* the number of sold shares, compared with last year increased by 12.8 times, and their cost by 103.4 times. The total market capitalization of branded companies reached 703.7 billion *tugriks.*

The index of prices and tariffs on consumer goods increased by 14.2 per cent compared with the same period last year, by 0.9 per cent compared with the previous month. Among the goods for which the price increased included garments, fabrics, footwear.

In Mongolia, 16 banks, 114 non-bank financial organizations operate. They support the activities of all industries and are willing to issue loans. If in 2005 the interest rates of loans accounted for 30.6 per cent, today it is 16.8 per cent-19.2 per cent.[12]

A growth has been observed in the foreign trade sector. The foreign trade turnover amounted to 3127.8 million US dollars, including export of 1469.3 million US dollars, and import of 1658.5 million US dollars. Thus, there was a negative balance of foreign trade of 189.2 million US dollars. At the same time, the volume of trade turnover increased by almost 30.2 per cent compared to the same period last year. The leading positions are taken China and Russia, followed by the Republic of Korea, United States, Japan and Germany.[13]

The growth of export goods, which amounted to 22.1 per cent, was caused by the increase in supplies of traditional Mongolian export goods abroad: mineral resources of 247.1 million US dollars, precious and semiprecious stones, metals and items made of them of 2.3 million US dollars, ferrous metals of 0.7 million US dollars, while knitwear exports decreased by 25.5 million US dollars, the export of unprocessed *cashmere* increased by US $1.6 million and 'Comb Out' *cashmere* by US $20.3 million. With regard to copper concentrate which is the main export product, the volume of its supplies in physical equivalent increased by 1.0 per cent or 4.6 thousand tons, compared to last year. The average price for one ton of copper concentrate increased from US $1012.5 to US $1293.2, which means a growth of 27.7 per cent.[14]

The import of mechanical engineering, electrical and electronic goods increased by US $103.2 million, minerals by US $93.1 million, food products by US $30.0 million, but the import of textile goods decreased by 14.9 US million dollars compared to last year.

The Russian-Mongolian trade turnover, which during the period under review amounted to US $528.8 million and grew by 30.8 per cent, continues to show a positive trend. The Mongolian exports on meat and meat products, textiles and leather goods amounted to US $29.4 million (a 33.0% growth).

As for Russia, it delivered to Mongolia goods worth US $499.4 million (a 30.7% growth). The products that were exported were mainly oil products, foodstuffs, electricity and construction materials.

At the end of September 2007, the number of unemployed people, officially registered at the labour exchange, has reached 32.3 thousand, which is an 8.2 per cent (3 thousand) less than last year. Since the beginning of the year, 39.1 thousand people have been officially given placements, out of whom 12.1 per cent in public institutions, and 87.9 per cent—in commercial enterprises.[15]

The indicators of socio-economic development of the country and the state budget for 2008 were reviewed at regular meetings of the government. The members of the Cabinet of Ministers, after discussing the documents, decided to put them before the parliament. The significant feature of these projects is that they stipulated implementation of large investment projects and measures. Among the main parameters are the followings: to ensure real economic growth by 9.4 per cent, bring the share of GDP per capita to the level of US $1574, to hold inflation at the level to 10 per cent, increase foreign exchange reserves up to US $1 billion 580 million, expand the export by 13.0 per cent and positive foreign trade balance to the level of US $49.4 million, industrial production growth by 9.2 per cent, to continue the programme of providing childcare benefits to each family, newlyweds and newborns, to increase the amount of pensions by 15 per cent and salaries of civil servants by 20 per cent.

Commenting on these programme documents, the Minister of Finance N. Bayartsaikhan noted that by the projected calculations the GDP of the country for 2008 will reach 5.4 trillion *tugriks*. According to the project estimates, in 2008 the investment to the volume of 441 billion *tugriks* will be made to implement the concrete major projects.

From 1 October 2007, the salary of civil servants has increased by 30 per cent. According to "the draft of the fundamental directions" the trend of enhancement of incomes of the government employees will continue and it is expected that the salary will rise up to another 20 per cent by the end of 2008. As a consequence, the average monthly income of the civil servants will reach 300 thousand *tugriks*. Additional increments for the pensioners are also expected.

The head of the Finance Ministry mentioned about the construction of a new international airport in the valley of Hushugt as one of the large-scale investment projects, the cost of which is estimated to US $250-270 million.

In general, during the period under review Mongolia's economy developed steadily, there have been additional income in the state budget, increase in trade turnover, production and sale of products, which would enable the government to fulfil the tasks it undertook in 2007 with respect to the socio-economic sphere.

Thus, regional interactions towards Mongolia would be more complex, although their ultimate effectiveness is difficult to forecast. That is why Russia and China have shown interest in strengthening the regional component of their foreign policy ambitions. Regional influence, together with increasing scope of global interaction has the prospect of turning these regions into a peculiar multi-vector anvil for a more useful dialogue of world economy, its diversity and stability.

So, the Russian-Mongolian-Chinese relations have a promising addition in the form of a regional component of global interaction. This once again assures that today's diverse world is becoming more accessible for dialogue between nations and their ethnic groups, and the opportunities for more penetrating action of various interest groups are being explored more openly.

The regions are showing the ability to use their potentialities and realize their capabilities in the vast space, by introducing options that are original, workable and stable at the same time.

Notes and References

1. To avoid terminological misunderstandings it should be noted that Switzerland is called a "confederation" solely due to loyalty to historical tradition, while its legal system and practice of political and administrative activities are undoubtedly federal.
2. This allegation proves, for example, the historical experience of the German Union of 1815-1866, which was disintegrated as a result of the war between Prussia and Austria.
3. L.B. Vardomskii, S.V. Golunov, Ed. Bezopasnost' i mezhdunarodnoe sotrudnichestvo v poyase novykh granits Rossii, *Moscow-Volgograd, 2002*. p. 522.
4. Sergei Luzyanin, "Vostochnaya politika Vladimira Putina". Vozvraschenie Moscow: AST, Rossii na "Bol'shoi Vostok" (2004-2008), "*Vostok-Zapad*", 2007, p. 342.
5. *Ibid.*
6. *Ibid.*
7. Bruce Harland, *Collision Course: America and East Asia in the Past and the Future,* New York, 1996; *East Asia in Transformation: Towards a new international order*, Singapore, 1995.
8. Statistical collection of the National Statistical Office of Mongolia, *Data on socio-economic development of Mongolia for 9 months in 2007*, Ulan Bator, 2007.
9. *Ibid.*
10. *Ibid.*
11. *Ibid.*
12. "The outcome of the socio-economic development of Mongolia in 2006", Ulan Bator: the Embassy of the Russian Federation, 2007.
13. *Ibid.*
14. *Ibid.*

25

Strategic Significance of Siberia for Russia

Ajay Patnaik

Since the conquest of Siberian Khanate in 1580 that signalled the supremacy of Moscow over the Golden Horde's former realm, Siberia has been vital to the spread Russia's influence beyond its boundaries and to the expansion of Russia's frontiers. Russian forts and garrisons in southern Siberia helped them to keep a watch on Kazakhs and Oirats, who were involved in a number of clashes with the Russians in the late 17th century. Siberian towns of Tobolsk and Tare were also instrumental in sustaining Russia's trade with Bukhara, which had come under pressure with the coming of the Kalmyks to the Caspian steppe and interruption of traditional caravan routes from Astrakhan and Kazan to Bukhara.[1] From fur and gold in Tsarist and early Soviet times, Siberia's importance as a huge resource rich region came into full play in the later part of the Soviet period. Siberia today contributes 77 per cent of Russia's oil, 85 per cent of its natural gas, and 80 per cent of its coal. Siberian raw materials account for 14 per cent of Russia's GNP.[2]

Siberia, even during the peak of the Cold War, was instrumental in linking Russia to West Europe. In the post-Soviet period, while Russia seeks to expand its reach in the energy markets of Europe it is also looking at diversifying to other regions of the world—the Asia-Pacific in particular. Siberia can act as another bridge to the North-East Asia, as well as help strengthening Russia's links with Central Asia.

European Dilemma

Europe is Russia's largest energy market. Russia supplies nearly a quarter of Europe's gas consumption, mainly on the basis of Siberian gas. As an economically prosperous region, Europe's demand for energy would grow substantially in the future and Russia would remain one of the most important sources. However, Europe's relations with Russia have not been smooth in the past few years. The expansion of NATO and EU to Russian borders evokes fears of containment and encirclement of Russia. The latest American move to place missile shield in Poland and the Czech Republic is bound to sour relations with some of the East European members of the European Union. Europe's sustained criticism of Russia's democratic and human rights records has increased the divide.

Russia's relationship with Ukraine and the Baltic states of the former USSR remain troubled. Russia would, under the circumstances, be weary of over dependence on European market, when the political relations are under strain and the access is through countries that are not friendly to Russia. There was pressure from the European countries when Russia demanded market prices for energy supplies to Ukraine. Demands were raised in Europe to minimise dependence on Russian energy. Simultaneously, the Western outcry over the Yukos affair gives Russia enough reason to feel that too much reliance on the European market can be a potentially damaging to its interests. Symbolic of Russia's displeasure with the West was the annulment in 2004 of the tender results of 1993 under an agreement for the development of the Sakhalin-3 oil and gas project led by the consortium of ExxonMobil and ChevronTexaco as well as Rosneft.

The loss of use of Baltic and Black Sea ports has further hampered Russia's energy exports to Europe. Russia has been taking steps to overcome the difficulties of transit through former Soviet republics and Soviet-bloc countries. The Nord Stream gas pipeline (before 4 October 2006 known as North European Gas pipeline) is a new proposed route for Russian gas exports to Europe under the Baltic Sea, bypassing transit countries.

Though it is very difficult for Russia to weaken its links with European energy market in the foreseeable future, Russia has started working out strategies to diversify to markets that are less likely to hurt Russia. At present European Union countries purchase bulk of Russia's oil exports. Yet, European market has relatively less of an impact on the development of the Siberian region since markets are distant and the region cannot take advantage of the economic growth in Europe. One important region, which can not only provide markets for Russian energy, but also help Siberia's socio-economic development, is the North East Asia (NEA)—China, Japan and the two Koreas. Russia, especially its Siberian and Far Eastern regions, can benefit from the economic growth in the NEA countries that border Russia. These countries can also provide Russia an extension to the larger Asia-Pacific region.

East Siberia and the North-East Asian Region

A report by Moscow-based investment bank Brunswick UBS, titled *Russia: One Foot in Europe, One in Asia* summed up, "The important point for Russia is that the economies to its eastern borders are likely to become bigger than its western neighbours in the next couple of decades. Since they are each big importers—and expected to become more so—of many of the raw and semi-processed materials that form the backbone of Russia's exports, Russia is looking at a huge ready market just beyond its borders".[3]

Russia's North-East Asian neighbours have also been vying to take advantage of the opening up of markets and resources in Russia's Siberian and Far Eastern regions to the outside world. Japan after initial hesitation over disputed islands saw greater economic opportunities in a more prosperous local economy in Siberia and Far East. For China, the scope for Chinese goods, labourers and entrepreneurs in this part of Russia opened up. Additionally, relatively poorer peripheries in China and Japan, like Northeast China and Hokkaido, could be helped by cross-border ties with Siberia and Far East region of Russia. Chinese were also enthusiastic about energy cooperation with Russia as the breakthrough that could propel regional cooperation forward. The urgency arose from the priority given in 2003 to development of Northeast China, emphasizing reform of the outdated industrial complex. Russia, according to Rozman, continues to be appealing as a geopolitical partner.[4]

However, according to Dimitry Trenin, a Russian strategic analyst, Japan is a more promising partner, even if Russia strengthens friendship and maintains controlled use of Chinese resources for the development of Siberia and the Far East. The idea is to balance against China in the region by getting Japan involved. This was probably one of the considerations, apart from Japan's willingness to invest huge sums, for Russia favouring its oil company Transsibneft's efforts for a pipeline completely across Russian territory that would terminate at the sea and supply mainly to Japan. This pipeline would carry oil from Taishet in East Siberia to Nakhodka (Sea of Japan). The opening up of 20 billion barrels of oil in the East Siberian fields (equivalent to proven reserves of the US) is of great significance to Japan which is totally dependent on imported energy. Moscow can hope that the energy co-operation with Japan would create the basis for improving relations in other fields and the territorial issue that has marred Russia-Japan ties so far would not become a stumbling block.[5]

Whatever might have been the geopolitical considerations for the pipeline to Japan, the official position, however, has been that this option is not at the cost of energy cooperation with China. Then Russia's Deputy foreign minister, Alexander Alexeyev told ITAR-TASS on 31 December 2004 that the key aim with the pipeline was "to expedite development of East Siberia and the Russian Far East". This project is to expand cooperation with partners in Japan, China and Asia-Pacific countries. To indicate that energy co-operation with China is going to deepen in the future, Russia promised to double its oil exports to China from 6.46 million tons in 2004 to 15 million tons in 2006.[6] Russia has shown interest to invite Chinese investors to discuss a possibility to finance construction of a special off-shoot (to Daqing in northern China) from the main pipeline going to Nakhodka.[7]

East Siberia is a bridgehead to connect Russia with the other two countries of North East Asia—South and North Koreas. South Korea is emerging as a strong player in the region. Primorskii Krai in Russian Far East exports fish to South Korea and there are plans for latter's investment in marine culture in the Krai. There was an agreement in 2003 to assemble South Korean cars in Far East for use of local residents following government clampdown on used Japanese-car market. There were about 14,000 Russian workers in South Korea in 2004 assembling furniture, much of which is sold in Russia. Unlike China, which encourages Chinese labour migration to Siberia and Russian Far East, South Korea's strategy has been to hire workers inside Russia and supporting resettlement of Koreans from Central Asia. South Korean investment by 2005 were reported to have sustained 80 per cent of the light industrial production in Primorskii Krai, providing nearly 10,000 jobs in textiles and packing. This benefited mostly women in small towns who faced severe unemployment.

North Korea could be a source of labour for the labour-deficient Siberia and Far East region of Russia. In 2000, North Korea contracted to send construction, agricultural and other workers. In the hope that North Korea would reconstruct the Trans-Korean railroad, Russia has already started to extend rail connectivity to the North Korean border by creating a link line to the Trans-Siberian railroad south of Vladivostok. Russia's plans to supply cheaper energy produced at Bureia hydropower station (Amurskaia oblast) to Russian Far East (Primorskii Krai) through a high voltage electric circuit could also make cheaper energy accessible in future to bordering North Korean areas. A cheaper electric power option could also reduce North Korea's dependence on nuclear energy programme, which is dividing the NEA region as well as arousing international concerns.[8]

According to Sevast'ianov, the Asia-Pacific region will remain one of the main focuses of Russian foreign policy due to its increasing economic potential to contribute to the development of the Russian Far East and Eastern Siberia. On 27 May 2004, Putin made special emphasis on implementing trans-border regional cooperation. Russia is actively participating in APEC and the ASEAN Regional Forum, apart from playing a role in the ongoing Korean Peninsula security negotiations. Addressing the delegated to the APEC Summit in Bangkok in October 2003, Putin announced that Russia was prepared to contribute to a new energy and transportation configuration in the Asia-Pacific. He urged foreign business to invest in the gas and oil industry in Siberia.[9]

Russia's growing potential in the Asia-Pacific is also demonstrated, according to Sevast'ianov, by the ongoing international debates on routes for the Eastern Siberian oil pipeline and alternative ways of connecting Trans-Siberian and Trans-Korean railroads.[10] Export of large quantities of oil and gas would require development of hydrocarbon resources in East Siberia and Far East, which have a special strategic significance as "the Eastern gates" of Russia to dynamically developing markets in NEA and Asia-Pacific.

Emphasising the potentiality of energy resources in Siberia and Far East, another scholar, Boris Saneev, underlines that the resources of this region are yet to develop substantially. For example, he states, East Siberia produces only natural gas, that too in small quantities, with annual production of only 4-4.5 billion cubic meters (bcm). Far East produces 3.2-3.4 bcm of gas and 1.6-1.7 million tons of oil.[11] In addition, the recession in East Siberia and Far East has led to an excess of electricity capacity of 30-40 billion kilo watt hours (kwh), which is likely to increase to 50-60 billion kwh after the completion of plants under construction. This excess electricity can be exported to NEA via high-voltage transmission lines, which can also help integrate the electric power system of Siberia and Far East, thus improving the reliability of power supply to the consumers in these regions. Saneev is also of the opinion that there is a strong possibility of creating an Eastern hub of global electric power system. An international consortium has already been created to develop Sakhalin shelf oil and gas. Cooperation in East Siberia is being promoted by negotiations between Russian and China on the exploration of oil and gas fields in the Siberian platform, with participation of other countries of NEA. Negotiations are also going on for export of electricity to China, Korea and Japan.[12]

While East Siberia opens the doors for Russia to its North East Asia neighbours, Siberia on its western side is the gateway to another sub-region of Asia that includes parts of Kazakhstan, Mongolia and China. As Russia looks to intensify its contacts with Central Asian countries through initiatives such as the Eurasian Economic Community and Common Economic Space, the Siberian region could make an important contribution to Russia's Central Asian strategy.

West Siberia and Trans-Altaic Cooperation

In the post-Soviet period Russia's economic links with Central Asia has substantially weakened. To revive and expand the linkages, Western Siberia has to play a major role. Despite the difficulties, trade between Western Siberia and Kazakhstan's regions at present account for 60 percent of the total trade turnover between the two countries.[13] In the Soviet period, due to Turk-Sib railway, West Siberia was an important market for goods from Kazakhstan and Uzbekistan. The majority of business activity in Altai region in West Siberia relied on buying raw materials from and on selling Russian goods to the Central Asian republics.

During that period, 30 per cent of Altai Krai's output was sold in Central Asia, a reason why Altai Krai in West Siberia suffered most. Many industries were hard hit, particularly light industry, chemical industry and machine-building for the agricultural sector. All the major textile companies in Altai Krai used to rely on cotton purchased from Uzbekistan. At present, light industry has lost its once significant status in the Krai's industrial structure. The share of light industry dropped from 13.2 per cent in 1991 to 3.8 per cent in 1995. Production of cotton fabric fell from 208,713,000 cubic meters in 1992 to only 9,156,000 cubic meters in 1995. The share of workers in the light industry declined from 9.6 percent of the total workforce to 6.1 percent between 1991 and 1995.

Central Asia was primary market for agricultural machinery produced in Western Siberia. Loss of this market following Soviet disintegration badly affected machine-building industry for the agriculture sector, which comprised 30 per cent of all machine-building and metal work in Altai Krai. Actual production capacity in 1995 stood at only 7 per cent for tractors, 4 per cent for ploughs and around 1.5 per cent for combine harvesters. Towards the end of the 1990s, industrial output of Altai Krai factories that had links with Central Asia fell by 80 per cent compared with 1991. In the same period, 15,000 jobs were lost at these factories. For that reason, the Altai Krai administration took a number of steps to revive contacts with the countries of Central Asia.

It was at a meeting during the September 1998 international exhibition and cross-border trade in the Altai city of Rubtsovsk that the idea for a quadrilateral cooperation project in Greater Altai was first voiced. It was also here that Altai Krai finalised its cooperation agreement with Pavlodar and East Kazakhstan oblasts. Another important step was taken in May 2002, when Altai Krai administration held talks with representatives of Kazakhstan's commercial bank (Kazcommerzbank) and the agricultural industrial investment bank (Djardemargo) from East Kazakh oblast. Agreement was reached on Kazakh investment in Altai Krai's food industry.[14]

West Siberia can play an important role in the revival of the economies of Central Asia and help Russia-Central Asia relations in general. There has been some effort to re-establish these links, like tractors made in Altai are again being sold to Uzbekistan and foodstuff from the latter is being imported to Altai. West Siberia can also be pivotal to the creation of a more integrated sub-region around Altai Mountain, which is also referred to as 'Greater Altai Region'.

The 'Greater Altai Region' includes four countries – Russia (Altai Krai and Altai Republic of Siberia), Kazakhstan (East Kazakhstan Oblast), Mongolia (Bayan-Olgiy and Kodbos) and Chian (the Altai Prefecture of XUAR). Altai republic and Chita oblast of Russia border China. These two along with Tuva, Irkutsk oblast and Buryat republic of Russia border Mongolia. Altai Krai, Altai Republic, Omsk oblast and Novosibirsk oblast of Russia border Kazakhstan.

Russian border regions can become active economic players, with raw materials and labour that are in demand by their neighbours on the other side of the border. The strategy for the Economic Development of Siberia approved by the Russian Ministry for Economic Development in June 2002 pointed out that economic development is contingent upon cooperation with the neighbouring states within an institutional framework. Joint projects in the areas of trade, ecology, labour and infrastructure were priority areas. The strategy underlines the economic potential of Western Siberia as a gateway to Central Asia and China. One of the key goals outlined in the strategy is to expand Siberia's foreign trade with former Soviet republics, especially Kazakhstan.

Putin, who until recently was a reluctant advocate for a greater regional role in foreign economic and other relations, looks at western Siberia as 'a locomotive for regional integration', according to analyst Oksana Antonenko. The influence of Western Siberian regions on Russia's policy vis-a-vis Central Asia is based on a combination of economic and traditional inter-community ties across the border.[15] At a meeting in 1997 October of the *Siberian Accord*, an inter-regional association, Altai Krai's administration proposed creating an international business centre called Siberia-Central Asia in order to facilitate contacts between businesses operating in the Greater Altai region. The proposal received the full support of the inter-regional association.

The *Siberian Accord* is making a contribution to building relationships between western Siberia with neighbouring states, especially in the area of economics and trade, seeking access for Siberian goods to foreign markets, creation of favourable conditions for foreign investment and development of tourism. At the 2000 annual meeting of the *Siberian Accord*, the proposed new highway between Russia, China, and Mongolia via Siberia was discussed. The then Governor of Altai Krai, Alexander Surikov, stated that immigration of Russian-speaking minorities from the former Soviet republics into the region should be encouraged.

The "Greater Altai" initiative foresees a multilateral integration project covering the whole area around the Altai Mountains and harmonisation of relevant local legislations of the four bordering regions on a multilateral basis. Ecological and environmental schemes have already led to extensive co-operation among them.[16] At a

Conference on the development of the region in Urumchi in 1998 the Altai Declaration was jointly released by the official representatives of Altai Republic, East Kazakhstan oblast, and the XUAR and Bayan-Olgiy of Mongolia. The Declaration called for a concerted effort to protect the Altai mountain natural reserve and set up a cross-border network of natural parks. The declaration also stipulated that the four states should enact a treaty on the steady development of the Altai region, to be called the *Altai Convention.*

During summer and autumn of 2000, a series of conferences on economic aspects of cross-border integration in Altai took place in the four regions (supported by respective local authorities). A Conference in Altai Krai in July 2000 launched the *Altai Mountain Forum*, which holds regular meetings. Following these initiatives, a political and ideological concept for 'Greater Altai' as a cross-border grouping of the given regions was approved by the local authorities of the four regions on 1 November 2000 at an international Conference on Greater Altai organised by Altai Krai administration in Barnaul. In the final declaration at the Conference, it was noted that 'Greater Altai' is an indispensable part of the "new Asia" based on inter-regional cooperation.

In July 2000, a Conference in Altay town in China's Xinjiang-Uighur Autonomous Region adopted a *Declaration on the Development of Transnational Cooperation in the Altai Mountain Region.* The Chinese authorities outlined their interest in cooperation with Altai region of Russia including collaborative development of a cattle-breeding hill pasture and a project on the general restructuring of cattle trade (creation of a joint tannery and fur business, among others). There is also prospect of establishing a joint mineral-extraction project (there are small deposits of copper, gold, lead, mercury, nickel, zinc and semi-precious stones there). In Chinese Altay and Mongolian Altay there are some coal reserves. Representatives of XUAR called for joint prospecting and search for deposits.

The most important aspect is the proposal to develop jointly a transport infrastructure in the Altai region. There is a 55 km impassable stretch on the western side of Russian border with China. At the Conference there was proposal for constructing a direct motorway along this part of the Russia-China frontier via the Kanas border crossing. A direct transport route would facilitate trade between the south Siberian region and western China. This proposed route might constitute a Russian alternative to the 'Great SilkRoute Project' which involves the construction of a main transport corridor via Central Asia, connecting Europe with China while bypassing Russia.[17]

Bilaterally, Altai Krai and XUAR established official links through an agreement in September 1998. Subsequently, during then Chinese Prime Minister Zhu Rongji's visit to Moscow in February 1999, four agreements were signed, one of which concerned cooperation between the above two regions. During a visit of Altai Krai Governor to Xinjiang in April 1999, agreements were signed on the trading of Chinese cotton for Altai timber and on the purchase of Chinese paper-production equipment for factories in Altai.

Opening of the Russia-China border has brought new opportunities for direct contact between Altai and Xinjiang. Xinjiang is regarded as China's western gateway to Central Asia, Russia and Europe, as well as its new centre of economic growth and cross-state and regional cooperation. One of the largest provinces of China, it is sparsely populated. Xinjiang's economy has been growing at nearly 8 percent. Its capital Urumchi is a growing international trade centre. According to Chinese statistics, cited by Nozkhin, Xinjiang-made products account for only 10 percent of the goods that China exports through the region and the XUAR uses 20 percent of the products that is imported via this route. Thus, Russia's trade with Xinjiang is rapidly helping to initiate a trade alliance with the whole of China.[18]

Russia is also showing a lot of interest for cooperation between Siberia, Central Asia and Mongolia. After Soviet Union, manufacturing links and other connections along the northern perimeter of the Altai Mountains involving Mongolia, Kazakhstan and Russia was lost. Mongolia has approached Russia to modernise the western section of the road, which stretches from the Altai Republic to Kodbo and beyond. This would be part of Millennium Road Project, a plan to construct new roads and to modernise existing ones in the Trans-Mongolian network, which will link east and west Mongolia. The Russian government is considering Mongolia's proposal for soft loan and use of Russian companies to do the construction. Modernising roads in western Mongolia will certainly play an important role in increasing trade and investment between neighbouring countries.

Mongolia has also proposed that the authorities in Altai Republic become involved in the reprocessing of Mongolian silver and metallic-ore deposits, which are situated in northwest Mongolia near the Russian border. This is an attractive proposal from a financial perspective. There is much cooperation between the Russian border regions and Mongolia. The *Siberian Accord* is devising plans to set up an association for cross-border cooperation between Mongolia and all Siberian regions.[19]

During his visit to Siberia, Putin participated in a meeting on *Social and Economic Development in the Siberian Federal District* on 26 April 2006. One important issue among others that he highlighted was that of improving the transport infrastructure in Siberia. "It has been noted in the past that this region is crossed by international transcontinental corridors. This enable Siberia to act not just as one of the links in the transport chain connecting European Russia to the Far East, but also gives it the real possibility of playing a much greater part as a bridge linking Europe – via Russia – to the Asia-Pacific region. We must not forget that the Asia-Pacific region is probably the fastest-growing region in the world and this creates huge opportunities for Russia to open up new markets and make use of its national advantages."

He further added, "In conclusion, I would like to note particular significance of cross-border and inter-regional cooperation in the Siberian Federal District. This is a powerful growth resource for all of Siberia. I ask you to speed up work on modernising the border infrastructure and on improving the legal foundation for inter-regional cooperation"[20]

Conclusion

Siberia has historically been instrumental in expanding Russia's boundary and influence. Its rich resources have contributed not only to Russia's economic growth, but also to its connectivity with the outside world. In Soviet times, Siberian energy linked Russia with West European markets. Siberia then was closely integrated with Central Asia and Mongolia. Today Russia feels the weight of NATO and EU expansion to its western borders. Though Europe is Russia's single largest energy market, Russia does not feel secure with overdependence on this region. Political and transit considerations further compel Russia to diversify its energy partnership. Eastern neighbours like China, Japan and the two Koreas, along with Central Asia and Mongolia could provide Russia a larger alternative space for economic engagement. No strategy of containment of Russia can succeed if Russia develops strong co-operative relations with its eastern and southern neighbours.

To achieve this objective, Siberia is an important strategic area for Russia. On both flanks, Siberia can link Russia to North East Asia as well as Trans-Altaic regions. Most of the countries involved on the other side of Siberia are strong economic powers. They can open up a vast market for Russian energy and bring in huge capital for investment in Russia. Kazakhstan can open up Russia to other countries of Central Asia, which have traditionally been close with Russia. The role of Siberian region, its resources and infrastructure orientation, is of critical significance if Russia were to reach out to the Asia-Pacific and Central Asian regions. It is the tri-junction, where Russia's economic linkages with Europe, North East Asia and Greater Altaic Region converge. Russia can ignore this region at its own peril. Realising the strategic significance of this region, Russia has taken a number of initiatives to use the advantages that Siberia offers to make Russia an important actor in an emergent Asia. The success of Russian efforts to link Siberia to its Asiatic neighbours would also contribute to regional prosperity in North East Asia, Mongolia and Central Asia.

Notes and References

1. Michael Khodarkovsky, *Russia's Steppe Frontier. The Making of a Colonial Empire*, 1500-1800, Bloomington: Indian University Press, 2002, p. 148
2. V. Pokshishevsky, Geography of the Soviet Union, Moscow: Progress Publishers, 1974; Oksana Antonenko, Oksana Antonenko, "Russia's foreign and Security policy in Central Asia: The regional perspective", *Russian Regional Perspective*, International Institute of Strategic Studies, 1, No. 2 (London: 2003).
3. John Chan, *ibid.*
4. Gilbert Rozman, *ibid.*, p. 20; Sergei Sevast'ianov, "The Russian Far East's security perspective: Interplay of internal and external challenges and opportunities", *Siberia and the Russian Far East in the 21st Century: Partners in the "community of Asia"*, Slavic Research Centre, Hokkaido University, Sapporo, 2005. The construction of 4,130 km pipeline from Taishet in Eastern Siberia Nakhodka, a port city on the Pacific coast opposite Japan, at a cost of $16 billion would take 80 million tons of oil every year from Siberia to Japan, and potentially to west coast of the USA. This pipeline would carter to also China and other markets in

the Asia-Pacific region. Japan promised $14 billion finance for the pipeline and another $8 billion for other oil and gas projects in the Russian Far East. John Chan, *op. cit.*

5. Both Russia and Japan have been making efforts to expand mutual ties in security, economic, education, culture and other spheres. In the defense area, the Russian Navy made their held the first joint search-and-rescue exercise with the Japanse in 1998, held in the Vladivostok area. Another breakthrough happened in September 2000 when Japan's Maritime Self-Defense Force ships (the first ever foreign Navy ships in the post-Soviet area) visited Kamchatka Peninsula. Finally, in August 2003, the Japanse Navy took part in a strategic exercise held in Russian Far East waters.
6. John Chan, *op. cit.*
7. Sergei Sevast'ianov, *op. cit.*
8. Construction of an electrical generating station of 340 mw with a line crossing the Amur river from Blagoveshchensk is the centrepiece of an integrated electricity grid from North East Asia that was discussed in the spring of 2003. If North Korean nuclear crisis were to be resolved, there could be larger station carrying 500 mw from the Vladivostok to North Korea. Rozman, *op. cit.*, pp. 19-20.
9. Sergei Sevast'ianov, *op. cit.*, p. 31.
10. Sergei Sevast'ianov, *ibid.*
11. The highest concentration of explored reserves in the regions is in the Sakhalin shelf in the Far East and the southern areas of the Siberian platform in East Siberia. Surveys estimate initial recoverable reserves on the Siberian platform at more than 3,600 billion cubic mts of gas and 1,300 million tons of oil, and those on the Sakhalin shelf at more than 820 billion cubic mts gas and 260 million tons of oil. The largest explored fields on the Siberian platform have the potential to deliver more than 30 million tons of oil a year, and more than 60 billion cubic mts of natural gas a year by 2010-15. The gas and oil of Siberia and Far East will cover regional energy demands and guarantee a reliable supply of 30-35 million tons of oil a year and 60-65 billion cubic mts of gas a year for export to NEA. Boris G. Saneev, "Russia's energy politics and northeast Asia", hyperlink http://nira.go.jp/publ/review/2001winter/saneev.txt
12. Boris G. Saneev, *ibid.*
13. Oksana Antonenko, *op. cit.*
14. Oleg Barabanov, "Greater Altai: A proposed alliance of the regions bordering Central Asia and Siberia", *Russian Regional Perspective*, 1, No. 2, International Institute of Strategic Studies (London: 2003)
15. Oksana Antonenko, *op. cit.*
16. Oksana Antonenko, *ibid.*
17. Currently, the Altay Prefecture of the XUAR has two border crossing points with Kazakhstan (the one at Timunai is permanent, and another

is temporary). There are also two seasonal crossing points on the Chinese-Mongolian border. Because these crossings have bilateral status, Russian citizens and goods cannot cross there. As a result, trade between Southern Siberia and Western China is conducted via long circuitous routes and the intersection where China meets southern Kazakhstan. Sergei Nozkhin, "The Altai Region: Old neighbours, new partners", *Russian Regional Perspective*, 1, No. 2, International Institute of Strategic Studies (London: 2003)

18. One percent of Russia's trade with China is with Xinjiang, while Russia accounts for 5-8 per cent of Xinjiang's trade turnover. Chinese economists predicted more than a billion trade between Russia and Xinjaiang. Between 1985-99, the weight of goods that passed through the 16 border checkpoints of the XUAR increased by over 200 per cent per year. The volume of cargo crossing the border increased 12-fold from 1991 to 1999. Sergei Nozkhin, *op. cit.*
19. Oleg Barabanov, *op. cit.*
20. Full text of the speech is available on President's website, *http://www.kremlin.ru/eng/speeches/2006/04/26*

26

Russia and the Changing Geopolitics of Central Asia: Situating the Kyrgyz Republic

Ruby Roy

Introduction

"Kyrgyzstan and Russia have traditionally deep historical ties. Our country was part of the Soviet Union and in our post Soviet development we have established good, political, economic, trade and cultural relations. Half a million Russians live in Kyrgyzstan now and Russian has the status of official language. More than 300,000 Kyrgyz citizens work in Russia. We have much in common with Russia.[1]

This is a very poignant remark which puts the entire Russo-Kyrgyz relation in proper perspective. When we think of Russia in Central Asia Kyrgyzstan becomes a natural point of reference as a traditional friend. Kyrgyzstan or the Kyrgyz Republic is one of the smallest among the Central Asian Republics (CARS). It seems to have acquired a certain image in international affairs – that it does not have a prominent strategic profile as compared to its regional neighbours, Uzbekistan and Kazakhstan; it is seen as relatively more peaceful in the region, right from the beginning it has been associated with democratic polity. In fact, it has been defined as an 'island of democracy'. Democracy became a matter of strategic identification. A Kyrgyz diplomat made a very realistic assessment of this aspect— "Kyrgyzstan has almost no strategic resources. But we do have an international image as an Island of Democracy', in Central Asia. We mustn't jeopardize that".[2]

But Kyrgyzstan has a self definition of its identity. According to which the Republic is an 'emerging democracy and an ancient people but a young nation'.[3]

Russia always maintained good working relation with the Central Asian Republics. This is specially visible in Russia-Kyrgyz relation. However, it must be remembered that Central Asia is not a monolithic region. In terms of size, geostrategy, degree of Islamic impact and Russian influence, they vary from Republic to Republic. They even have different perception of strategic partnership. Like, Kyrgyzstan will never become member of any military alliance (e.g., NATO) which does not include Russia. For this tiny Republic China is also important because its on the border.

The Post Soviet Space

Geo political and strategic issue does not remain constant but are subject to dynamic changes. Central Asia has always been vulnerable to such changers for a variety of reasons, essentially because of its location. This become clear in 1991 and in 2001. Russian policies towards the Kyrgyz Republic has to be understood against the basic geo political changes that took place in the region since the last decade of the twentieth century. Disintegration of the Soviet Union had completely changed the security architecture of region. The Russian Federation due to its internal problems could not retain the continuity of her geo political interest in the region. In fact, it was as late as 1993-94 that the Russia Foreign Ministry refereed to the Common Wealth of Independent States (CIS) as being an area of Russia's vital interest.[4] Lack of a substantial policy resulted in an unprecedented American geo political offence in the region.[5] For the first time 'USA was able to impact its political presence in the new post Soviet Republic of Eurasia all the way to the frontiers of China and as well to dominate the Persian Gulf on the southern fringes of Eurasia'.[6] This observation is a clear indication of the fact that US foreign policy saw this region[7] as part of a greater area.[8] Now extra regional powers started competing with each other for strategic benefits and "numerous actors ranging from businessman, diplomats, oil companies have been attracted to the wealth and power in the region".[9] However, geography and history makes Russia the most important power in the region. This naturally gives Russia a lot of geopolitical weight in the region. After all "geography represents a basic permanent factor in a country's foreign policy."[10] And these natural factors cannot be wished away by the west. This is the reason why Russian foreign policy is defined in terms of geopolitics and security. Political forces in Russia as well as its citizens view the strengthening of their country's geo political influence as essential for national security in the military sphere.[11] Eminent Russia political personality Y. Primakov acknowledged the very big role geo political factors play in this country's foreign policy.[12]

The Soft Underbelly

The CARs along with the countries of the Caucasus form the strategically crucial southern rim of Russia the 'soft under belly' as famously described by Winston Churchill. The CARs are located on the borders of Iran, Afghanistan and China. These were sensitive borders even during Soviet days both from political and military stand point because of the contraband operations and border incursions. In the post Soviet space the region still retain this quality.[13] Former Russian Minister Igor Ivanov admitted that the threat for Russia hides in the Caucasus mountain region and its Asian border. A major source of threat is Afghanistan. Therefore, one of the major foreign policy task of Moscow is to address regional security matters.

In this geo political context Kyrgyzstan's location acquires critical importance. This was further heightened by the post September 11, 2001 developments in the region. Kyrgyzstan is situated in extreme south-eastern part of the region. It is on the border of China and this gives the Republic a lot of strategic importance. The most critical situation arises out of the relentless separatist struggle by the Uyghurs in Xinjiang on the border of Kyrgyzstan and Kazakhstan, for an independent state. They have well organised resistances groups in many countries, including Kyrgyzstan. The Kyrgzstan, Uyghur Unity (Ittipak) Association and others in Bishkek are capable of endangering the security of the region.[14] Undoubtedly there is growing Chinese influences in the CARs. But there is strategic understanding between Russia and China in the Post Cold War period and this trust was revived in the Shanghai Co-operation Organization (SCO).

New Politico-military Challenges

The 'war on terror' highlighted the importance of geopolitics of a country. The new geo political factors that emerged in the region at the outset of the twenty-first century heightened the strategic importance of Kyrgyzstan. September 11, 2001 is a watershed in international relation for several reasons. A very important factor was that radical movements became the pressure point for all countries, hence *international coalitions* to combat terrorism became necessary. This was an important reason behind the improvement of Russia-USA relation for a brief while. The 'war on terror' in Afghanistan famously called 'Operation Enduring Freedom' was conducted from Central Asia. American forces landed in Uzbekistan and Kyrgyzstan. It was apparent that US 'focus on Eurasian convergence zone became one of the most spectacular changes in Asia and the Pacific region in 2001.[15] Consequently the region under went dramatic shift geo politically – what emerged was *two types of security structures* – the indigenous Collective Security Treaty (CST) group led by Russia and the military bases of USA. As a result CARs came to occupy that critical strategic space where a resurgent Russia meets an ever expanding USA. This is most pronounced in Kyrgyzstan where the US forces are still concentrated.

'War on terror' conducted from this region imparted valuable strategic lessons. It became clear that – terror attacks of September 11, 2001 prove that today national security can be threatened by conflicts and events happening far way from the borders of the sovereign state. Also that threats from now onwards will not be geo-politically limited.[16]

It also showed that the region could be linked to a pivotal area, from where US military campaigns could be conducted, in other directions, like Middle East or South Asia and others. Gradually the US military bases became part of a string of military installations across South and Central Asia, that are pivotal to the US campaign and terrorism.[17]

US bases in Central Asia was accompanied by a sharp rise of indoctrination of the local people. For example, Radio Free Europe, Radion Liberty have increased the number of its broadcasts in various parts of the region including Uzbekistan, Kazakhstan, Tajikistan, Kyrgyzstan and in the Farsi language. Important fact is that military bases generally 'tend to become entrenched institutions due to different internal reasons both civilian and military and lobby to maintain or perhaps to expand themselves.[18] As a result of America's power projection in the region, Russia-Kyrgyzstan gave priority to the military aspect in their bilateral ties.

US military base at Manas in Kyrgyzstan covers 1000 hectors. Strategically Central Asian bases enable USA to control vast areas in the region including air space above Afghanistan. Fall our of militarization clearly means – arms race, rival blocks, spheres of influence and uneasy security scenario in the region.

Strategic importance of the region was growing even prior to September 11. Since then the region's strategic significance has grown by orders of magnitude. The most tangible and visible manifestation of its new found importance is the scramble for military bases there. There seems no scope for unilateral withdrawal of US forces from Central Asia seeing the presence of Russian military forces.[19]

Religious Extremism and Drug Trafficking

The crucial changes that occurred were, *militarization,* growth of *religious fundamentalism and drug trafficking*. Therefore, the remark that "Others who might fill nay vacuum left by Russia are Islamic Fundamentalist intruders".[20] Growth of extremism in the Former Soviet Union (FSU) countries is directly linked to the collapse of the USSR. But the scenario got aggravated after September 11. End of Soviet Union meant end of 'real socialism' which created an ideological void in the region. This had the potentialities of retarding nation building process, as political ideology is an important component of political culture. Consequently, religious extremist views found and easy ascent here. Therefore, in the post Soviet space, rightist forces got a tremendous thrust. Islamic Radicalism is a product of the cold war. New threats of transnational terrorism based on religious extremism is a destabilizing factor in CARs. Spread of this is most critical in the Fergana Valley which includes South Kyrgyzstan, Uzbekistan and parts of Tajikistan. In fact, an interesting development in Central Asia concerns not Pan-Turkism but the flowering of Islam as an important Socio-cultural force in the ideological vacuum created after the disintegration of U.S.S.R.

Emergence of Islamic fundamentalist Taliban militia in 1990s added a new dimension to the post cold war security concerns of states contiguous to Afghanistan.[21] Taliban were alleged to be involved in supporting militant Islamic groups from Chechnya to Kashmir. They support violent groups seeking to overthrow the secular regimes in CARs.

The Hizb-ut-Talimir al-Islami (HT) or the party of Islamic liberation is key extremist group of current concern. It became very active by 2003. It's aim is separate Islamic enclave in parts of Fergana valley, including south Kyrgyzstan patterned on similar structures in Chechnya and Kadar zone in Dagestan.[22]

Kyrgyz civil society is deeply concerned about this danger. Intellectuals realize that religious extremism is essentially an ideological problem therefore, the Kyrgyz 'must combat it ideologically'.[23] Religious leaders along with the law and order authorities also take effective measures. Imams of all mosques in Osh, police and national security services meet in the Al-Bukhari Mosque at Osh, every month and discuss ways and means of meeting the challenge.[24]

Today the most dangerous threat arises from a nexus of religious extremism and drug trafficking. This again is linked to the collapse of Soviet Union. A recent analysis admitted that "The disintegration of the Soviet Union in December 1991 threw open the floodgates of drug trafficking from Afghanistan across Central Asia to Russia and further west to Europe. Overnight, Russia lost control over nearly 5,000 km of former Soviet borders in Central Asia and the Cancasus..."[25]

Drug trafficking along with terrorism is an extremely serious threat to the security and stability of Eurasia. The region is not a major producer of narcotics but it is a major transit link of the global narcotic industry. The use of CARs for active drug-trafficking is a fairly recent development because it all began during the last decade. During Soviet days the borders were closed. The drug route then was from Afghanistan via the open Iranian border-Turkey-Balkan states – and Western Europe.[26] Today, the main narcotics and weapon smuggling routes are believed to be Khorog-Osh bighway the so-called 'highway above the cloud'.[27] According to unconfirmed reports, the US military transport aviation is used for the delivery of drugs from Afghanistan to the American Airbase Ganci (Manas) in Kyrgyzstan and Incirlik in Tukey.[28] Increasing use of CARs as major transit route has led critics to forecast that the region is 'set to become a global hub for drug trafficking.'[29] Significantly, the drug trade is found particularly in areas which have acute internal problems like, Southern Kyrgyzstan and Tajikistan.

To make matters worse regional economies are getting criminalized, as substantial portion of these economies are being controlled by drug money.[30] At times, it is used to finance local uprisings. A good example is the recent flowery revolution in Kyrgyzstan, which brought down the Akaev government. Centre of the Kyrgyz Tulip revolution was Osh. It is commonly known that drug lords financed the revolution as well as the march from Osh to Bishkek.

Meeting with the Military Challenge

Russia has been watching Kyrgyzstan carefully ever since the arrival of US troops. The Kyrgyz Republic has become a central focus of Russia's security, military and law enforcement authorities. Russia and the Kyrgyz Republic have traditional close political ties.[31] Kyrgyzstan has been generally supportive of Kremlin's policies in the region. The new Government headed by Kurmanbek Bakieyv also continues to do so. The new Kyrgyz government will continue implementing all international agreements and accords including those signed with Russia on the Kant military airbase. Russia has been watching Kyrgyzstan carefully even since the arrival of the US troops. Naturally, Russia-Kyrgyz defence ties are most important in their relation. Defence Minister Sergei Iranov[32] made it clear that the western presence in Kyrgyzstan would not affect defence relation between Moscow and Bishkek as "Russia does not intend to use Kyrgyzstan as an arena for any sort of confrontation.[33] This is in tune with the post cold war trend. The military consideration in strategic planning which was a hall mark during cold war days is missing in Russian policy now.

For meeting new security challenges, Russia has plans to establish new military bases abroad, in particular in Kyrgyzstan. In fact, Russia maintains its military presence in all Cis countries. As Ivanov put it, "we are acting above all one the interest of our national security".[34] Geopolitically, Russia is seen as the 'heartland' and the heartland cannot be defended without a strong 'periphery'. So the peripheral Southern States are areas of Russia's vital interest', as it is like an outer security ring for Russia Borders are defining features of national interest and always susceptible to security threats. This has become more critical presently due to US military bases and the eastward expansion of NATO. For ensuring national interest Russia chose to deepen bi-lateral ties and build a viable integrated core within the CSTO and the Eurasian Economic Community for a unified defence area and economic co-operation respectively. May be Russia is promoting an Eurasian block. Therefore, Moscow seemingly views Kyrgyzstan as a sort of security out post of Russian led post soviet groupings in the heart of Central Asia.

Both the countries tried to boost military ties. Russia's main defence priorities rotated around the Kant airbase in North Kyrgyzstan:

- Kant airbase in Bishkek which has collective Rapid Deployment Force (CRDF) financed by CIS members but mostly by Russia and Russian Servicemen form the backbone of CRD7.
- Russian base at Ozero military test range where new types of naval weapons are tested Ozero is in Issykal district.
- Russia maintains a small military post for seismic monitoring in Kyrgyzstan. This post plays an important role in sustaining the international nuclear non-proliferation regime. Kant airbase alongwith the military base at Tajikistan enables the Russian Air Force to cover the Fergana Valley. Russia is now looking for a second military base at Osh to meet security threats in the volatile region.[35]
- Russia and Kyrgyzstan have signed supplementary agreements on status of the Kant Airport. This endorsed Russian plans to expend the Kant military airbase; raise troops from 500 to 700 and enhance equipments; increase SU-25, SU-27 fighter places from 20 to triple the number.

Both Russia and Kyrgyzstan face threat from trans-border terrorism. Russia wants to build a security hub in Bishkek. Ivanov also described Bishkek as an emerging "Capital of military structures" of many post-Soviet groupings. The Kyrgyz authorities have acknowledged Russia's role in 'strengthening Kyrgyz defense against international terrorists and extremists'.

The 'New Foreign Policy Concept', passed by the Bakiev Government (January 2007) identified 'Russia as a strategic partner'. And that 'co-operation with Russia is one of the main conditions for the peaceful and sustainable development of Kyrgyzstan'.[36]

This Republic's foreign policy has been moulded essentially by two factors, Kyrgyzstan is a small relatively resource poor remote nation and requires considerable external assistance, it lies in a volatile corner of the globe, vulnerable to a number of security challenges.

A small state with little to offer except a strategic location, Kyrgyzstan's foreign policy has blended a pro-Russian orientation, with a tilt to the West and increasing inclination to China. As a Kyrgyz diplomat said 'for Kyrgyzstan the option is foreign policy' is not or and or but and – and. But in recent times there has been a distinct anti-western mood at the popular level. This is particularly against USA. Local analysts[37] acknowledge this trend in popular mood because of American activities on the world stage. They attribute this anti-American mood to the US led war in Iraq. Certain sections, especially the 'religious minded' strongly resented US actions in Iraq.[38]

The Kyrgyz people resented American interference in their internal maters, like, in the Tulip resolution of 2005. As a matter of fact, there is popular resentment against USA's democracy promotion. Resistance to democracy promotion is actually viewed as resistance to 'American intervention'.

The most systematic and forceful resistance to Western democracy has come from Russia under Putin. His "supporters have cast his campaign pro-democracy groups as a security imperative asserting that the United States is trying to encircle Russia with pro-Western governments and subvert its political order".[39] The CARs, therefore, feel strengthening interaction with Russia best way to avoid American intervention in their internal politics.

Final Remarks

Russia's Central Asian policy emerged with substance in late 1990s. The defining phase began from President Putin's phase. Russia's policy thrust was towards strengthening regional security and coalition with surrounding countries China, Iran, Turkey etc. This alone can check America's unilateralism and militarization of Central Asia.

The new geo-political and security factors that followed in the post-Soviet space was a new focus on state security issues which were further aggravated by the terrorist attacks of September 11, 2001. The American military bases in Central Asia to counter this is actually meant for projecting American presence as preponderant. This would mean a counter balances to Russia and China as well as keep a watch on the Persian Gulf region. For the USA, Russia, China and Iran are 'potential adversaries'. New tensions are bound to arise as Russia, China and Iran feel they are being encircled and come to some sort of strategic understanding in the region. This would mean 'a triangular relationship that has Russia, China and Iran as the three sides with the energy rich Central Asia boxed in. In fact this is becoming America's geo-strategic nightmare especially after its colossal failure in West Asia.[40] Thus excessive militarization may lead to a situation, which might look like a cold war version 2.[41]

Notes and References

1. Roza Otun Bayeva, Foreign Minister in President Baikev's cabinet soon after the Tulip Revolution, March 2005, in Kyrgyzstan. This statement was made during her visit to Moscow. *Times of Central Asia,* April 7, 2005, p. 3.
2. International Crisis Group (ICG) Report No. 22, p. 6.
3. At the 50th Session (October 1995) of U.N. General Assembly, some countries took the opportunity to describe their own identity. Nuxit Kilot and David Newman ed., *Geopolitics at the end of the Twentieth Century,* Frank Cass, London, 2002, p. 22-3.
4. Sergei Kortunov, 'Russia's National Identity: Foreign Policy Dimension', *International Affairs,* Vol. 49, No. 4, 2003, p. 105.
5. *Ibid.*
6. Zbigniew Brzezinski quoted in Boris Rumer ed., *Central Asia in Transition,* M.E. Sharp, NY, London, 1996, p. 11.
7. A common definition of region refers to a set of countries linked by geography and one or more common traits, such as level of development; culture or political institutions. David Lake and Patrick M. Morgan, ed. *Regional Orders: Building Security in a New World,* Pennsylvania State University, 1997, p. 11.
8. Details—Bruce W. Jentheson, American Foreign Policy: The Dynamics of Choice in the 21st Century NY. 2004, First edition 2000, p. 164.
9. Remarks by a Geneva based journalist, Quoted in *Amu Darya, The Iranian Journal of Central Asian Studies,* Summer 2002, Vol. 6, No. 12, pp. 258-9.
10. Nichola J. Spykman, "America's Strategy in World Polities in Colin S. Grey ed *The Geo Politics of Nuclear Era,* New York, 1997, p. 1.
11. David E. Albright and Semyen J. Affater ed. *Ukraine and European Security,* St. Martin's Press, I.N.C. New York, 1999, p. 194.
12. Primakov held several sensitive diplomatic past including of Russia's Foreign Intelligence in early 1990s. M. Mesbahi, 'Russian Foreign Policy and Security in Central Asia and the Caucasus', *Central Asian Survey,* 1993, 12 (2) p. 187.
13. George T. Kennan, *At a Century's Ending Reflections,* W.W. Norton and Co., New York. 1996., p. 325.

14. I owe this information to Dr. Abanti Bhattacharya, Researcher Institution of Defence Studies, New Delhi.
15. Yang Bojiang, and others "Changes and Challenges in Asia and Pacific", *Contemporary International Issues,* Vol. 12, No. 3, March 2002, p. 1.
16. *Hindu*, June 1, 2003, p. 10.
17. Pauline Jones Luong, 'The Middle Easternization of Central Asia', *Current History,* Vol. 102, No. 666, October 2003, p. 339.
18. Rajan Menon, 'The New Great Game in Central Asia', *Survival*, Vol. 45, No. 2, Summer 2003, p. 189.
19. Stephen Blank, "Scramble for Central Asian bases", *Times of Central Asia*, April 9, 2003.
20. Charles S. Dick, "The Military Doctrine of the Russian Federation and Ukraine", *Journal of Slavic Military Studies,* September 1994.
21. The 1992 Military Doctrine of Russia briefly mentioned International Terrorism. The SVR (Foreign Intelligence Service) was the first public body to point out the Islamic threat in Afghanistan and Central Asia in its 1994 Report.
22. *Times of Central Asia* (TCA), April 7, 2005, p. 41.
23. Conservation with Prof. Asanov, Dean, Osh State University.
24. *TCA*, July 15, 2004, p. 4.
25. Vladimir Radyubin, "Russia: Victim of Narco-aggression" *The Hindu*, February 4, 2008, p. 12.
26. *Economist,* February 7, 1999, p. 40.
27. *Eurasia Insight,* January 3, 2008.
28. Niklas Swanstrom, "The Southeast Asia and Chinese Connection to drug trade in Central Asia", *Central Asia and Caucasus Analyst,* August 27, 2003.
29. *The Hindu*, February 4, 2008.
30. Nicole J. Jackson, "The Trafficking of narcotics, arms and humans in post-soviet Central Asia, *Central Asian Survey* (CAS) 24 (1) March 2005, p. 41.
31. Sergei Blagor, "Russia boosts military ties with Kyrgyzstan", *Asia Times,* June 15, 2002.
32. Russian Defence Minister Sergei Ivanow to the press, peoples' Daily Online. April 6, 2005.
33. Kyrgyzstan is Becoming One Big Military field", *Current Digest,* Vol. 54, No. 27, July 31, 2002, p. 19.
34. *Ria Novosti*, June 19, 2003, p. 4.
35. "Russia Seeks A Base", *International Herald Tribune,* May 25, 2005, p. 3.
36. *Eurasia Net Partner Post from RFE/RL.* January 3, 2008.
37. Deputy Director, OSCE Academy and Director of Bishkek's Research Centre on Politics, Religion and Security. Daniel Sershen. "Kyrgyzstan: An Anti-Western Mood Gains Strength", *Eurasianet,* May 22, 2007.

38. *Ibid.*
39. Thomas Carotherts, "The Backlash Against Democracy Promotion", *Foreign Affairs,* March/April 2006, p. 57.
40. Details Vikram Sood, "Global Problems and Regional Issues", *The Hindu,* August 15, 2007.
41. Vikram Sood, "The Great Game 21st Century Vision, *Indian Defence Review*, 22-23 July/September 2007, p. 70.

List of Contributors

Ajay Patnaik, Professor, Centre for Russian and Central Asian Studies, School of International Studies, Jawaharlal Nehru University, New Delhi

Alexei K. Kirillov, Senior Researcher of Institute of History, Siberian Branch of Russian Academy of Sciences, Novosibirsk

Anita Sengupta, Fellow, Maulana Abul Kalam Azad Institute of Asian Studies, Kolkata

Boris V. Bazarov, Director of Institute of Mongolian, Buddhist and Tibetan Studies, Siberian Branch of Russian Academy of Sciences, Ulan Ude, Mongolia.

Denis Ananev, Research Assistant, Institute of History, Siberian Branch of Russian Academy of Sciences, Novosibirsk

Evgeny T. Artemov, Historian, Institute of History and Archaeology, Ural Branch of Russian Academy of Sciences, Ekaterinburg.

Evgeny Vodichev, Historian, Institute of History, Siberian Branch of Russian Academy of Sciences, Novosibirsk.

Felix N. Yurlov, Professor, Institute of Oriental Studies, Academy of Sciences, Moscow.

Jatinder Khanna, Researcher, Centre for Russian and Central Asian Studies, Jawaharlal Nehru University, New Delhi.

Kulbhushan Warikoo, Director, Central Asian Studies Programme, Centre for South, Central Asian & South East Asian Studies, School of International Studies, Jawaharlal Nehru University, New Delhi.

Madhavan Palat, Historian, Formerly associated with Centre for Historical Studies, Jawaharlal Nehru University, New Delhi

Marina N. Baldano, Head of the Department of History, Ethnology and Sociology, Institute of Mongolian, Buddhist and Tibetan Studies, Siberian Branch of Russian Academy of Sciences, Ulan Ude, Mongolia.

Mikhail V. Shilovskii, Russian History Chair of the Novosibirsk State University and Unit Head of Institute of History, Siberian Branch of Russian Academy of Sciences, Novosibirsk.

Natalia Ablazhei, Senior Researcher, Institute of History, Siberian Branch of Russian Academy of Sciences, Novosibirsk.

P.L. Dash, Diretor, Centre for Eurasian Studies, University of Mumbai.

Phunchok Stobdan, Senior Fellow, Institute of Defence Studies and Analyses, New Delhi

Rashmi Doraiswamy, Professor, Academy of Third World Studies, Jamia Millia Islamia, New Delhi.

Ruby Roy, Researcher, Formerly associated with Institute of Defence Studies and Analyses, New Delhi

Sharad Soni, Assistant Professor of Mongolian Studies at the Central Asian Studies Division, Centre for South, Central, Southeast Asian and Southwest Pacific Studies, School of International Studies, Jawaharlal Nehru University, New Delhi

Sreemati Ganguli, Fellow, Maulana Abul Kalam Azad Institute of Asian Studies, Kolkata.

Stephane Dudoignon, Permanent Research Fellow, Turkic and Ottoman Studies, CNRS, Paris.

Suchandana Chatterjee, Fellow, Maulana Abul Kalam Azad Institute of Asian Studies, Kolkata

Sudha Mahalingam, Member, Petroleum and Natural Gas Regulatory Board, New Delhi.

V.V. Alekseev, Director of Institute of History and Archaeology, Ural Branch of Russian Academy of Sciences, Ekaterinburg.

Viktor I. Dyatlov, Historian, Department of World History and International Relations, Irkutsk State University, Irkutsk, Russia

Vladimir Lamin, Director of Institute of History, Siberian Branch of Russian Academy of Sciences, Novosibirsk.

Vladimir Yu. Malov, Senior Researcher, Institute of Economics and Industrial Engineering, Siberian Branch of Russian Academy of Sciences, Novosibirsk.

List of Russian Translations

The following articles were translated from their original Russian version to English by Susmita Bhattacharya, Fellow, Maulana Abul Kalam Azad Institute of Asian Studies, Kolkata.

- The Integration of Asiatic Russia: The Historical Experience and Today's Problems
  V. V. Alekseev
- Northern Asia and Northern America in terms of Colonial Administration (XVII-XVIII c.)
  Denis Anan'ev
- Siberia as a Part of the Russian Empire: Economic Development, State Interest and Private Capital
  A.K. Kirillov
- Siberian Regionalists on the Place of the Region in Civilizational Development of Eurasia
  M. V. Shilovskii
- Asiatic Vector of Soviet Economic Policy
  E.T. Artemov
- The Asian Part of Russia: New Step of Industrial Development
  V. Yu. Malov
- Transborder Character of Transport Communications
  V.A. Lamin
- International Transport Corridors of Eurasia: Socio-economic and Geopolitical Dimensions
  M.N. Baldano
- Siberia: Scenarios of Colonisation and the Demographic Landscape
  N.N. Ablazhei and E.G. Vodichev
- Chinese Migrants and Migrantophobia in Contemporary Russia: Stereotypes and Mechanisms of their Formation
  Viktor I. Dyatlov
- The Transborder Regions of Siberia and East Asia: The Problems of Regional Paradiplomacy
  Boris V. Bazarov

Index